A Concise History of the World since 1945

States and Peoples

W. M. Spellman

First published 2006 by
PALGRAVE MACMILLAN
Houndmills, Basingstoke, Hampshire RG21 6XS and
175 Fifth Avenue, New York, N.Y. 10010
Companies and representatives throughout the world

PALGRAVE MACMILLAN is the global academic imprint of the Palgrave Macmillan division of St. Martin's Press, LLC and of Palgrave Macmillan Ltd. Macmillan® is a registered trademark in the United States, United Kingdom and other countries. Palgrave is a registered trademark in the European Union and other countries.

ISBN-13: 978–1–4039–1787–4 hardback
ISBN-10: 1–4039–1787–6 hardback
ISBN-13: 978–1–4039–1788–1 paperback
ISBN-10: 1–4039–1788–4 paperback

This book is printed on paper suitable for recycling and made from fully managed and sustained forest sources.

A catalogue record for this book is available from the British Library.

A Catalog record for this Book is available from the Library of Congress.

10   9   8   7   6   5   4   3   2   1
15   14   13   12   11   10   09   08   07   06

Printed in China

For Nanci Meyer

CONTENTS

WITHDRAWN
ACKNOWLEDGMENTS

The idea for a concise, topical history of the period since 1945 was prompted by my experience teaching in an interdisciplinary humanities program at the undergraduate level. The module focused on the reading of key primary texts, but students often lacked familiarity with the broader political and cultural context in which the readings were composed. In any short introductory survey, one is deeply indebted to specialist scholars in what continues to be a dynamic period in world history: A sampling of some of the recent literature that has informed my thinking is provided in the "Further Reading" section. I am grateful to colleagues who have explored some of the topics with me, including Grace Campbell, Barbara Reynolds, Dee Eggers, and Bruce Larson. Mark West helped to frame the two main tensions at the core of the text, while Jeremy Black first suggested that I bring the project to the attention of Terka Acton at Palgrave. The three anonymous readers for the press offered valuable advice and timely criticism. Margaret Costello provided solid editorial feedback – and not a few stylistic recommendations – on the typescript, while my students in the first year 'World Since 1945' colloquium helped to shape some of the topics covered in the book. A number of colleagues at the University of North Carolina, Asheville, made it possible for me to complete this project; special thanks are extended to the Provost, Mark Padilla, for affording me time to write during a period of transition at my home institution. As always, members of my family offered support in the form of time and tolerance that I probably did not deserve; these are gifts that should never be undervalued by any self-respecting author. The book is dedicated to a friend of many years.

TIMELINE

POLITICS

1945	United Nations (UN) established
1947	Truman Doctrine and Marshall Plan
1947	India and Pakistan win independence
1948	State of Israel established
1948	Berlin blockade
1949	North Atlantic Treaty Organization (NATO)
1949	Republic of Indonesia established
1949	Communist victory in China
1950	Outbreak of Korean War
1953	Death of Stalin
1955	Warsaw Pact
1956	Suez crisis
1956	French withdrawal from Vietnam
1956	Soviet invasion of Hungary
1957	Ghana first sub-Saharan African nation to win independence
1957	Great Leap Forward begins
1960	Eighteen African nations secure independence
1961	Berlin Wall erected
1962	Cuban missile crisis
1964	Palestine Liberation Organization (PLO) founded
1964	American Civil Rights Act passed by Congress
1966	Great Cultural Revolution begins
1967	Arab–Israeli war
1968	Soviet invasion of Czechoslovakia
1974	Richard Nixon resigns presidency
1975	End of Vietnam War
1975	Helsinki Agreement
1976	Death of Mao Zedong
1979	Soviet invasion of Afghanistan
1979	Iranian revolution
1980	Founding of Solidarity union in Poland

1985   Gorbachev assumes power
1989   Fall of communism in Eastern Europe
1989   Tiananmen Square massacre
1991   Dissolution of Soviet Union
1992   War erupts in former Yugoslavia
1994   Democratic elections in South Africa
1998   Hindu nationalists win Indian general election
2001   Palestinian intifada begins
2001   Islamist terrorist attacks in New York and Washington
2001   Overthrow of Taliban
2003   US and British invasion of Iraq

ECONOMICS AND DEMOGRAPHICS

1945   International Monetary Fund (IMF) and World Bank chartered
1950   World population passes 2.5 billion
1950   European Coal and Steel Community (ECSC)
1953   China's first Five Year Plan
1957   European Economic Community (EEC)
1973   First oil crisis
1976   World population passes 4 billion
1978   Deng Xiaoping begins market reforms in China
1993   World Trade Organization (WTO)
1993   European Union (EU)
1994   North American Free Trade Agreement (NAFTA)
1997   Asian bubble crisis
1999   World population passes 6 billion
2001   China enters World Trade Organization
2002   EU adopts euro currency
2003   China's exports to US reach $150 billion
2004   EU accepts ten new member states

SCIENCE AND TECHNOLOGY

1947   Transistor
1951   Hydrogen bomb
1953   Double helix structure of DNA

1954	First commercial electricity generated by atomic reactor
1955	Polio vaccine
1957	Sputnik launched
1958	Boeing 707 jetliner
1960	Birth control pill
1961	First man in Space (Yuri Gagarin)
1962	First satellite television transmission
1963	Measles vaccine introduced in US
1967	First heart transplant
1967	First coronary artery bypass
1969	First moon landing
1970	Pocket calculator
1974	CAT scan
1977	Last recorded case of smallpox
1977	Apple personal computer
1977	Magnetic resonance imaging
1979	Three Mile Island nuclear reactor accident
1979	First baby from artificial insemination
1980	First 24-hour cable news broadcast
1981	IBM personal computer
1986	Chernobyl nuclear reactor accident
1991	World Wide Web
1993	First satellite global positioning system
1997	Sheep cloned from adult cell

INTRODUCTION: DYNAMIC TENSIONS IN RECENT GLOBAL HISTORY

This is a book about the human experience since 1945, focusing on two central points of tension or debate. The first involves the struggle between two political and economic systems: centralized socialism with its authoritarian political order on the one side, and free-market capitalism with its open, democratic political life on the other side. This first tension or debate remained at the forefront of world history from 1945 until the late 1980s, making its mark on cultural and intellectual life, shaping international relations, and abetting an enormous, and enormously expensive, military arms race. The Soviet Union and the US were the principal nation-states engaged in this debate, although both "superpowers" were joined, sometimes reluctantly, by a host of allies and surrogates around the globe. The Soviet system, with its centralized economic planning and high levels of social control, began to unravel with the fall of the Berlin Wall in 1989 and finally collapsed in 1991, ending more than three decades of Cold War with the US. The sudden demise of the Soviet Union suggested to some sanguine observers that the "end of history" had arrived and that a "new world order" of peace and expanding democracy was in formation.

Although at one level the capitalist democracies seemed to have triumphed over socialist authoritarianism, the story is in fact far more complicated and ambiguous. Despite the failure of communism, postwar Western democracies actually adopted their own enhanced forms of social and economic control during the Cold War, and these controls remained in place, and in some instances expanded, during the 1990s. The emergence of the welfare state in Western Europe and North America after World War II, for example, sharply enhanced central government power over both individuals and the economy. Indeed large-scale government social programmes, led by regulation-wielding bureaucrats, became commonplace elements of democratic culture after 1945. In addition, free-market capitalism was subject more extensively to the regulatory (some would say intrusive) hand of the state. Economic life continued to be driven by market forces, but the national security requirements of the state played an increasingly important role in the fields of trade and tax policy, scientific research, and industrial development. In fact the Cold War contributed mightily to the growth of a symbiotic relationship between the military and large private industry in the West, as well as to the expansion of central government surveillance and information-gathering capabilities.

Inherent in both of these developments was the potential for an even greater amplification of the state's role in the lives of citizens. By the late 1990s it became clear that the breakup of the Soviet Union had not ushered in the anticipated new world order. Indeed, Western-style democracy stood as the exception rather than the rule in global politics. Much of the Muslim world remained in the grip of authoritarian rule, while for one-fifth of the world's population living in China, the communist political elite jealously guarded its monopoly on power, even while beginning an unprecedented flirtation with capitalist economics. And the economic gulf between the world's wealthiest nations and their poorest neighbors continued to widen. At the beginning of the twenty-first century, as fear of organized terrorism increased in the Western world, the cost of military preparedness and the implications of a broader surveillance culture for democratic freedoms became topics of much heated discussion.

The second tension or debate addressed by this book involves the interaction between the forces of cultural fragmentation and affirmation of difference, and the competing integrative forces of what has come to be termed "globalization," or world culture. The postwar world witnessed both the proliferation of new nation-states and the celebration of separate peoples, together with their varied material, cultural, and religious traditions. Unhappily this affirmation of difference sometimes took an ugly turn, engendering strident ethnocentrism and bloody regional conflicts. The dissolution of communist Yugoslavia; the fraying of national sensibilities in Nigeria, Rwanda, and Sudan; and violent opposition to Russian authority in Chechnya, were each symptomatic of the rising power of separatism in a world of multiethnic states. At the same time, however, a global system of finance, commerce, and communications, dominated by the West and carrying with it many of the cultural assumptions of the West, eroded the texture of cultural difference, placing enormous stress on peoples and communities struggling to maintain unique patterns of life.

Despite the rhetoric emphasizing the value of multiculturalism and diversity, rhetoric that was especially pronounced in the West during the 1980s and 1990s, the fact is that the world has become significantly *less* diverse in the wake of global trade, modern transportation, instant communications, and the influence of Western material culture. The result has been an intense debate between those who seek to preserve individual cultural identity, personal community, or national autonomy, and those who champion the values of global commerce, culture, and universal rights. The latter group sometimes views its position as healthy inclusion, while its opponents are portrayed as narrow-minded and divisive exclusionists. For many thoughtful opponents of globalization, however, the primary danger of "world culture" involves the growth of multinational business and financial networks whose allegiance is to no state, while for others, the most troubling feature of the post-Cold War world is the unrivaled military, economic, and cultural influence of one power: the US.

This second tension overlapped the first chronologically, but it became the primary focus of global history after the fall of Soviet communism in the early 1990s. Indeed one might argue that the tension or debate between particularism and the developing world culture, or between regional difference and global uniformity, constitutes the fundamental fault line around which much of contemporary culture and civilization is arranged. Its reach was enormous, affecting everything from the status of women, environmental protocols, and educational practice, to the role of religion in state building and the debate over universal principles of justice, including definitions of human rights. By concentrating on these two dynamic tensions in recent world history, and adopting a thematic approach to our consideration of the period since 1945, this book seeks to bring a wide range of seemingly disparate developments into sharper focus.

Of course no survey text, topical or otherwise, can hope to cover all aspects of the human experience since 1945. And no historian can claim to be above the clash of interpretations regarding the significance of recent global developments. The interpretive model presented here is designed principally to facilitate reflection, discussion, and further debate. It makes only modest claims as a synthesizing narrative, for I am aware that all organizing principles are conditioned by time, place, and personal biases. Although uncomfortable with recent scholarly criticism of historical narrative as little more than subjective fiction, I am sensitive to the fact that when attempting to address essential themes in the thought and culture of the recent past, each of us is limited by our lack of perspective and engagement in a variety of issues that constantly demand our attention. In other words, we are often too close to events to be able to evaluate their larger significance in a dispassionate manner; too often we make sweeping judgments on the basis of events that may, in the long run, prove to be less than central to the main contours of global history.

While acknowledging these limitations, however, it is helpful to be reminded that we all do history, all the time. Our days consist of millions of perceptions of individuals, places, and things. But the *story* that tells us what those images and perceptions mean is provided by us as we arrange the events of our days into a narrative. In a very real sense, we write our own lives, assigning meaning and significance to some events, forgetting others, creating a history of our own existence out of the raw material of perception. Since the 1980s, traditional political history – largely the story of male elites – has been complemented by a growing volume of social history, fruitful examinations of the lives and experiences of common women and men. Through these histories, from the personal level to the national and world stage, we attempt to come to an understanding of who we are, what we are doing, and how to live. Unlike the journalist who attempts to relate the facts about a contemporary event, the historian seeks to uncover the shared social context of a past era, and to use that social context to uncover meanings that are both true to those who lived them, and which make sense to a reader who is embedded in the current social *milieu*. Like it or not, we are all engaged in this latter process. We tell stories about the past, and we attempt to give those stories meaning in order to better understand events in our own lives.

This brief volume is divided into three parts. Some of the chapters address state issues, while others focus on peoples without reference to territorial boundaries. Unlike most surveys of the period, I have tried not to privilege developments in international politics. To do so would be redundant in light of the many fine studies of recent political history now available and noted in the "Further reading" section. More importantly, to highlight politics would place the Western states at the center of the narrative, for the developed West undoubtedly had an inordinate impact on the shape of the contemporary political world. Instead, I have elected to provide a more thematic analysis of the past half-century, devoting equal attention to influential intellectual, religious, and social trends. These had their origin with peoples, not states, and many first emerged or had the greatest impact in regions of the globe whose political influence may have been limited, but whose interaction with the West was both dynamic and transformative. Chapters 1 and 2 will address some key political developments under the heading of "The bipolar world order," but even here the text is careful to treat events from the perspective of states and peoples who lived outside the boundaries of the superpower countries. This is especially the case in Chapter 2 where the "problem" of neo-colonialism is addressed. Chapter 3 explores some of the main challenges facing the international community in the post-Cold War world, paying particular attention to the rise of non-state terrorism and efforts to combat it. The focus then shifts in Parts II and III, where we will investigate a range of broadly defined material, cultural, and intellectual topics that can best be understood with reference to one or both of the book's core tensions.

Part II, "Globalization and its discontents," devotes two chapters to leading issues in the postwar debate between cultural difference and greater integration. Chapter 4 examines the prolific breadth and influence of international business, finance, and capitalist economics generally. During the final two decades of the twentieth century, the advent of the corporation as a dynamic agent of cultural homogenization, not to mention the power of the investing community to influence the well-being of regional and national economies, prompted both applause and spirited political opposition around the world. Chapter 5 looks at the multiple challenges posed by voluntary and involuntary international migration during a period when the number of sovereign nation-states grew dramatically. In the first two decades after the war, international migration typically involved the orderly procession of peoples from former colonies to the old imperial centers, or movement across one border into a neighboring state. More recently, however, migration patterns have reflected both larger shifts in the global economy and a higher incidence of involuntary flight due to domestic political crises. Legal and illegal Latin American migration to the US, and South Asian migration to oil-producing Arab states, illustrate the former phenomenon. Not only is the formal imperial connection absent in this growing South–North passage, but cultural and linguistic differences oblige newcomers to negotiate aspects of their identity that differ from the mainstream. The debate between proponents of assimilation and defenders of tradition often hinges on the perceived value of immigrant labor to the host nation, with the majority culture tolerant of immigration during good economic times and less accommodating when the domestic job market slumps.

Here it is essential to reemphasize that most of the world's population lives outside of the prosperous and demographically stagnant West (increasingly referred to as the North), and that economic disparities between rich and poor countries continue to grow at an alarming pace. This may be the most significant – and troubling – development in recent global history. The simple fact that population growth was (and remains) most dramatic in countries whose economies are least able to cope with the added pressure on resources is one of many reasons to highlight regions, and idea systems, outside of the West in any history of the global community since 1945. The tension between globalization and particularism, between integration and the defense of difference that is at the heart of this study, cannot be understood outside of a discussion of what some scholars have termed the "North–South divide" between developing states and the economically dominant countries located north of the equator. Although discussion of this problem was largely muted in the industrialized world at the beginning of the new century (or wished away by proponents of market-based solutions to regional poverty), this cleavage promises to be one of the central, and perhaps least tractable, dilemmas facing the international community in coming decades.

In Part III, "Body and spirit," our attention turns first to the engines of change in the material world, and then to humankind's ongoing interest in the transcendent and in the affirmation of human rights. During the past half-century, the contributions of scientific research to world health and nutrition, and the role of technology in changing (some would say "improving," others "degrading") the quality of life, have been fast paced, conspicuous, and often unanticipated. These developments, and the place of scientific research and technological innovation in both the Cold War and in the process of globalization, are discussed in Chapter 6. The following chapter interrogates some of the major world religions within the context of modern civil society. Too often relegated to a few lines or an unobtrusive subsection in general histories of the period, religious allegiance frequently transcended the claims of the nation-state and in some quarters fostered powerful – and occasionally violent – political action against the state. The widespread notion in the West, inherited from the eighteenth-century Enlightenment, that the capacity of religion to inform action would wane as science, industry, and consumer culture gained momentum, has not been borne out by events of the very recent past. If anything, organized religion has reasserted its place as a preeminent force in contemporary world politics, and in the personal lives of billions of people.

Often related to religion, but not exclusively dependent upon a religious worldview, is the question of human rights. Assumed to be universal and easily defined by Enlightenment thinkers, recent discourse over what constitutes human rights – and how those rights should be protected – has been contentious and divisive. And inseparable from the human rights debate is the changing status of women since World War II. Arguably more than anything else, women's quest for social, political, economic, and religious parity has accentuated the predicament created by principled attempts to reconcile universal standards or fundamental rights with respect for divergent cultural traditions. Changes in the status of women and minorities in the Western world after World War II, together with universalist claims put forward by the United Nations regarding "essential" human rights, often came up against the myriad values and beliefs of non-Western cultures.

The book concludes with some reflections on the unprecedented, and perhaps unhealthy, pace of change in the post-World War II world, how the centuries-old rhythms of life, already unsettled by the onset of industrialization in the West during the nineteenth century, are now being recast around the globe. It also considers the extent to which the territorial state as we have known it since the advent of modern nationalism in the wake of the American and French Revolutions is best suited to address the multiple challenges of the twenty-first century. For good or ill, most of the readers of this book have abandoned the habits of thought that informed earlier generations, and now expect their world to be changed, to be *otherwise*, almost as a matter of course. Whether or not this rapidly changing world will be better, or even sustainable, and whether the state is adequately equipped to guide peoples in a manner that will ensure the survival of their increasingly fragile planet – these, I would suggest, are very much open questions at the start of the new millennium. I hope that by introducing some of these issues within the context of recent world history, the book will afford students and the general reader a perspective on the past that expands the definition of that which is worthy of our attention.

Part I
From bipolar to multipolar world

1

THE COLD WAR IN GLOBAL CONTEXT, 1945-1991

KEY TOPICS

Triumph and disquiet: the human prospect in 1945
Early superpower tensions
Expanding the circle of conflict

The Khrushchev era, 1955–1964
From detente to denouement
Power and principle

TRIUMPH AND DISQUIET: THE HUMAN PROSPECT IN 1945

Millions of Westerners look back on the year 1945 with a sense of accomplishment and pride. For many who were alive during the 1940s, and especially for those who participated in World War II, the hard-fought military victory over fascist Germany and imperial Japan signaled a resounding affirmation of Western-style democracy, individual freedom, and the rule of law. In the case of Nazi Germany, state-sponsored bestiality on a scale never before witnessed had been decisively eradicated, while in the Pacific theater the insatiable territorial ambitions of the Japanese military had been thwarted. During the war, two major ideological adversaries, the US and the Soviet Union, played down their many differences in order to defeat a common enemy. The scale and tenacity of the fighting on numerous fronts around the globe guaranteed that millions of people were directly involved in the conflict, while the sacrifices of colonial peoples in Africa and Asia suggested to many in the West that empire could no longer be justified. Although the cost in human lives and physical destruction had been enormous (approximately 60 million soldiers and civilians lost their lives between

1939 and 1945), a colossal scourge had been lifted. Soon, it was hoped, a peaceful world would be restored, civilian pursuits again taken up, and a new international order established on the solid foundations of shared experience in battle. The formation of the United Nations Organization (UN) by 50 states in San Francisco in the summer of 1945 augured well for a new era of international cooperation, one where the mistakes made after the close of World War I would be avoided.

The fragile West

The feeling of triumph over evil was especially compelling for those who had witnessed the many trials of parliamentary democracy during the first half of the twentieth century. Before 1914 the prophets of progress were applauding the achievements of Western civilization. Highly competitive European nations experienced increased material affluence at home and unprecedented influence abroad. Advances in industry, housing, transport, medicine, and public education all seemed to indicate that the Western world had indeed unlocked the secrets of political stability and material abundance. And then, quite suddenly, the illusions were shattered in the mud-encrusted trenches of the Western Front. Some ten million Europeans lost their lives during World War I, and those four years of butchery spelled disaster for the German, Austrian, Ottoman, and Russian empires. An entire body of buoyant ideas and assumptions about human nature, progress, reason, the place of technology in modern culture, and humankind's ability to avoid future disasters all came under scrutiny. "War is hell," wrote the English poet Siegfried Sassoon from the trenches, "and those who institute it are criminals."

From the point of view of Woodrow Wilson, America's idealistic wartime president, World War I had been a "war to end all wars," a noble struggle "to make the world safe for democracy." It did neither. Following a Carthaginian peace in which the fledgling German Weimar republic was obliged to accept responsibility for the misdeeds of Kaiser Wilhelm II and his wartime government, a decade of German resentment against the victors set the stage for the rise of belligerent and hate-filled Nazism. Instead of extending the principles of democratic self-government to their respective colonies, Britain and France enlarged their empires by taking control of former Ottoman territories in the Middle East. The US, having become the world's leading creditor nation at the conclusion of the war, refused to join the new League of Nations and instead withdrew into isolationism during the 1920s, while in Russia a revolutionary communist government rejected the very foundations of the Western political and economic order. Some of Europe's leading intellectual and artistic figures, including Evelyn Waugh, Ezra Pound, D. H. Lawrence, George Bernard Shaw, and Salvador Dali, despaired of modern mass democracy and longed for the emergence of a "natural leader" who would be invested with wide powers to do good. The start of a worldwide economic depression in late 1929 merely confirmed the verdict, reached separately by fascists and communists, that political pluralism and parliamentary democracy were doomed to extinction.

Democracy on the defensive

That collapse seemed imminent during the 1930s. While the world's democracies appeared dithering and incapable of lifting their people out of the economic crisis, dynamic leadership in the fascist states and in the Soviet Union projected the image – if not the substance – of national unity and overriding purpose. Perhaps most importantly, these regimes seemed to place food on the table by guaranteeing full employment. Or at least this was the picture offered for international consumption by finely tuned offices of propaganda. The noted American historian Carl Becker, in a pensive 1932 essay entitled "Liberalism: A Way Station," wondered whether the values emerging out of the Enlightenment, like the autonomy of the individual and freedom of expression, once thought to be in harmony with universal natural laws, constituted no more than a temporary rest stop on the road to another, more efficient if less emancipating form of social, economic, and political organization. Historian Roland Stromberg has written that in normal times "Hitler would never have found a political career through the usual boring channels; but he could fish in the troubled waters of post-war Germany, where the old order had fallen and everybody was groping for a new one." Without question the emerging totalitarian order in Hitler's Germany and in Stalin's Soviet Union imposed a new sense of collective purpose for many, but at a very high price indeed.

Tragically, it would take another global conflict, and the senseless deaths of additional millions, before the myth of the leader principle was fully extinguished (at least in the West) and to restore widespread support for democratic government. The Algerian-born French novelist Albert Camus, reflecting on the deceits of dictators, wrote that "none of the evils that totalitarianism claims to remedy is worse than totalitarianism itself." Three years after the close of the war George Orwell published *Nineteen Eighty-Four* (1948), an influential reverse utopia where claims to absolute truth in politics invariably result in the evisceration of the human spirit. When Soviet Communist Party Secretary Nikita Khrushchev denounced the terror regime of Joseph Stalin in 1956 at the Twentieth Party Congress, he had no intention of relaxing one-party rule, but the revelations did stand as sober testimony to monstrous crimes committed in the name of the alleged communist utopia. By that date most of Europe's communist parties had broken with their imperious mentors in Moscow.

An optimistic view

Four and a half decades later, with the peaceful collapse of the Soviet system, first across Eastern Europe in 1989 and then in Russia in 1991, the memory of World War II was recast by some Western scholars in terms of the success of enduring liberal values over collectivism, including the primacy of individual rights and freedoms over the coercive power of the state. Under this reading of history, the struggle against Nazi totalitarianism that concluded in Western Europe in 1945 had now reached a successful resolution with the failure of Soviet-style communism across the entire continent. In particular, the remarkable economic transformation of Western Europe in the half-century since the end of the war, with men and women living longer, healthier, wealthier, and more comfortable lives than anyone could have imagined in 1945, seemed to legitimize a certain level of confidence. Victory in 1945 became an important preamble to a broader triumph of Enlightenment political and economic values, first with the end of Europe's colonial empires in the 1960s and 1970s, and then with the downfall of communism during the final decade of the twentieth century.

A pessimistic view

There was another reality in 1945, one that found little comfort in the singular fact of military victory over Germany and Japan. History's most costly conflict had raged for six years in Europe, beginning with the Nazi invasion of Poland in September 1939, and for eight years in China, inaugurated by the invading Japanese in 1937. It had involved the majority of the world's nation-states, and it drew no distinctions between combatants and civilians. Indeed one-half of all those who died in the war were unarmed innocents, what contemporary military jargon antiseptically refers to as "collateral damage." Conventional – and finally atomic – bombs dropped from distant aircraft led to the slaughter of millions of noncombatants in large cities. Most of Germany's major cities were leveled, and the same was true for key urban centers in Japan. Only an emergency shipment of grain to Japan after the war averted mass starvation, while in Europe nutritional deficiencies were commonplace. Not only cities, but farms, manufacturing plants, sewage systems, and transportation networks had been severely damaged, leaving manufacturing capacity in Europe at 20 percent of prewar production levels. In Central Europe, desperate people searched the rubble for food and shelter while relief agencies struggled against the odds to meet multifarious and complex needs.

The Soviets, who had endured the brunt of the fighting against Nazism, suffered almost half of the total fatalities in the European theater. Virtually everyone left alive in European Russia, Ukraine, and Belorussia in 1945 had lost either a friend, a neighbor, or loved one during the previous four years. In the battle for one Russian city, Stalingrad, over one million Soviets had died – more than the total war dead from Britain and the US combined. Soviet productive capacity, especially in the agricultural sector, was decimated by the German invasion and occupation. Indeed Soviet agricultural output did not reach prewar levels until 1952. In addition, the Holocaust claimed the lives of 6 million European Jews, while a similar number of Slavs, gypsies, communists, pacifists, homosexuals, and disabled persons perished at the hands of the Nazis. Whereas World War I had been mainly a European conflict, World War II was truly global in reach. Approximately one million Bengalis died as a result of war-induced famine in India in 1943, and the same fate struck the Vietnamese in 1945. In China, the death toll from the protracted struggle against Japan was upwards of 15 million. The sands of North Africa were occupied and fought over by the principal combatants, tropical Pacific islands were scenes of terrible carnage, and the world's oceans were transformed into battle sites where merchant ships and their civilian crews became legitimate targets. No one was secure in a total war environment where technology and industrial production were focused on the twin goals of physical destruction and psychological demoralization.

The eclipse of Europe

Perhaps most importantly, the dominion of Europe came to an abrupt and inglorious close as Soviet and American forces entered the rubble that was Berlin in April 1945. Science, industry, and technology had raised Europe to the pinnacle of global power at the start of the twentieth century, and these same factors hastened its fall. For the previous four centuries, from the moment that the indefatigable Genoese navigator Columbus had reached landfall at Hispaniola in 1492, to the establishment of the British and French mandates in the Middle East during the 1920s, the projection of Western power, Western culture, Western religion, and Western ideas around the globe had defined the parameters of early modern society and then the modern world. The Americas, South and East Asia, Australasia, and Africa had each in their turn come under the dynamic and destructive influence of the Europeans. The unmatched success of European civilization during those 400 years, the creation of great empires, and the integration of non-Western peoples into the European economy, served to shrink the global community, to abridge cultural isolation and autonomy, and to involve distant lands and peoples in the dynastic conflicts of European kingdoms. During these centuries of pivotal change, the world became both interdependent and increasingly "Europeanized."

But now, having turned against itself in what some have described as the Second Thirty Years' War (1914–45), that proud tower had suddenly imploded. "What is Europe now?" Winston Churchill queried. "It is a rubble heap, a charnel house, a breeding ground of pestilence and hate." In May of 1945, British and American troops occupied newly liberated lands in Italy, France, and parts of Germany. To the east, the Soviet Red Army was in command of six nations: Hungary, Bulgaria, Romania, Yugoslavia, Poland, and Czechoslovakia. Stalin's forces also controlled eastern Germany. Between 20 and 30 million Germans were displaced, homeless, and on the move. Many had been uprooted by the fighting, suffering deportation, political persecution, forced labor, and enemy attacks from the air. In addition, there were over eight million foreign workers in the German Reich in 1944, and most of these were there under duress. The brutality of the war had been carried out with scientific and calculated efficiency. In the case of Germany, what had once been Europe's best-educated and most scientifically advanced nation had descended almost overnight into a state where killing became bureaucratized and routine. The sheer physical destruction was only paralleled by the moral bankruptcy associated with the Holocaust.

Intellectual disquiet

For some, the overwhelming horrors of the war transformed the texture of the argument in favor of self-government. No longer to be celebrated as a product of the Enlightenment confidence in human nature and human potential, democracy had become a compulsory defense mechanism, an emergency survival strategy. The English literary scholar C. S. Lewis spoke for many when he confessed that he was a democrat owing to the existence of original sin. Human beings are "too wicked to be trusted with more than the minimum power over other men." Existentialist writers and activists like Albert Camus and Jean-Paul Sartre spoke of the need for commitment in the face of an absurd universe, one where meaning had to be fashioned by a deliberate act of will. Colonial peoples pointed to the destruction of the Japanese empire as precedent for the end to European empire. How could the victors call for self-determination in postwar Europe and deny the same opportunity to non-

Westerners? The road to renewal in 1945 was circumscribed by the sobering lessons of the previous three decades, and more immediately by the grim reality of the Nazi extermination camps at Buchenwald, Belsen, and Auschwitz. So far, the twentieth century had been the bloodiest in human history, and it had yet to reach its chronological midpoint. For millions of people around the world, 1945 was a year of want and a time of acute mental anguish: civilization itself had arrived at a moral and material impasse.

EARLY SUPERPOWER TENSIONS

The bitter and costly geopolitical conflict between the US and the Soviet Union known as the Cold War became *the* dominant feature of international relations for almost 45 years. But the ideological and territorial divisions which hardened into the Cold War were anything but fixed in 1945. Thucydides, the ancient Greek historian, had cautioned that wartime alliances, like the one that united the Greek city-states against the Persian threat, were inherently unstable, the product of mutual fear of a common enemy. The subsequent Peloponnesian War and the fall of Athens to Sparta appeared to confirm the gloomy thesis. But perhaps the claim was unwarranted when applied to Europe in 1945. For a moment in the spring and summer of that year, the differences separating the bourgeois West from Bolshevik Russia did not appear insurmountable. The US had supplied the Soviets with abundant arms and supplies after 1941, and Stalin had disbanded the Comintern, the organization founded by Lenin to promote world revolution. Both US and Soviet leaders agreed on the need for reconstruction, and both states firmly opposed European imperialism. Surprisingly, noncommunist political parties, which dwarfed the communists in terms of membership, were allowed to operate without hindrance for some time in the Soviet-controlled zone of occupied Europe. In Hungary, for example, only 17 percent of the electorate supported the communist candidates in elections held in November 1945. Noncommunists participated in coalition governments across postwar Eastern Europe. In France, Italy, Belgium, and Greece, communist parties enjoyed considerable strength, with party members even holding cabinet rank. In Britain, a new Labour government committed to the establishment of a wide-ranging socialist economic program replaced a respected wartime coalition headed by Conservative Prime Minister Winston Churchill. And at the newly organized UN, the 11-member Security Council was designed around the principle of establishing global consensus. Britain, France, China, the US, and the Soviet Union held permanent seats on the Council, where all important decisions required a unanimous vote. Here, it was hoped, old-style power politics would be superseded by healthy debate and consensus building. Thus the ideological divide separating East and West, the historic tension between communist and capitalist systems, appeared somewhat permeable in the immediate aftermath of the terrible conflict.

A second front

It was obvious to all observers in the summer of 1945 that the difficult work of rebuilding broken economies and shattered lives would necessitate a high level of postwar cooperation and trust within the Grand Alliance. But earlier differences over the prosecution of the war did not bode well for subsequent peacetime collaboration. There was no denying that a host of serious disagreements existed between the inter-Allied forces. First and foremost was Stalin's deep suspicion that the opening of a Western front against Germany had been repeatedly delayed by the British and Americans until June 1944 in order to undermine Soviet human and material resources. From the moment that Britain and the Soviet Union had agreed a pact of mutual assistance in July 1941, Stalin had called for an assault by British forces into occupied France in order to relieve the enormous pressure on the Red Army in Russia. Churchill, recalling the debacle of a failed amphibious landing at Gallipoli in Asia Minor during World War I, was hesitant to mount a premature attack against well-entrenched German forces in Normandy. He thought it would be the better part of wisdom first to secure North Africa as a staging point for an eventual return to the continent. Once the crossing into Italy was successful, enough German troops would be bogged down in defending the peninsula to make a Normandy landing more propitious. Only at a meeting in Tehran, Iran, in November 1943, after Churchill proposed yet another southern strategy – this time an attack on the Balkans – did Stalin receive assurances from Roosevelt and the British Prime Minister that the planned offensive would be centered on France. By this date the Red Army had already begun the process of dislodging the Germans from Soviet territory. Historians continue to debate the rationale for the joint Churchill–Roosevelt position on invading Western Europe; what mattered in 1945, of course, was how the deeply paranoid Soviet dictator chose to understand events.

Eastern Europe

The second area of disagreement involved Stalin's insistence that future Soviet security mandated the formation of friendly governments to the immediate west of the USSR. The Soviets had incurred staggering human losses during the war: 7.5 million soldiers, and perhaps as many as eight million civilians, had died at the hands of the Nazi enemy. When we add deaths related to malnutrition, forced labor, and physical dislocation, a total of 20–25 million Soviet citizens perished during the four-year confrontation. By way of contrast, Britain and the US suffered a combined one million fatalities in all theaters. Since the overwhelming majority of Soviet war dead were males, the country experienced an acute drop in the overall birthrate. Together with the widespread destruction of farms, livestock, agricultural machinery, factories, and homes during the period of German occupation, it is hardly surprising that the Russians demanded secure frontiers. The Nazi invasion, while certainly more destructive than its predecessors, merely reinforced the popular perception that from Napoleon to Kaiser Wilhelm to Hitler, Russia's sorrows originated in the West.

For Stalin, friendly states meant subservient client states, especially in terms of their political, economic, and military organization. During a summit meeting in the Crimean city of Yalta in February 1945, the Soviet dictator called for the imposition of a harsh peace against Germany, particularly in the areas of reparations and postwar political reconstruction. And while he promised Roosevelt and Churchill that free elections would take place in Poland at the close of the war (the principle of free elections which was extended to all of Europe in the subsequent Declaration on

Liberated Europe), Stalin had no intention of allowing the formation of Western-style liberal democracies in Soviet-occupied countries. Most of these countries were fiercely nationalistic and anti-Russian, but their military establishments were no match for the battle-hardened Red Army. At a July 1945 summit in Potsdam, Germany, Stalin confronted two new, and untested, leaders: Clement Attlee of Britain and Harry S. Truman of the US. Here, the Soviet leader refused to follow through on the controversial elections issue.

Deepening Western suspicions

The US had emerged from the war as *the* dominant global power, with a monopoly on atomic weapons, military mastery in the air and on the seas, the strongest private-sector economy, and the most advanced manufacturing base. The continental US had not been attacked during the war, and its immediate neighbors had never posed a threat to national security. In 1945 the American economy accounted for nearly 50 percent of the world's gross national product (GNP). Russia, on the other hand, may have been a major military power in May 1945, but economically it was poor, backward, and seriously disadvantaged in terms of useable physical plant. It had relied heavily on American Lend-Lease assistance in order to prosecute the war against Germany, and just before the Potsdam meeting Stalin requested massive postwar reconstruction loans from the US. This economic weakness was offset somewhat by the rapid postwar demobilization of American troops in Western Europe, made necessary by political opinion at home and involving a reduction in personnel from 12 million to 1.4 million by 1947. The Soviet military, close to 11 million men in 1945 and reduced to 3 million by 1948, was thus in a strong position to enforce Moscow's dictates on its zone of influence. In addition, wartime physical and human devastation in Russia was offset by the fact that Stalin ruled an empire that comprised one-sixth of the world's land mass, rich in natural resources, and with a population of some 200 million people who understood the consequences of disloyalty, or even suspicion of disloyalty. Thousands of Soviet prisoners of war returned home in 1945 only to be exiled by Stalin to forced-labor camps or executed for fear that they had been contaminated by anti-Soviet ideas during their imprisonment. By 1953 an estimated five million of these internal exiles were living and working in Soviet labor camps, and approximately half a million political murders had been carried out. Even Marshal Georgii Zhukov, the military commander who led the defense of Moscow and later conquered Berlin, was re-assigned to postwar commands distant from the seat of power. Stalin reached the pinnacle of his control in 1945; many Soviet citizens viewed their leader as a national hero despite his brutal domestic policies, and victory in what became known as the "Great Patriotic War" intensified the cult of personality that had developed around the dictator.

Iron curtain speech

In the minds of some policy makers in the West, including those within the new Truman administration, an effective countervailing force was necessary in order to prevent the extension of Soviet power – indeed, possible Soviet hegemony – across the European continent. It had not been forgotten that the Bolsheviks had stated publicly during the interwar years that their ultimate goal was the downfall of capitalism and the establishment of global communism. Stalin had no master plan for global hegemony, but the perception was growing in the West that he did. Now, with the war over, balance-of-power politics was poised to trump Wilsonian internationalism and the hope for greater postwar cooperation. Lend-Lease funds were no longer available after the defeat of Germany, and by early 1946 the prospect of future American loans to the Soviet Union had evaporated. In a now famous speech delivered at Fulton, Missouri in March 1946, former Prime Minister Churchill warned his American audience that with respect to the Russians, "there is nothing they admire so much as strength, and there is nothing for which they have less respect than for military weakness." Referring to the establishment of an "iron curtain" across the European continent, Churchill counseled that security could only be found in an alliance among the Western democracies, including the US. The speech encapsulated the broader ideological division now guiding policy makers on both sides of the political divide. For the Western democracies, Soviet expansion into the European heartland meant the repudiation of the 200-year-old Enlightenment project, with its emphasis on individual rights, the sanctity of property, freedom of thought and expression, self-government, and religious pluralism. Some policy makers in the West maintained that the Soviet state mirrored its tsarist predecessor in its attempt to extend Russian imperial influence into the Middle East, the Balkans, and Central Europe.

The communist perspective

Stalin's dictatorship was a brutal caricature of Marx's vision of the final stage of human history, and there was no denying that the Soviet command economy, the collectivized farms, and the stultifying bureaucracy together constituted a problematic path to the alleged goal of human equality. But from the Russian, and later Chinese communist perspective, it was the West that had the long and undistinguished record of international aggression and imperialism. And with the defeat of Japan in August 1945, the US had become the unrivaled power in the Pacific Basin, establishing a string of military bases with distinctly offensive capabilities. For Stalin, the hostility of the capitalist West toward all newly formed communist states demonstrated that a strong defensive posture was crucial if the Marxist alternative were to survive. The rhetoric of working-class solidarity, however hopelessly miscast in predominantly agricultural societies like Russia and China, was put forward as a bold alternative to the ruthless class warfare characteristic of all capitalist societies. Stalin argued that the heavy hand of the state was necessary in nascent communist states so long as the forces of international capitalism stood united in their opposition to the dream of a classless society. The precipitate cutoff of US military aid to the Soviet Union in 1945 provided the most immediate evidence of the West's unswerving hostility. One month before Churchill's "iron curtain" speech, Stalin and Soviet Foreign Minister Vyacheslav Molotov stated publicly that the Western democracies had become enemies of the Soviet state.

The German dilemma

At the geographical center of the embryonic Cold War was Germany, prostrate and leaderless. An interim joint occupation of the country had been agreed by the Allies as early as November 1943 when Churchill, Roosevelt, and Stalin met in Tehran. In February 1945, the "Big Three" issued a "Declaration on Liberated Europe" that called for free elections across occupied Europe, allowing each country to determine its own future form of government. The physical cost of total war was difficult to calculate, but something of its punishing nature was readily apparent to troops occupying Germany. Hitler had exhausted the natural and human resources of occupied countries in his racist bid for mastery, while massive Allied bombing crippled the productive capacity of the world's first industrial continent. Food and housing were in short supply, transportation networks were fractured, and economic collapse was the norm everywhere. In the absence of a formal peace settlement with Germany, a dangerous power vacuum emerged in May 1945.

Earlier in the war the British and Americans had agreed with the Soviets that the political disintegration of the Nazi regime was essential to the future security of Europe. Churchill spoke of detaching the industrial Rhineland of Germany from any future Central European successor state, while as late as September 1944 Roosevelt's Secretary of the Treasury, Henry Morgenthau, argued for a postwar German state that was predominantly agricultural. All of the Allies agreed that every remnant of National Socialism had to be destroyed. Although many Nazi officials were able to escape punishment by disappearing into the refugee population, the most influential leaders were tried and convicted by an international tribunal held in the city of Nuremberg in late 1945. Most of those convicted were executed. But the animosity directed against German citizens during the war changed appreciably at Yalta in February 1945. Churchill and Roosevelt now agreed that a punitive peace that left Germans bitter and resentful would only serve to advance Soviet interests on the continent. They opposed Stalin's call for reparations from Germany in the form of money, industrial plant, and forced labor, focusing instead on the need for reconciliation and reconstruction. At a meeting in the Berlin suburb of

Potsdam in July 1945, Stalin, Truman, and Attlee agreed to the details of dividing Germany into temporary occupation zones. A similar model was imposed on the capital city of Berlin, located deep in the heart of the Soviet zone. Although initially designed as a stopgap measure until a lasting structure could be devised for the entire country, these divisions would remain in place until the end of the Cold War some 40 years later.

The Soviet decision to remove natural resources and relocate whole manufacturing plants from eastern Germany to Russia played an important role in prompting the West's decision to unite the French, British, and American zones of occupation in 1947, inaugurating a *de facto* partition of the country. Alarmed over the escalating cost of administering their zone and providing relief for a people that in many cases had been reduced to a barter economy, the Western powers, all of whom had embraced parliamentary political systems and capitalist economic structures, were eager to bring their portion of Germany into the community of prosperous democracies. Free provincial elections were called in 1947, and the two dominant political parties, the Social Democrats and the Christian Democrats, looked to the West for economic aid and political support. When Allied foreign ministers finally came together in February 1947 to conclude peace treaties for the defeated Axis countries, no agreement was reached over Germany. While neither side desired partition in May 1945, the goal of internationalism in the heart of Europe fell victim to a sphere-of-influence perspective that was informed by a deepening culture of distrust.

The Marshall Plan

Crucial to the overall Western strategy of rebuilding Europe's war-torn economies was the implementation of the so-called Marshall Plan, named after American Secretary of State George C. Marshall. In a speech before the Harvard graduating class of 1947, Marshall addressed the issue of continued postwar dislocations on the European continent, inviting all affected nations, including the Soviet Union and its satellites, to construct a comprehensive plan for economic recovery built around the promise of coordinated American financial assistance. And although the

Soviets attended the first planning meeting held in Paris at the end of June 1947, Stalin eventually rejected the offer and prohibited Eastern European client states from participating. Ostensibly, the Soviets took exception to the Plan's requirement that the US have some supervisory role over and access to the budgetary records of the receiving countries. These conditions were interpreted by Stalin as a violation of the principle of national sovereignty. The additional requirement that Marshall Plan money be used to purchase American products struck the Soviets as yet another attempt to extend the influence of the capitalist system. The Cominform, the propaganda wing of the Soviet state, denounced the Marshall Plan as a sinister ploy to "establish the world supremacy of American imperialism." In response, Moscow announced the establishment of the Council for Mutual Economic Assistance in January 1949 to coordinate the rebuilding of those states under Soviet control.

Sixteen nations, all outside the Soviet sphere of influence, eagerly accepted Marshall Plan funds. Each stepped forward to receive a substantial aid package from the Americans, and the Organization for European Economic Cooperation (OEEC, later to become the OECD) was created to supervise the generous grants. By 1952, the year when the Plan ended, over $13 billion in grants and credits had been extended to participants, and the enormous infusion helped to restart Europe's industrial base while also serving to modernize the agricultural sector. As new factories were built and farms restored, production levels and agricultural output rose to exceed prewar levels by the early 1950s. In West Germany, for example, the funds facilitated a remarkable resurrection of the industrial economy, where production levels climbed to more than 50 percent over prewar levels. The contrast between life in East and West Germany became obvious to all who visited both zones, and the situation reflected very poorly upon the Soviet system. Under directions from the Kremlin, the Red Army began to install pro-Soviet communist regimes in every state under its control. By 1948 the Baltic states of Latvia, Lithuania, and Estonia, together with the occupied countries of Eastern Europe, were compelled to adopt Soviet-style political systems and state-dominated command economies.

Overall, Western European states realized growth rates of 5 percent per year by 1952. The US also reaped significant long-term benefits from the Marshall Plan. Almost two-thirds of postwar European imports originated in America, and the reemployment of Europe's laboring population translated into the rapid stabilization of Europe's democratic political systems. The effort to undermine the appeal of the communist alternative through economic revival had passed a crucial test, but the success of the Marshall Plan for Western Europe also served to exacerbate the ideological divide with the East. Communist parties in the West lost influence as prosperity returned, while communists in the Eastern bloc states silenced all opposition political voices, jailed clerics who dared to challenge state orthodoxies, and censored the press with stultifying regularity.

The Truman Doctrine

While the Soviet presence in Eastern Europe was irreversible, short of a major military clash that few in the West welcomed, President Truman and his advisors were eager to foil potential Soviet influence elsewhere. Formal and highly secretive information-gathering and espionage organizations, led by the Central Intelligence Agency (CIA) and the National Security Council (NSC) – both established in 1948 – faced off against their Soviet counterparts in an ever expanding theater of operations around the world, but most immediately along the southern rim of Eurasia. The first crisis occurred in Iran, where British and Soviet troops had been stationed during the war and where, in the summer of 1945, the Soviet Union encouraged a secession movement by the communist-controlled Tudeh Party in the far northern province of Azerbaijan. Strong British and American opposition to this meddling led to the grudging withdrawal of Soviet forces in May 1946. The oil-rich regime of Mohammed Reza Pahlevi received strong backing from the British and the Americans, with the Truman administration providing essential military hardware and technical support to the monarchy. In Turkey, fear of growing communist influence, and in particular Western resentment over Stalin's clumsy demand for Russian access to the eastern Mediterranean via Turkish waters, led to a swift and dramatic American response. In August 1946, after the Soviets called for joint Russian–Turkish control over the Turkish Straits and the cession of Turkish-held lands in the Caucasus, US naval forces were dispatched to the eastern Mediterranean by President Truman, who announced that a portion of the ships would remain permanently on station in the area.

Further to the west, a communist guerrilla insurgency against the pro-Western monarchy in Greece, begun after the withdrawal of German occupying forces in November 1944, led the American president to announce a sweeping change in US foreign policy. During the summer and fall of 1946 the Greek government made repeated appeals to Britain and the US for financial and material assistance against the rebels. In February 1947, Britain (which had intervened in the Greek conflict) put the US on notice that it could no longer continue to provide the Greek authorities with economic or military support. The winter of 1946–7 in Britain had been the coldest on record, and government spending on food and fuel depleted modest reserves. The British government had already received an emergency loan from the Americans of almost $4 billion in 1946, and it now found itself unable to maintain its far-flung international commitments. It was a watershed acknowledgment of the coming end of what had been the world's largest empire, requesting that the Americans assume the burden of repulsing communist insurgency from afar. Truman responded in March 1947 in an address before a special joint session of the US Congress. In his speech, the president stated that "it must be the policy of the United States to support free people who are resisting attempted subjugation by armed minorities or by outside pressures." Congress, convinced that communist insurgency represented a threat to US strategic interests, immediately voted to increase military aid for both Turkey and Greece, although neither government had come to power through the votes of "free people."

In the two years that followed, the US spent nearly $700 million in shoring up the Greek army and in providing valuable economic assistance. By 1949 the communists had been defeated, but not before American military trainers had begun to work closely with Greek forces in the field. The articulation of the "Truman Doctrine" played a major role in helping to refocus American public opinion concerning the West's erstwhile wartime ally. While the Greek communists were in fact being supplied by neighboring Yugoslavia without the support of Stalin, Truman's actions put the

Soviet Union on notice that the US would not withdraw from Europe as it had after World War I. A program of global "containment," first articulated by George Kennan, a seasoned State Department policy planner and former deputy chief of mission at the American embassy in Moscow, was now underway.

Berlin airlift

One of the first tests of the new policy took place in Berlin, the former German capital located in the heart of the Soviet-controlled sector. In July 1948, Stalin closed off road and rail access to the Western-controlled portions of Berlin, isolating 2.5 million inhabitants. For the next 11 months, the US organized 277,000 airlifts into the city, an average of one plane every three minutes, bringing essential fuel, medicine, and foodstuffs, and circumventing the Soviet land blockade. The Western allies stated their intention to continue the airlift indefinitely, and more ominously, 60 American strategic bombers capable of dropping atomic weapons on Russian cities were reassigned to bases in Britain. A military showdown seemed imminent. The Soviets finally reversed their policy, but not before the Western powers decided to unify their three zones in West Germany into a new state: the German Federal Republic. Elections were held on August 14, 1949, and the pro-Western Christian Democratic Party led by Konrad Adenauer emerged victorious. The Soviets responded in October 1949 with the formation (without elections) of the German Democratic Republic, inaugurating what would become a nearly 40-year division of the country into capitalist and communist components. The pledge taken by both sides at Potsdam that Germany would not be permanently partitioned now seemed both naive and impractical.

NATO

An important part of containment policy involved the building of traditional alliance systems. In the wake of the Berlin crisis, the governments of Western Europe asked for assurances from Washington that American military might would be employed on their behalf in the event of Soviet aggression. Britain, France, the

Netherlands, Belgium, and Luxembourg had already entered into a defensive military alliance known as the Brussels Pact Organization in March 1948, but given the huge Soviet advantage in available ground forces in Europe, America's large nuclear "umbrella" appeared to be the only credible guarantee against a potential communist incursion. The Truman administration concluded that the US needed to make a more formal commitment to the defense of Europe along conventional military lines. Enough Republican members of Congress were convinced that Europe's economic recovery would be enhanced by this additional security, and in April 1949, the US joined in a regional defense pact with Canada, Iceland, France, Britain, Italy, Portugal, Norway, Denmark, Luxembourg, Belgium, and the Netherlands. At the heart of this new security alliance, called the North Atlantic Treaty Organization (NATO), was a commitment by each signatory to come to the defense of any member state should it be attacked.

The agreement was accompanied by an American pledge of $1.5 billion in military aid for the member states in Europe. Although there were only 100,000 US troops in Europe in the spring of 1949, NATO instantly transformed American foreign policy, ending nearly two centuries in which the Atlantic Ocean was seen as a welcome divide between the new world and the old, and ensuring that the US would not disengage from European affairs as it had after World War I. Even Greece and Turkey joined the new pact in 1952, making these weak and volatile countries potential flashpoints in the emerging Cold War regime. Finally, in 1955 West Germany, now restored to full sovereignty, joined the NATO alliance and began the process of rebuilding its military. By this latter date, the division of Europe had assumed what appeared to be an irrevocable character. With the exception of Ireland, Switzerland, Spain, and Sweden, every European country had "taken sides" in the unfolding bipolar struggle.

The nuclear arms race

Soon after the US employed atomic weapons against Japan, Stalin ordered an intensive acceleration of the Soviet wartime program of research and development. In the summer of 1946, the Americans called for UN supervision of nuclear research around the world, but Stalin refused to support the proposal. Lacking American financial assistance after the war, Stalin insisted on greater exertions from his own people, and the Soviet consumer economy was further neglected in favor of heavy industry and the military. Uranium was extracted from mines in East Germany and Czechoslovakia (with little attention paid to the safety of workers who toiled in the mines), and the Russian scientific community, assisted by German researchers, became part of the overall Soviet defense establishment. Their work put an end to America's atomic monopoly in July 1949, just as the NATO alliance was established. Four years later both countries had developed hydrogen bombs, devices with a destructive capacity 1,000 times more powerful than the weapons which had incinerated Hiroshima and Nagasaki.

At first only the US had the ability to deliver these weapons in overwhelming force thanks to its fleet of long-range bombers, and Eisenhower's hard-line Secretary of State, John Foster Dulles, built American defense strategy around the doctrine of "massive retaliation" during the early 1950s. Under this dangerous strategy, the threat of nuclear attack would neutralize Soviet conventional strength on the European continent while saving American taxpayers the cost of maintaining expensive ground forces overseas. But the policy was based on the absence of Soviet bases in the Western hemisphere or long-range bombers capable of reaching American cities, and the lack of intercontinental ballistic missile delivery systems (ICBMs). By the mid-1950s the two latter technologies had been developed. In October 1957 the Soviets stunned the West by launching the first man-made satellite, called Sputnik, into orbit; competent observers quickly recognized that rocket power capable of sending an object into space could also deliver them anywhere on earth. The age of the ICBM had begun. Satellite technology for surveillance and missile guidance, again inaugurated by the Soviets in 1957, rounded out the early advances related to weapons of mass destruction.

By the close of the 1950s, the two superpowers each had the previously unimaginable capacity to put an end to global civilization in an instant. For the first time in its history, the continental US was vulnerable to surprise attack from a potential enemy thousands of miles away. Over the next 20 years, both sides spent billions of dollars "enhancing" their stockpiles of weapons and "improving" delivery systems. In Western Europe, the amassing of medium-range nuclear missiles by the Americans led to fears that the continent would be incinerated in the event of a conflict between the US and the Soviet Union. Indeed in 1959 Khrushchev's regime made this possibility explicit. Sadly, but perhaps inevitably, nuclear weapons technology proliferated beyond the superpowers, with France, Britain, China, India, and (while still unacknowledged) Israel all joining the nuclear club by the 1970s. The cycle of weapons development, deployment, and numerical escalation transformed every regional superpower confrontation into a potential global crisis.

EXPANDING THE CIRCLE OF CONFLICT

The first phase of the Cold War ended with the promulgation of the Truman Doctrine and the adoption of the policy of containment as the basis of America's posture toward the Soviet Union. Abandoning any thought of a possible rollback of the existing Soviet sphere of influence, Western diplomatic and military strategy, led by the US, would now focus on resisting communist expansion around the globe. And the goal of securing reliable allies who embraced the anticommunist position trumped whatever concerns might be raised over the forms of government or the human rights record of these potential allies. During the next 40 years, diplomatic backing of and military assistance to anticommunist regimes often placed the US and its European allies in an awkward position respecting their professed stand for individual freedom, political democracy, and civilian rule.

Communism in China

The defeat of Japan in August 1945 brought about the collapse of an enormous East Asian empire and created a dangerous power vacuum in a number of strategic areas. Japan's main islands were occupied by American forces, while the Soviets took charge in Manchuria. On the Korean peninsula, a temporary partition was organized between the two emerging superpowers, but elsewhere in the former Japanese empire there were rival claimants to postwar political power. The subsequent struggles to establish claims to political legitimacy inevitably became part of the nascent Cold War discord. East Asia, which prior to the rise of Japanese imperialism had been part of the larger European-dominated world system, was now to find itself drawn into the Washington–Moscow rivalry.

The inaugural setting for this ideological struggle was China, an enormous nation which had suffered greatly from civil conflict between the Nationalist government and rural-based communist insurgents since the late 1920s. In this vast and densely populated land, the Nationalists under Chiang Kai-shek enjoyed the financial backing of the US by virtue of their strong anticommunist credentials. But Chiang's forces had fared poorly during the years of Japanese occupation, and despite the infusion of American military aid beginning in 1942, the Nationalists did not win a single significant battle against the Japanese and had essentially hunkered down in the mountains of the interior.

In the rural areas along the coast, however, and subsequently in distant north-central China, an alternative movement under the leadership of Mao Zedong had won the support of increasing numbers of resistance fighters. As early as the 1920s Mao had insisted (in opposition to classical Marxist–Leninist theory) that the revolutionary potential and leadership capacity of the peasantry was enormous. The communists successfully cultivated the oppressed peasantry by working to lower rents and by attacking exploitative landlords. The results of this campaign to win the backing of rural workers were impressive. By 1945 Mao stood at the head of a communist (mostly peasant) army of over one million men. In contrast, the Nationalists were so poorly organized that the US sent troops to hold some crucial Chinese ports while also (remarkably) charging the Japanese to stay in place until Nationalist administrators and soldiers could arrive. Despite this disarray, few observers thought that the communists were capable of winning over the entire country. Even the Russians were skeptical of Mao's ability to prevail, and on the day before Japan accepted the Allied terms of surrender, Stalin concluded a treaty of friendship with Chiang's government, calling upon Mao to join forces with the Nationalists. In January 1946, both sides signed a ceasefire and began discussions to form a unity government. It was all to little effect. The Communist People's Liberation Army (PLA) held enormous sweeps of territory across China, and Mao's continued call for fundamental land reform, something that the Nationalists had never taken seriously, translated into enormous political advantage for his movement.

While the Americans continued to send military and financial resources to Chiang Kai-shek's Nationalist government, by 1947 it had become obvious that the corruption and complacency of the anticommunist side could not be reversed. Despite continued warnings, Nationalist military leaders preferred to rule the provinces in a highhanded manner reminiscent of the old warlord system. Frustrated by the lack of progress, US forces were withdrawn from China, and American-sponsored mediation efforts between the two sides, led by General George C. Marshall, were abandoned. By the spring of 1948 the Nationalists' military situation on the mainland had become untenable, and in 1949 Chiang withdrew to the island of Formosa (Taiwan). Within two years of this stunning military victory, achieved without the support of the Soviet Union and against an American-armed opposition, Mao officially announced the formation of the Communist People's Republic of China. Since his momentous victory occurred barely one year after a Soviet takeover in Czechoslovakia and the Berlin blockade, and in the same year that the Soviets successfully tested an atomic bomb, many Western observers and pundits drew strong linkages between Mao's successes and a purported worldwide communist conspiracy led by the Soviet Union. Suddenly, events in East Asia appeared to be intimately connected with developments in the heart of Europe.

In truth, relations between Mao Zedong and Stalin were anything but cordial. Stalin's earlier support for the Nationalists was driven by his desire to prevent the formation of a unified and politically powerful China. Such a state, with three times the population of Russia, might pose a future challenge to Moscow's self-proclaimed leadership of the communist world. As late as 1948, Stalin was cautioning Mao against a final assault on Nationalist forces in the cities of South China, advice that was ignored by the Chinese communists. The Soviet ambassador to China even remained with the Nationalist government until the end of the mainland conflict in 1949. Sadly, the mirage of worldwide communist solidarity is what continued to drive both American foreign policy and the domestic political rhetoric of the major national parties. When Mao, desperate for foreign aid to begin the process of rebuilding China's shattered economy after almost 20 years of military conflict, arrived in Moscow in 1950 and signed a Treaty of Friendship with the Soviet Union, the proponents of containment theory in the US lamented the "loss" of China as a significant defeat for the free world. But from the Chinese perspective, the unfavorable terms of the treaty with Russia (the Chinese were forced to recognize Mongolian independence under Soviet protection) did little to affirm the supposed solidarity of Marxist–Leninist states.

Korean domino

The Manichean worldview of both sides in the evolving bipolar conflict reached its first flashpoint on the occupied Korean peninsula less than a year after the creation of the People's Republic of China. Like Germany, Korea had been partitioned after the conclusion of World War II, and the Soviets and Americans had failed to reach agreement on terms for the reunification of the peninsula. After separate governments were installed (both of which claimed sovereignty over the whole of Korea), the respective American and Soviet armies had withdrawn. This was in 1948; what they left behind was a highly volatile situation in which neither side was prepared to make tangible concessions to the other. The leader of the US-backed state, the authoritarian Syngman Rhee, engaged in hyperbolic saber-rattling on a regular basis, vowing to achieve national unification by force if necessary, while his communist counterpart in the North, Kim Il Sung, similarly proclaimed the mantle of leadership over the entire peninsula. Military and financial assistance flowed into both Koreas over the next two years, and on June 25, 1950 a North Korean army of some 100,000 men, with the implicit endorsement of the Soviet Union, crossed the 38th parallel on a course to "liberate" the people of the South from their "reactionary" nationalist government.

Stalin and Kim II Sung were gambling that the Truman administration would not intervene to save the dictatorial Rhee regime. But the American response, conditioned by recent developments in

China, Soviet testing of an atomic bomb, and by memories of the appeasement of fascist aggression in 1930s Europe, was immediate. Advocates of containment within the Truman administration insisted that a credible reaction must include military intervention on behalf of the beleaguered South. The President told reporters that the Korean situation represented "the Greece of the Far East" and his advisors were convinced that the invasion was a Soviet-led test of American resolve in the Pacific. Communist forces scored impressive early victories, capturing the southern capital city of Seoul two days after the initial incursion. Truman dispatched American forces from nearby Japan, under the command of General Douglas MacArthur, and the Security Council of the UN (minus the Soviets, who were protesting the exclusion of communist China from the UN) voted to legitimize the defensive intervention. In addition, American naval forces entered the Straits of Formosa in order to prevent a possible Chinese communist invasion of the Nationalist-controlled island of Taiwan. In a sharp reversal of policy, the Truman administration was now prepared to assist Chiang's rump Nationalist state. Unexpectedly, the first military clash of the Cold War began thousands of miles away from its point of inception in central Europe.

What began as a limited defensive action in Korea quickly escalated into a full-scale war. After the South Korean army retreated to a small area around the southern coast, MacArthur's forces quickly reversed the tide of battle with a daring amphibious landing some 200 miles behind enemy lines at Inchon, north of Seoul. Within two weeks, UN troops, with token manpower contributions from 20 nations that joined the main American complement, took to the offensive, driving the enemy back across the line of partition at the 38th parallel, and killing or capturing nearly half of the invading army from the North. Pushing forward on the strength of an ambiguous UN resolution to "take all appropriate measures to insure a stable situation in the whole of Korea," MacArthur's army captured the Northern capital of Pyongyang and, after two months of fighting, approached the border of China.

At this critical juncture, after repeated warnings from Beijing to the Americans, some 200,000 battle-hardened Chinese "volunteers" entered the conflict, pushing the UN army back into the South and setting the stage for a protracted and bloody stalemate along the original line of partition. The fighting continued for the next three years, with the United States incurring over 100,000 casualties as leader of the UN army. Chinese and North Korean dead and wounded reached an estimated one million soldiers, and the same ghastly count applied to South Korean combatants. North Korean cities suffered heavy damage from American bombers, and before an armistice was signed in 1953 (soon after the death of Stalin), the posture of the United States toward both China and the Soviet Union had hardened into one of deep animosity. China's intervention in a war that had been sanctioned by Moscow convinced many policy makers in the West that Beijing was now acting in concert with Soviet foreign policy. America's defense budget escalated, new air bases were constructed at key locations around the world, and the doctrine of containment and strategic alliances with anticommunist regimes (irrespective of their domestic behavior) became the centerpiece of American military thought and action for the next 25 years. Back in Western Europe, America's swift intervention in Korea dispelled any doubts about the integrity of the NATO alliance or the willingness of the US to act with its strategic allies.

Red Scare

During the late 1940s and throughout the 1950s, fear of an alleged global communist conspiracy seriously impaired domestic political freedoms in the US. The "Red Scare" of the early 1950s, fueled in part by heightened anxiety over the apparent failure of American foreign aid to stem the tide of communist revolution around the globe and revelations of espionage and betrayal on the part of prominent Americans, forged a climate of suspicion and recrimination in America. Led by Wisconsin Senator Joseph McCarthy, whose unsubstantiated allegations of communist infiltration at the US State Department and within the popular entertainment industry led to widespread blacklisting and ruined careers, the hysteria over clandestine communism gripped the country. In magazines, novels, and on television programs, the Cold War theme, replete with international spies and espionage, took center stage. In 1954

McCarthy, who drew no distinction between the administrations of the Democrat Truman or the Republican Eisenhower when it came to coddling traitors, finally overextended himself when he alleged that the armed forces were saturated by communists. In December, 1954 McCarthy's Senate colleagues censured him, but the wave of suspicion and anxiety over national security persisted. Anti-communist frenzy on the domestic front during the early 1950s strengthened the hard-line position adopted by the State Department under the leadership of John Foster Dulles, who spoke intemperately of "rolling back" communism.

Southeast Asia

The Philippines, liberated from Japanese occupation in 1944, secured full independence from the US in 1946. But in the wake of the Korean conflict, long-term leases on military bases and airfields were extended to the Americans, and a defense treaty pledged US assistance in the event of communist aggression. Similarly, the US entered into a mutual defense pact with Australia and New Zealand in 1951, signaling the end of a half-century of British protection for these European-settler countries in the South Pacific. The shadow of one great empire was replaced by the protective military and financial umbrella of another, a country that for most of its history as an independent nation had eschewed the temptations and the burdens of global power.

While the Americans played the predominant role in postwar Japan and South Korea, the British, Dutch, and French returned to their former colonial holdings in Southeast Asia. In the case of Britain, the reversion was essentially a temporary measure designed to facilitate the creation of independent, pro-Western, and anti-communist governments. The Dutch and the French were less realistic. Dutch troops reoccupied Indonesia in late 1945, ignoring the fact that nationalists had declared independence after the Japanese withdrew. A bloody four-year struggle ensued, with leaders in the Netherlands intent upon keeping their oil and mineral-rich colony. Only threats from the US to stop all Marshall aid payments to the Netherlands put a stop to the conflict. Dutch troops withdrew in 1949 and the Republic of Indonesia was formed in 1950 under the leadership of Sukarno.

In 1946, French soldiers and administrators returned to their prewar imperial holdings in Indochina, hoping to resume their suzerainty over the region's people and resources. But they were immediately confronted by an indigenous guerrilla movement led by the communist leader Ho Chi Minh. Unlike Mao, Ho Chi Minh had traveled widely, especially in Europe, and he had embraced Marxism while living in France during the 1920s. But he shared with the Chinese communist leader an unshakeable conviction that national liberation and the triumph of communism were inevitable. Ho established a League for the Independence of Vietnam during World War II from a base in China. The League was composed of a variety of nationalist groups, and under Ho's leadership they worked, ironically, with American intelligence operatives in an effort to organize underground resistance to Japanese occupation of Vietnam. After the ousting of the Japanese in 1945, the communists declared an independent Republic of Vietnam, but the French refused to recognize the claim. In 1946 French troops ordered Ho's forces to evacuate the city of Hanoi in the North; when they refused, the French attacked, driving Ho's communist fighters into the rural countryside and setting the stage for what would become a bloody 30-year guerrilla war against Western domination.

The US had originally looked upon French operations in Indochina as a misguided attempt to restore an old-style empire. But in 1950, in the wake of the Chinese Revolution and Soviet sponsorship of North Korean aggression, the Truman administration changed its position. Although the Soviets had given Ho little encouragement or material support, the communist guerrilla insurgency in Vietnam was now labeled as part of a larger pattern of worldwide Marxist belligerence directed by Stalin. By 1954 the Americans were paying for a large percentage of French military costs in Indochina. As in the case of Chinese communism, the Americans failed to recognize and act upon the serious differences that existed between Ho Chi Minh and the leadership in Moscow and Beijing. Having "lost" China, hard-line American policy-makers resolved not to repeat the debacle in Southeast Asia.

But the infusion of American material assistance failed to achieve its objective. In early 1954 French forces suffered a humiliating defeat at the hands of the communists, with 11,000 French troops surrendering a strategic redoubt at Dien Bien Phu. The French now conceded that they could not win the war; they had already suffered 100,000 casualties and domestic popular opinion turned decisively against the undertaking. Although of little economic value in terms of its global influence, Vietnam attracted the attention of the super-powers when peace negotiations were opened in Geneva between communist and noncommunist representatives from Vietnam. The US, the Soviet Union, and China all sent delegates to the confer-ence, and once again a disputed land was partitioned pending UN-supervised national elections set for 1956. Under pressure from the Soviets, Ho Chi Minh accepted the terms of the accord, confident that the communists would win an overwhelming majority in nationwide balloting. Significantly, the US declined to sign these Geneva Accords on the future of Southeast Asia. Two years earlier Secretary of State John Foster Dulles had constructed a new defens-ive alliance for the region, the Southeast Asia Treaty Organization (SEATO). Its terms included a pledge from the US to defend Laos, Cambodia, South Vietnam, Thailand, and the Philippines against communist insurgency.

Washington intervenes

The elections in Vietnam never took place. The US proceeded to recruit a nationalist leadership for the South, provided military training and funding for a new South Vietnamese army, and quickly forged a pliable client state thanks to the infusion of almost $1 billion in the period ending in 1960. Repeating many of the errors of the Nationalist leadership in China, the leader of the new state, the American-educated Ngo Dinh Diem, refused to counten-ance land reform for the majority peasant population, preferring instead to ally himself with the country's largest landowners. An influx of almost one million refugees from the North, most of whom were Christians fearing persecution under Ho Chi Minh's govern-ment, compounded the many challenges already facing the untested leadership in the South. With American acquiescence, Diem refused to hold the previously agreed elections in 1956, opting instead to solidify his own power base by strengthening the army and police as instruments of domestic control. The communists in the North effectively characterized the authoritarian Diem regime as nothing more than a corrupt instrument of Western imperialism.

Conditions in the North, meanwhile, were anything but ideal. Ho Chi Minh ordered the collectivization of agriculture, outlawed opposition parties, and exercised violent coercive measures against anyone who resisted the implementation of state-imposed communism. Yet in spite of this heavy-handed agenda, the communists were able to play the national liberation card to full effect against the American-backed Saigon government. By 1959 the guerrilla war against the South was resumed and thousands of Diem's officials in the countryside were assassinated by communist insurgents. Within the space of a year the communists were close to victory, and the newly elected American president, John F. Kennedy, made a crucial decision to redouble military and economic support for the corrupt and authoritarian Diem regime.

The successful communist revolution on the island of Cuba (see below) played a significant role in the American commitment to remain engaged in Vietnam, as Fidel Castro's victory was interpreted as a major breach of the containment policy. President Kennedy was unwilling to allow a similar reversal in Southeast Asia. By 1963, over 16,000 American military advisers were stationed in South Vietnam. Their efforts were in vain. Diem's government was torn by factions and failed to win the loyal support of the majority population. Acting with the tacit consent of American officials, in November 1963 a group of army officers seized control of the government and assassinated Diem. Within days of this brutal action the American president himself was felled by an assassin's bullet. The new president, Lyndon Johnson, inherited a rapidly deteriorating and chaotic situation in Saigon. Over the next two years, leading military figures in the South struggled for mastery as ever greater portions of the countryside fell to communist forces. The social and economic disorder visited upon the civilian population, both North and South, was without precedent in the history of the region.

An undeclared war

It was within the context of this deteriorating political situation that the first American combat troops arrived to prop up South Vietnamese forces. In August 1964, after reports that the North Vietnamese had fired on an American ship that was on patrol in the

Gulf of Tonkin, President Johnson won from Congress sweeping authorization to use "all appropriate means" to thwart North Vietnamese aggression. In the years that followed, American land forces and enormous air power were employed against Ho's guerrilla army. American jet aircraft dropped more ordnance on North Vietnam than had been dropped on Germany during the entire course of World War II, but control of the air was of little significance against highly mobile and deeply committed guerrilla forces. By 1967 there were over half a million American troops in Vietnam, but the additional firepower did little to stem the growth of communist resistance. Increasing opposition to the war in the US, the first televised war where Americans could witness the disconnection between the optimistic assessments of political and military leaders and the horrors on the ground, did not augur well for the corrupt and incompetent Saigon government.

Recognizing the strength of the opposition to his war policies, Johnson chose not to seek reelection in 1968. The new president, Richard Nixon, began to recall combat troops and instead focused on intensive bombing campaigns, including strikes against communist redoubts in Laos and Cambodia beginning in 1969. But the expansion of the conflict precipitated massive popular protests in major cities and on college campuses across the country. After National Guard troops opened fire on antiwar protestors at Ohio's Kent State University in May 1970, killing four and wounding fifteen others, the demonstrations intensified. Resistance to the draft increased, and some members of Congress attempted to stop all funding for the war in Cambodia. Over the next two years it became apparent that the president's plan for "Vietnamization" – the strengthening of the South Vietnamese military coupled with the withdrawal of American forces – had not revived the fortunes of the South. The bombs continued to rain down on a war-weary population, destroying both the natural environment and the credibility of the Saigon government. Two years after the departure of the last American soldiers in 1973, South Vietnam fell to the communist North. During that same year, the communist Khmer Rouge in Cambodia overthrew the American-backed government of Prince Norodom Sihanouk, and the noncommunist government of Laos was ousted by communist guerrilla fighters under the direction of the Pathet Lao Party.

Sino-Soviet split

Perhaps the larger tragedy of Vietnam from the American perspective was not the fall of the South, but the inability of American policy makers to take timely diplomatic advantage of a serious ideological and diplomatic split between communist China and the Soviet Union during the 1960s. As we have seen, US hostility toward Mao's revolutionary government intensified after the outbreak of the Korean War. Military and economic assistance flowed to Chiang Kai-shek's government in exile on Taiwan during the 1950s, and the US successfully defended the right of the Nationalists to hold the Chinese seat on the UN Security Council. The Americans imposed a trade embargo against the mainland and forbade US citizens from traveling to China. Recognizing an opportunity, Stalin provided economic, technical, and military support to Mao's regime in return for Chinese acknowledgment of Soviet leadership in the family of communist nations. The Soviets also lobbied hard for the recognition of communist China in the UN, insisting that Taiwan was just a renegade province propped up by American military power. For the Eisenhower administration, Soviet assistance for the Beijing government demonstrated the validity of the thesis, forcefully promoted by Senator Joseph McCarthy, that Moscow was indeed leading a broader world conspiracy against free peoples.

American policy makers failed to appreciate the level of disappointment that Mao felt in China's relationship with the Soviets. Beijing had turned to Moscow because of the perceived threat from the US: America's postwar rebuilding of Japan, military and diplomatic support for Taiwan, intervention in Korea, and its growing involvement in French Indochina all suggested to Mao that his communist state was under siege. But after Stalin's death in 1953, the Soviets appeared less than enthusiastic about their communist neighbor to the east. Khrushchev was keen to extend the Soviet Union's relationship with nonaligned developing countries, particularly India and Egypt. In 1959, the Soviets extended a loan to India that was larger than any offers previously made to China. That same year, Khrushchev withdrew an offer made in 1957 to assist the Chinese with their nuclear program. The Russian leader was in the midst of an effort to engage the US in nuclear arms control negotiations, and further assistance to the Chinese in this area was bound to hamper relations with the Americans. Mao, who remained firmly committed to the Marxist–Leninist position that conflict with the capitalist West was inevitable, viewed these Soviet summit meetings with the Americans as a betrayal. He felt that an understanding between the US and the Soviet Union would leave China susceptible to further challenges to its sovereignty by the American imperialists.

In 1960, just as the number of American military advisors to South Vietnam was escalating due to the continuing perception in Washington that a communist monolith was sweeping across Southeast Asia under the direction of Moscow and Beijing, Khrushchev ordered all Soviet technicians out of China. Later that year, at a meeting of world communist parties held in Moscow, the Chinese delegates alleged that the Soviets had fallen into apostasy. Increasingly bitter exchanges followed, and by 1962, when the Soviets declared their neutrality over a border conflict between India and China, relations plunged to a new low. Not only did the Chinese openly criticize Khrushchev's handling of the Cuban missile crisis in 1962, alleging that Moscow had abandoned a fellow communist state, but during the following year Mao's government condemned the Russians for providing military hardware to China's enemy, India. When China proudly tested its first atomic bomb in 1964 (without Soviet assistance), the Beijing leadership projected itself as an alternative forerunner in world communism. Russian exchange students were expelled from China in 1966, and in 1969 military clashes between the two communist powers along their lengthy common border prompted Moscow to redeploy thousands of troops from Eastern Europe to the Far East. In 1969, in the midst of the Cultural Revolution, some Chinese leaders feared that the Soviets were planning a preemptive strike against China's nuclear facilities. The Soviet military buildup continued into the early 1970s, spurring the Nixon administration in the US to revisit 25 years of Cold War policy toward China.

Ironically, the American presence in Vietnam provided the lone opportunity for China and the Soviet Union to cooperate in what was an otherwise stormy relationship. But in 1979, four years after the fall of South Vietnam, even that common experience was undermined as the USSR supported Vietnam in its brief war with China. The American president's insight into the depth of the Sino-Soviet rift, and the possibility of exploiting that rift, was never fully appreciated by earlier administrations. Nixon's breakthrough visit to Beijing in February 1972 – the first time that an American president had set foot on Chinese soil – afforded the Americans an unprecedented opportunity to put an end to the costly Cold War in Asia. Presidents Ford and Carter continued the process of normalizing US–China relations, culminating in the visit of Chinese communist leader Deng Xiaoping to America in 1979.

THE KHRUSHCHEV ERA, 1955-1964

Lacking any constitutional procedure for succession, Stalin's death in 1953 was followed by two years of collective leadership before the first secretary of the Communist Party, Nikita Khrushchev (1894–1971), emerged as the top Soviet official. Khrushchev's 1956 denunciation of Stalin's regime at a secret session of the twentieth annual Soviet Party Congress; the arrest and execution of Lavrenti Beria, Stalin's head of the dreaded secret police; the release of thousands of Stalin's victims from Soviet jails; and the announcement that the Soviet Union would seek "peaceful coexistence" with its neighbors raised modest hope in the West that meaningful confidence-building measures could be undertaken. The first summit of Western leaders with their Soviet counterpart since the end of World War II took place in Geneva during July 1955, and while no formal treaties were signed at the meeting, pledges by all participants to continue the dialogue suggested that a new era in Soviet diplomacy was underway.

Soon after his momentous speech before the Party Congress, Khrushchev dissolved the Communist Information Bureau (Cominform) which had been erected by Stalin to insure the obedience of European communist parties to the official Soviet line. Since 1947 the Soviet "satellite" states had mirrored the repressive political order in Moscow, where large cadres of secret police were given extensive powers to root out dissent, where the press and education were tightly controlled, and where arbitrary judicial systems made a mockery of the rights of the accused. The economies of these states were nationalized, and under Stalin grain and manufactured goods had to be sold to the Soviets in order to compensate for Russian deficiencies. Only Yugoslavia managed to escape the heavy hand of Stalinism, but even here the communist regime of Josep Broz Tito was a barely disguised dictatorship with strong nationalist roots.

In the late 1950s some of these subject countries anticipated that greater regional autonomy might be possible under the leadership of a Soviet statesman who dared to question the notion that truth in the communist world emerged only from the offices of the Kremlin. In Poland, labor unrest prompted broad-based criticism of Soviet policies. Władysław Gomułka, jailed in 1951 by the pro-Soviet leadership in Poland, was released from custody in 1955 and elected general secretary of the Communist Party the following year. Gomułka proceeded to grant both greater toleration to the Roman Catholic Church and wider economic freedoms to ordinary citizens. In a hastily arranged visit to Warsaw, Khrushchev threatened the use of force unless Poland complied with Soviet directives, but when the Polish government began to arm workers in anticipation of an invasion, Khrushchev backed down, agreeing to limit Soviet military activity in Poland and endorsing modest economic reforms.

Crackdown in Hungary

In Hungary, similar calls for greater autonomy from Moscow met with a very different response. Strongly nationalistic, most Hungarians applauded when the communist reformer Imre Nagy (1896–1958) permitted the formation of a multiparty political system and invited noncommunists into his government. But when Nagy called for Hungary's withdrawal from the Warsaw Pact in 1956, Khrushchev responded by ordering Soviet tanks and troops into the country. Thousands of Hungarians were killed during the crackdown, over 200,000 others fled to the West, and Nagy was hustled out of the country by the Russians and eventually hanged for his political indiscretions. The general assembly of the UN condemned the aggression, but the Western democracies did not intervene. In fact, disagreements within the Western alliance were strong at this moment as a joint French and British invasion of Egypt's Suez Canal zone was strongly opposed by the US (see Chapter 2). It was an opportune time for Khrushchev to use force in Eastern Europe; military action in Hungary confirmed that the Soviets were not about to permit any dismantling of the buffer zone that had been erected between Russia and the West after World War II.

The Berlin Wall

The forceful suppression of the uprising in Hungary in 1956, together with the collapse of a planned 1960 summit with President Eisenhower, signaled a return to a more combative relationship with the West. The mercurial Khrushchev had enjoyed a successful visit to the US in 1959, but a May 1960 downing of an American U-2 spy plane over Soviet airspace discredited the American president in the eyes of the Soviets. The new American leader, John F. Kennedy, delivered a hard-line inaugural address in January 1961, and at his meeting with Khrushchev in Vienna five months later the two clashed over the future status of Berlin. The Soviets wished to end the anomaly of a divided city. Between 1945 and 1960 over two million disaffected East Germans had evaded communist authorities and settled in the West. The sight of thousands of East Berliners voting with their feet as they fled to the western part of the city was too much for the Soviets to abide, especially in light of Khrushchev's incessant boasting about the manifold benefits of Soviet-style communism. In August 1961 East German authorities constructed a 100-mile wall around the city, topped with barbed wire and manned by armed guards who were ordered to shoot anyone attempting to cross into the western half of the former capital. The wall instantly became a stark symbol of the deep divide between the communist and capitalist systems. The panicked construction of the Berlin Wall in August 1961 demonstrated that it was military force, not worker solidarity, that kept communism alive in Eastern Europe. America's inaction during the crackdown in Hungary may have demonstrated that Soviet control over Eastern Europe would not be challenged militarily by the West, but there was no guarantee that internal resistance would not resurface. For the Soviets, it appeared as though the entrenched forces of nationalism in Eastern Europe were every bit as much a threat to Soviet security as the military power of the NATO alliance.

To the brink: Cuba

Superpower rivalry informed events on every continent, and in the Caribbean, Central, and South America, the appeal of communism was strongest among those elements of the population who had suffered most under authoritarian, right-wing regimes. During the early 1950s the Americans had successfully overturned a reformist government in Guatemala after the leader of that country, Jacobo Arbenz, expropriated the extensive landholdings of the US-based United Fruit Co. as part of a larger land reform program. In 1953, when Arbenz agreed to buy military hardware from communist countries, the US Central Intelligence Agency (CIA) began training and equipping exiled opponents of the Guatemalan leader. A 1954 invasion led to the formation of a conservative, anticommunist dictatorship in the country, complete with the restoration of all lands previously owned by United Fruit. In addition to the CIA's role, the State Department, under directions from Secretary of State Dulles, had worked closely with the Guatemalan military in order to assure that Arbenz's attempt to distance his country from the US sphere of influence did not succeed.

In neighboring Nicaragua, General Anastasio Somoza's support for American Cold War policies won for his authoritarian regime both military aid and business opportunities for the wealthiest Nicaraguan landowners. The situation was similar in Cuba during the 1950s, where the dictator Fulgencio Batista banned the communist party and established close relations with the US in return for military aid and business investment. In this island nation of seven million people, a small Cuban middle class benefited greatly from their economic ties to the American colossus to the north. Sugar exports and the tourist trade stood at the heart of the relationship, but improved economic conditions for some could not compensate for the absence of political freedoms under a regime that did little to improve the lives of the majority population. Fidel Castro, a youthful lawyer and opponent of US influence in Cuba, attempted to overthrow the Batista government in 1953, but his effort failed and he was jailed for two years. When the US finally ended its military aid program to the repressive Batista government in 1958, the Eisenhower administration hoped that a broad coalition of moderate parties would be able to form a new government.

At this juncture, Castro and his reconstituted rebel army were able win enough support in the countryside to attack and secure the capital city of Havana. In the early stages of the revolt and subsequent assumption of political power, Castro succeeded in uniting disparate ideological forces: communists, socialists, and anti-Batista liberals, who together were interested in promoting social justice and land reform for the rural poor. US officials, pleased to see the end of the corrupt and ineffective Batista dictatorship, held out modest hope that the coalition would survive, especially in light of the fact that Castro himself had no clear agenda beyond his broad call for national renewal. Within three years of his initial victory, however, Castro had broken with most of his allies over the issue of free elections, erected a one-party state, implemented the first stages of a Soviet-style command economy, and turned to the USSR for essential foreign aid. Political dissent, press freedoms, foreign ownership of established business enterprises and landed estates – all were forbidden by the ruling junta. By the end of the Eisenhower presidency in 1960, Castro had seized the property of all US-owned businesses in Cuba, and the US had adopted a full embargo on trade with the island. As Castro turned repeatedly to the Soviets for technical advice, economic assistance, and trade partnerships, the new Kennedy administration prepared to fight the Cold War in its own hemisphere.

In April, 1961 a US-organized and US-funded group of 1400 Cuban exiles (trained in Guatemala and Nicaragua by the previous administration) disembarked from American naval vessels at the Bay of Pigs. Their assault was a debacle, with Cuban troops quickly defeating the rebel contingent on the landing beaches and Cuban authorities arresting rebel sympathizers. The US-sponsored 1954 Guatemalan invasion was not to be repeated in Cuba. In the aftermath of the failed invasion, Castro proclaimed his adherence to the Marxist–Leninist community of anti-imperialist nations, and while he did not secure the formal military alliance with the Soviet Union which he desired, Russian leader Nikita Khrushchev offered to introduce medium- and intermediate-range ballistic missiles in Cuba, on condition that the weapons be installed and controlled by the Soviets. Castro consented, and in the fall of 1962 the lethal hardware, together with thousands of Russian technicians and military personnel, began to arrive at its destination less than 100 miles off the southern coast of Florida.

Speculation continues to this day over the Soviet decision to confront the Americans in their own hemisphere. It is possible that Khrushchev hoped to use the missiles as a bargaining chip to eliminate the Western capitalist enclave in Berlin, or to remove American ballistic missiles stationed near the Soviet border in Turkey. But no single motive is apparent. What is clear is that the subsequent "Cuban Missile Crisis" brought the world's two superpowers to the edge of nuclear war a short 17 years after the defeat of Nazism in Europe. With the Cuba platform, America's major cities would now be vulnerable to a direct Soviet nuclear strike. In October the US began an air and naval blockade of Cuba and insisted that existing Soviet technology on the island be withdrawn. The president received NATO backing for his position, which went so far as to declare that a missile launched from Cuba against any nation in the Western hemisphere would result in American nuclear retaliation against the Soviet Union.

After a tense week of threats and counter-threats, and with 19 American warships prepared to stop and board Russian cargo ships traveling across the Atlantic en route to Havana, Moscow reevaluated its position. Khrushchev at last agreed to remove the weapons in return for a US pledge not to attempt the overthrow of the Castro government. The Soviet leader also requested the removal of the US missiles in Turkey, and while Kennedy refused to accept the latter request in public, the weapons in question were quietly removed from their forward positions in 1963. The world had narrowly avoided an unthinkable nuclear end to the Cold War.

FROM DETENTE TO DENOUEMENT

The Cuban Missile Crisis highlighted just how dangerous the bipolar world had become. In its aftermath both sides agreed to establish a teletype "hot line" that would afford the respective leaders direct access in the event of future crises, but it was becoming clear that more and better weapons only made the superpowers less secure. By the early 1960s each country had delivery systems capable of hitting their opponents' major cities within a half-hour from launch. Costly efforts were undertaken to devise effective interceptor rockets programmed to knock out an incoming missile before it reached its intended target. The Russians deployed an antiballistic missile system (ABM) around Moscow in the late 1960s and the Americans responded in kind with ABM plans for 15 cities. But the results were destabilizing, as each side struggled to increase its offensive capabilities in order to overwhelm any ABM system. These defensive measures were also countered by troubling offensive innovations, including the mounting of multiple warheads on a single missile, with each warhead capable of hitting a different target. This race to secure a durable technological advantage seemed interminable; by the mid-1960s the United States was spending roughly 5 percent of its gross national income on defense, while in the Soviet Union, where living standards continued to stagnate when compared to averages in the West, almost one-quarter of the country's economic output, and one-quarter of its workforce, was dedicated to the military. By 1974, the Soviets possessed over 1500 intercontinental ballistic missiles (ICBMs) capable of reaching the US, while the Americans had over 1000. Combined with hundreds of nuclear-armed submarines, long-range bombers, and tactical battlefield weapons, no one doubted that mutual obliteration would be the fate of both countries – and most likely Europe as well – should a nuclear exchange begin. The Cold War had reached a confounding stalemate.

Seeking a way out

The convergence of a number of factors motivated each side to exercise restraint while working toward a resolution of the un-winnable nuclear arms race. The fate of Germany had been a constant irritant since 1945. The first Chancellor of West Germany, Konrad Adenauer, was a staunch anticommunist who refused to re-cognize the sovereignty of East Germany and who would only discuss reunification on the basis of free elections. Tensions eased in the mid-1960s after Willy Brandt became foreign minister and then, in 1969, Chancellor. Brandt concluded treaties with the Soviets recognizing the division of Germany in return for freer access between East and West Berlin, and both East and West Germany became member states of the UN in 1974. By the early 1970s it was becoming apparent to American policymakers that the specter of communist world revolution directed from Moscow was a myth. The Sino-Soviet split; the strained relationship between Moscow and its communist satellites in Eastern Europe; the anti-Soviet posture of communist Yugoslavia; all illustrated the fact that nationalism and ethnic identity were every bit as powerful in the communist world as the call to international working-class solidarity. In addition, emergent communist and nonaligned states in Africa and South Asia were likely to be suspicious of Soviet aid if it implied political subservience to Moscow.

On the other side of the ideological divide, Soviet fear of America's military power was allayed by US reverses in the Vietnam conflict. By 1975 all three Indochinese countries – Vietnam, Cambodia, and Laos – had communist governments. In addition, Soviet anxiety over NATO and America's dominant role in that alliance abated in 1966 when the French withdrew their forces from this major Western military pact. The unwillingness of the NATO allies to contest a Soviet crackdown in Czechoslovakia in 1968 indicated to the Kremlin, now under the leadership of Leonid Brezhnev, that the status quo in Eastern Europe was secure. Under the so-called Brezhnev Doctrine, the Soviets stated their right to interfere in the internal affairs of other socialist states if the survival of those states was threatened. Meant to reaffirm Moscow's position on the status of Eastern Europe, the Brezhnev Doctrine was in fact a tacit admission that the Soviets had more to fear from their own communist subordinates than they did from the capitalist world. Western European states clearly wanted improved relations, not confrontation, with their Eastern bloc neighbors.

Limiting weapons

In 1963 the first British, American, and Russian agreement on nuclear weapons banned testing in the atmosphere, under water, and in outer space. Five years later, in response to growing worldwide concern and public pressure for action, most of the world's nations agreed to a comprehensive nuclear nonproliferation treaty. Those already in the nuclear club pledged not to assist other countries seeking these weapons. Although weakened by the refusal of India, Pakistan, Israel, South Africa, Brazil, and Argentina to sign the treaty, the two superpowers not only signed but agreed to hold future talks on limiting strategic arms. When Richard Nixon became the first American president to visit Moscow in 1972, the groundbreaking Strategic Arms Limitation Treaty (SALT I) was signed. It limited the deployment of defensive missile systems to each nation's capital city and their IBM sites. The treaty also placed numerical caps on certain types of intercontinental ballistic missiles, intermediate range missiles, and strategic bombers. Surveillance satellites were deployed successfully over both countries in order to verify compliance, and in an agreement reached at Vladivostok in 1975, the terms of SALT I were extended. Another SALT agreement was reached between Brezhnev and President Jimmy Carter in June 1979, but Carter withdrew the treaty from Senate consideration in the wake of the Soviet invasion of Afghanistan in December of that year.

The high-water mark of detente occurred in 1975, when representatives of the leading Western states and their communist counterparts met at the Helsinki Conference on Security and Cooperation in Europe (CSCE). In the final Helsinki Agreement, representatives from the Eastern bloc secured recognition of the legitimacy of existing borders across the continent. Each signatory acknowledged the inviolability of existing states in Europe and pledged noninterference in the affairs of its neighbors. In return, the West gained from the communist countries, including the Soviet Union, an admission that civil and political liberties were essential to just government. Enhanced East–West economic and cultural contacts were endorsed, and even when tensions between the US and the Soviet Union increased, as they did immediately after the Soviet invasion of Afghanistan, the gradual rapprochement between the two Europes continued.

Soviet weaknesses

During the 1950s and 1960s, the Soviet Union and its Eastern bloc satellites had undergone significant economic transformation. The centrally planned and highly bureaucratic communist economies emphasized heavy industry, military hardware, energy, and transportation projects, all of which brought millions of people into the cities. The successes were undeniable but limited in scope. The Soviet Union had become a formidable rival to the US in terms of its technological abilities and its military prowess, but by the 1970s it became increasingly apparent that military and industrial power had been achieved at the cost of forgoing improvements in the domestic consumer sector. The Soviet system lacked flexibility, local initiative, and the ability to innovate. Economic decisions were most often made by central planners in Moscow who were insensitive to problems on the factory floor, while weaknesses in the distribution system and inefficiencies in the workplace hampered quality and output levels. Workers in industry who were guaranteed jobs for life had little incentive to excel when rewards were not linked to productivity – not that higher wages mattered a great deal in an economy where consumer goods were in short supply and of poor quality. The same inefficiencies plagued the agricultural sector, where massive collective farms were so unproductive that the Soviets were obliged to import grain from the West. And with the exception of minerals and military hardware, the export market for shoddy Soviet-made goods was minuscule. Only the Party elite enjoyed ready access to better-quality Western consumer goods, a state of affairs that led to growing cynicism and disdain for the communist system.

In the decade before his death in 1982, Soviet premier Leonid Brezhnev offered neither vision nor constructive solutions to the domestic dilemma. Convinced that America was on the wane as a great power in the wake of Vietnam and Nixon's resignation under fire in 1974, Brezhnev felt emboldened to assist Marxist insurgencies in Angola and Ethiopia (see Chapter 2). The development of Russia's vast oil reserves and the robust sale of petroleum to the West during the 1970s helped to sustain an otherwise inefficient economy and fund Marxist rebels in Africa, but prices began to slump in the early 1980s. In 1979 Brezhnev plunged the Soviet military into Afghanistan, ostensibly to prop up the new communist regime there, but the conflict quickly degenerated into a nasty guerrilla conflict similar to the American experience in Vietnam. Over 100,000 Russian troops were sent to fight the Afghan rebels who, with generous assistance from the American CIA, effectively frustrated the Soviets for ten years and added to the strain on the struggling Soviet economy. In the wake of the Afghanistan invasion, President Carter stopped all American grain shipments to Russia, forbade the export of high technology, and prevented American athletes from participating in the 1980 Olympic Games hosted by Moscow. Closer to home, another challenge to Soviet influence in Eastern Europe erupted in neighboring Poland, when in 1980 striking workers, supported by the Catholic Church, founded the Solidarity free labor movement. After a year of indecision, the Polish communist government under General Wojciech Jaruzelski declared martial law, outlawed the Solidarity movement, and reaffirmed its close ties with the Soviet Union. Brezhnev was succeeded by two equally uninventive and elderly leaders, Yuri Andropov (1982–84) and Konstantin Chernenko (1984–5), neither of whom was able to extricate Soviet forces from the Afghan debacle. Dissident voices within the Soviet Union continued to be silenced, but the heavy hand of the state was unable to manufacture confidence in a regime that seemed unable to improve the lives of its citizens.

Detente in shambles

When a new American administration under the leadership of President Ronald Reagan took office in January 1981, the rhetoric of Cold War confrontation returned and bilateral relations worsened. Reagan referred to the Soviet Union as an "evil empire" that (against the evidence) remained committed to world domination. Soon after the crackdown in Poland, the US banned the export of equipment that was essential to the USSR's massive Siberian oil-pipeline project. Construction of the pipeline, the largest construction undertaking in Soviet history, was designed to provide energy to Western European states in return for technology and desperately needed hard currency. Now the US was intent upon undermining the entire enterprise, much to the chagrin of its allies in Western Europe. American military spending intensified sharply under Reagan, especially on research for a proposed missile defense system that critics dubbed "Star Wars," and which the Soviets argued was in violation of SALT I. Relations reached a low ebb in September 1983 when a Russian fighter jet shot down a Korean Airlines jumbo jet en route from New York to Seoul that had strayed into Soviet air space over Sakhalin Island. Two hundred and sixty-nine passengers were killed, including a US congressman. Instead of apologizing, Soviet authorities alleged that the 747 was actually a spy plane, an untenable position that led the Reagan administration to ratchet up the "evil empire" rhetoric. Even before the airline tragedy, Chernenko had stated at a meeting of the Communist Party Congress that the Americans were focusing "attacks of an unprecedented scale on our social system and Marxist–Leninist ideology" and that capitalism and communism "are waging an intense and truly global struggle."

During the winter of 1983–4, the Soviet leadership feared that Reagan might follow up his tough rhetoric with rash action. Concern over the possibility of an American surprise attack, although misplaced, was very much on the minds of the men in the Kremlin. On the symbolic Olympic front, Moscow reciprocated America's 1980 decision and withdrew from the 1984 Los Angeles games. As more and more resources were dedicated to the rekindled Cold War, living conditions in the USSR tumbled, a black market economy emerged under the protection of corrupt state officials, and the fabric of everyday life began to unravel for millions of people who had lost faith in the promise of communism. Even the Soviet Union's scientific and technological prowess was undermined when, in 1986, a nuclear accident at the Chernobyl power plant forced the evacuation of thousands of Ukrainians from their homes. Average life expectancy for Soviet women and men actually fell during the 1970s and early 1980s. When the leaders of the Central Committee of the Communist Party selected 55-year-old Mikhail Gorbachev to succeed Chernenko, the country's social and economic problems were both deep and widespread. The historian Jonathan Becker has written that since "the Soviet state itself emerged on the promise of social and economic progress, the legitimacy of the state and thus the unifying strength of the Soviet identity were to a large extent contingent on performance." And on this measure alone the Soviet experiment had failed miserably. For Gorbachev and his advisors, ending the Cold War with the US became both a political priority and an economic imperative.

Gorbachev and Reagan

Gorbachev moved quickly to replace Andrei Gromyko, who had been the USSR's hard-line foreign minister since 1957, with a close ally, Eduard Shevardnadze. Within three years, Soviet–American relations were recast. Gorbachev met Reagan in Geneva soon after the new Soviet leader assumed office, and this was followed by a second meeting in Reykjavik, Iceland in October 1986. Negotiations between the two leaders and their advisors continued apace, and in December 1987 both sides agreed to eliminate their stockpiles of intermediate-range nuclear weapons, many of which had been deployed in Europe during the early 1980s. And Gorbachev became the first Soviet leader to agree to on-site inspections designed to verify compliance. Speaking before the UN in December 1988, Gorbachev announced additional cuts in Soviet conventional forces and echoed the American call for a new era in foreign relations. Finally, in 1989 the Red Army was recalled from Afghanistan, putting an end to both a major drain on resources and a sharp ideological conflict with the Americans. In December, 1989, within weeks of the fall of the Berlin Wall, the new American president, George H. W. Bush, met with Gorbachev on a Soviet ship off the coast of Malta, and both men declared an end to the Cold War. Reflecting on those years of dangerous rivalry, Gorbachev confessed that "the reliance on force, on military superiority and the arms race that stemmed from it, did not withstand the test. And our two countries seem to realize it better than anyone else. To no avail was the ideological confrontation which kept us busy maligning each other. We reached a dangerous brink. And it is good that we managed to stop."

The change in bilateral relations over a few short years was remarkable. The staunchly anticommunist Reagan and the career Communist Party member Gorbachev established a frank and cordial working relationship, and this carried over into the Bush presidency. Even Britain's conservative Prime Minister, Margaret Thatcher, spoke highly of Gorbachev's abilities and of his desire to forge a new East–West relationship that was based on a recognition of common global interests. Gorbachev and his principal advisors wished to save the Soviet system, not undermine it, but they had come to the conclusion that the first step in this process lay in a drastic reduction of military spending. Only then could the Soviet

Union attract foreign investment and prompt domestic economic development. For his part, Reagan came to see the Soviet people in a different light thanks to his personal interactions with the new leaders in the Kremlin. Abandoning the "evil empire" bombast, the president gradually learned to appreciate the enormous sacrifices of the Soviet people during World War II, the aspirations of common Russians for a better quality of life, their concern (after the Chernobyl nuclear disaster) for the health of the environment, and their desire to put a stop to the senseless arms race. When Gorbachev made the momentous decision to lift the oppressive mantle of Soviet control in Eastern Europe, he was inviting both Europeans and Americans to revisit the failures of statesmen in 1945, to imagine a road not taken by the victors as they entered the city of Berlin. The metamorphosis of Soviet foreign policy was driven largely by a realistic appraisal of domestic dereliction, corruption, and incompetence, but it was not without its worthy side, a determination to make decisions based on elemental human aspirations, not tired ideology.

POWER AND PRINCIPLE

Committed first and foremost to abridging the expansionist drive thought to be inherent in capitalism and communism, respectively, both sides in the early Cold War discourse pursued their respective strategic goals with a signal disregard for the ideals that were purportedly embodied in their individual systems. On the Soviet, Chinese, North Korean, North Vietnamese, and Cuban side, the quest for a social and economic order devoid of exploitation and class conflict was forfeited in the name of party discipline, military preparedness, and the cult of leadership. The Marxian ideal of the classless society, one where human potential would at last be realized under conditions of genuine majority rule, was repeatedly sacrificed to accommodate the territorial and nationalist ambitions of the leadership elite. The very concept of the nation-state, so anathema to the Marxist ideal of international proletarian solidarity, emerged as the central focus of the communist bloc. The strained relations that emerged within the family of communist states after 1945, and in particular the embittered relations between the Soviet Union and China, bore witness to this awkward reality.

On the other side of the ideological divide, the US advertised itself as the defender of the Enlightenment tradition of liberalism, including the defense of individual liberty, the rule of law, government by consent, and national self-determination. Along with their West European allies, the Americans claimed the moral high ground over the Soviets by virtue of their respect for the will of the majority and the right of minorities to dissent without hindrance. Unfortunately, as Cold War suspicions intensified, and in particular as policymakers in the US interpreted nationalist revolts through the lens of containment theory, alliances predicated solely on a state's anticommunist credentials undermined America's reputation throughout the developing world. From Korea and Southeast Asia in the Pacific theater, to Guatemala and Nicaragua in Central America, the US adopted a policy of propping up undemocratic and sometimes brutal regimes in the interest of anticommunist solidarity.

Historians have differed widely over the origins of the Cold War. Some have asserted that the discord between the Soviet Union and the US after the defeat of fascism was the predictable outcome of great power relations. Throughout the course of the human experience major kingdoms and empires have tended to suspect each other, and while occasionally avoiding direct hostilities, rivalry and rhetorical sparring are simply part of the culture of distrust inherent in relations between states. What may appear to be essential to the defense needs of one side often strikes the other as insidious expansionism, while the formation of extensive alliance systems and friendship pacts merely serves to heighten the collective anxiety of the other side. Other scholars have defined the postwar US–Soviet antagonism in terms of the power of ideology to shape human action. In the West, many scholars lay the blame for the conflict squarely on the shoulders of Stalin. The Soviet dictator's paranoid fear of encirclement, combined with a longer tradition of Russian expansionism, determined the fate of postwar Eastern Europe and set the stage for decades of communist meddling and coercion in Asia, Africa, the Middle East, and Latin America. Revisionist historians have taken a very different approach, arguing that America's governing elite, convinced that democracy and free enterprise were under immediate threat, took a series of provocative steps against the Soviets, steps that obliged Stalin to respond in a manner that only served to intensify American apprehension. Without these provocations, revisionist scholars claim, the intensely pragmatic Stalin would have been less adventuresome, less apt to encourage communist revolution elsewhere around the globe. Mediating these two perspectives is difficult, even one decade after the end of the ideological conflict. During the Cold War, scholars were denied access to Soviet and Eastern bloc sources, thus every interpretation was at best incomplete. The work of examining recently opened archives continues and may shed new light on the Soviet perspective.

A few points can be made with some certainty, however. In 1945 two antithetical systems of political, social, and economic organization, both revolutionary in terms of the long sweep of global history, each viewed the collapse of Nazi totalitarianism and the end of colonial empires as an opportunity to rebuild along new paths of human organization. For the 200-year-old liberal democratic revolutionaries, humanity's best hope centered on the primacy of the individual. Freedom to pursue one's material goals in a market economy, to seek social change within a democratic polity, to differ from one's neighbor under conditions of free expression, both civil and religious – these were the benchmarks of civilized living; these were the inalienable rights for which so many millions had already sacrificed their lives during the bloodiest half-century in history.

For the more recent Marxist revolutionaries, the promises of liberal capitalism, of markets, of individualism, all rang hollow in light of the ongoing pattern of class conflict and economic inequality which characterized societies spawned by the Enlightenment project. According to this worldview, true human dignity and material sufficiency would never be achieved under the umbrella of liberal capitalism. Lenin had identified the natural tendency of capitalist states to foster a competitive culture which in the end would consume all of its proponents. For true believers in the communist model, it was time to escape from the grip of a system whose inherent dynamic was to guarantee the misery of the majority. The dialectic of great power rivalry, of ideological confrontation, informed not only military decisions, but also shaped economic priorities on both sides. It fostered what President Eisenhower lamented as the "military-industrial complex" in the West, and denied Soviet citizens a genuine consumer sector as Stalin doggedly pursued military parity with the US. Both sides were diminished in the process, no more so than in their failure to honor the aspirations embodied in the founding ideas of their respective systems.

2

THE END OF EMPIRE AND THE PROBLEM OF NEOCOLONIALISM

KEY TOPICS

Decolonization and its discontents
The South Asian precedent
Africa's hope and misfortune
Anticolonialism and nationalism
   in the Middle East

Southeast Asia
The overlooked empire: Russia
Assessing the colonial legacy

DECOLONIZATION AND ITS DISCONTENTS

In terms of the long sweep of world history, the period of Western colonial empire was relatively brief, although its economic, cultural, political, and intellectual impact on the global community was, and continues to be, enormous. Beginning in the late fifteenth century with Spanish and Portuguese claims in Central and South America and continuing (if we include the breakup of the Soviet Union) until the final decade of the twentieth century, the British, Dutch, Belgians, French, Germans, Spanish, Portuguese, Russians, and Americans built powerful imperial regimes that touched every continent and forged a series of dependent relationships that clearly advantaged the colonizer. A amalgam of power and ideology undergirded the West's physical occupation of large portions of the globe during these centuries, and it was a combination of European weakness, the spread of nationalist ideology to colonial peoples, and superpower opposition to traditional forms of colonialism that brought about the downfall of most territorial empires after 1945.

When compared with the decades, and in some cases centuries, involved in building these colonial possessions, the process of political and military decolonization occurred quite rapidly. By 1985, after a series of liberation struggles and peaceful negotiations, more than 80 non-Western countries had achieved political independence, and by the end of the twentieth century less than 0.1 percent of humans lived in territories ruled externally by foreigners. The withdrawal was all the more surprising in light of the fact that in 1945 nearly one-third of the world's population, some 750 million people, lived under the political control of a foreign, and predominantly European, power. And despite their weakened state in the aftermath of World War II, none of these powers was keen to withdraw from empire; if anything, the preservation of overseas colonies was thought to be key to Europe's postwar economic recovery. In many cases the controlling state was more than willing to use force in order to retain control over its overseas and transcontinental possessions. The Dutch in Indonesia, the French in Vietnam and Algeria, and the Portuguese in Angola and Mozambique all used their military in unsuccessful attempts to preserve their imperial ascendancy.

In large measure former colonial territories became sovereign nation-states in the three decades after the war, each striving for political stability and economic well-being in a global economy that was increasingly dominated by industrialized Western nations. Colonies that managed to secure independence in a peaceful manner typically began as constitutional republics, led by indigenous Western-educated rulers who could be trusted to protect foreign investment and established trade relations, as in India, or who agreed to strategic military partnerships, as in the Philippines, where the Americans were afforded long-term leases on key military installations. Most importantly, the vast majority of postcolonial states remained firmly within the worldwide capitalist system, trading with and borrowing from the developed West. First World development aid, for example, was often tied to the purchase of goods and services from the donor country, thereby creating a generous subsidy for companies in the developed states. And Third World economic diversification – key to building a balanced economy – was made more difficult as the sale of labor-intensive cash crops and raw materials became the principal means of servicing development loans from Western banks.

Neocolonialism

Whether or not political decolonization was synonymous with genuine national autonomy remains a contentious issue in scholarly circles. In the estimation of some critics, traditional territorial empire was replaced after World War II by a neocolonial relationship in which former colonies, now developing nation-states, were handicapped both by international economic forces that privileged developed countries, and by the extension of Western political and cultural forms that disparaged tradition and local practices. Many indigenous leaders in the Third World complained that political freedom after 1945 did not translate into true economic or cultural independence. Nominally sovereign nations in South, Southeast, and East Asia, together with Africa, struggled against enormous odds to improve the quality of life for their citizens against the backdrop of decades in which colonial economic development was distorted to fit the needs of the metropolitan power. Although many of these new states began as multiparty constitutional republics, their ongoing economic dependency undermined the credibility of democratic practice and led to a demoralizing pattern of military coups and authoritarian rule. By the close of the twentieth century, the income disparity between residents of First and Third World countries continued to widen, with poverty, overpopulation, and political disorder the common lot of many postcolonial states. It is within this context that critics caution us against thinking of decolonization as the inevitable result of the spread of democratic ideals after the defeat of Nazi aggression and Japanese militarism. Support for territorial empire remained a defensible political position in the democratic West as long as colonies were viewed as strategic and economic assets.

Empire as anachronism

Before World War II, there was broad consensus in the West respecting the appropriateness of white control over "inferior" black, brown, and yellow peoples. The pace of imperial conquest quickened after 1870 as industrially advanced European states like Germany, Britain, and France competed for ascendancy over less-developed but resource-rich areas of the globe. Imperialist ideology, buttressed by much pseudobiological thought, claimed that the white race had an inherent right to occupy foreign lands, if only in the interest of "progress." But control was predicated on the acquiescence, cooperation, or disunity of subject peoples whose productive capacity was dedicated to the service of the metropolitan power. In the European popular imagination, a handful of selfless imperial administrators, soldiers, businessmen, and missionaries brought the benefits of civilization to benighted millions in Africa, Asia, South Asia, the Caribbean, and the Middle East. They supervised the building of roads and railways, provided medical care, encouraged healthy trade relations, established schools and colleges, introduced the truths of Christianity, and maintained order and good government through willing surrogates. Their indigenous allies might eventually be capable of self-government at the local level, but genuine equality in a world of competitive nation-states was unlikely. By the start of World War I, Europeans held direct or indirect influence over 80 percent of the earth's land surface, and the expectation was that colonial empires would last for a very long time.

Europe's ascendancy over its far-flung colonies was impaired after World War I, even as new territories in the Middle East were brought under the administrative control of the British and French. American President Woodrow Wilson's insistence that the war was a noble conflict to "make the world safe for democracy," while simultaneously advancing the cause of national self-determination, carried great weight with colonial peoples who had fought alongside their imperial masters during the war. They witnessed the breakup of the Hapsburg, Hohenzollern, and Romanov empires and the formation of new states in their wake, and they saw former German colonies in Africa and the Pacific handed over to League of Nations supervision. But Wilson's rhetoric carried less weight with America's victorious European allies, none of whom reversed their long-standing colonial policies. Indeed the British and the French extended their overseas commitments after 1918, taking charge of

Muslim lands formally controlled by the Ottoman empire in the Middle East. And the new Bolshevik government in Russia reasserted the prerogatives of the tsars when it triumphed in a protracted civil war that was marked by breakaway movements throughout the empire.

World War II as catalyst

The end of political colonialism was the result of many factors, but the impact of World War II on European power was decisive. With few exceptions, states like France, Britain, and the Netherlands simply lacked the economic and military resources needed for the maintenance of overseas empire in the face of growing opposition both at home and in the colonies. The rapidity with which the Japanese had expelled the white imperialists from Vietnam, Malaya, Burma, the Philippines, and the Dutch East Indies during the early years of World War II bolstered nationalist aspirations throughout the colonial world. And although Japanese "liberation" turned out to be even more onerous than Western control, at the end of the war there was an expectation among many indigenous elites that independence was a logical next step, especially since the Japanese had announced plans for greater autonomy under an East Asian "coprosperity sphere."

Nationalist sentiment was also bolstered by the 1941 "Atlantic Charter" between the US and Great Britain, which called for an end to territorial expansion at the expense of other peoples, and by the charter of the newly established UN. The latter document called for member states "to take due account of the political aspirations" of all peoples, "and to assist them in the progressive development of their free political institutions, according to the particular circumstances of each territory and its peoples and their varying stages of advancement." In order to accelerate the process of decolonization, in 1960 the UN passed a "Declaration on the Granting of Independence to Colonial Countries and Peoples." This document proclaimed that "the subjection of peoples to alien subjugation, domination and exploitation constitutes a denial of fundamental human rights, is contrary to the United Nations Charter, and is an impediment to the promotion of world peace and cooperation."

With the important exception of the Soviet domination of Eastern Europe, the establishment of new colonial dependencies after 1945 was avoided by the Western powers.

In colonies where the metropolitan power had trained local elites as military officers, judges, and civil servants, the transition to self-rule was comparatively smooth. And where the imperial power invested in the development of the colony's economic and educational infrastructure, the chances for political stability and social order were greatly enhanced. This was the case in many of Britain's Asian colonies, and particularly in India. On the other hand, conditions in the French, Belgian, and Portuguese empires were less propitious. In these colonies little effort was taken to prepare the indigenous population for the demands of nationhood. Even when a small number of elites managed to gain access to education in Europe, they often returned home with a diminished sense of identity with their impoverished neighbors. Lacking that bond, their attempts to forge a common national identity based on geography were largely unsuccessful. In addition, economic development was often distorted in these colonies, with export-driven cash-crop agriculture frustrating efforts to diversify for a domestic market. Postcolonial Africa represents the greatest tragedy under these conditions. Even where the introduction of Western technology successfully reduced infant mortality rates through better hygiene, food and water, and medical care, the absence of appropriate educational opportunities meant that burgeoning birthrates compounded the problems faced by new states whose political leaders had promised a better quality of life after independence. South Asia and sub-Saharan Africa illustrate the two extremes of colonial experience and the range of implications for state sovereignty. For this reason it would be helpful to look at both regions in some detail.

THE SOUTH ASIAN PRECEDENT

India was one of the earliest (after Jordan and the Philippines) and certainly the largest European colony to secure full independence in the postwar era. And it was the first instance of a colonial power surrendering its claim to rule another country without having been defeated militarily. This vast subcontinent, twenty times the size of the British Isles, had been the centerpiece of the world's largest empire for over a century. Bounded on the north by the world's highest mountains, and on the east and west by two great bodies of water, India was a land of multiple languages and dialects, myriad local traditions, and boasted a remarkable history of absorbing new peoples. The birthplace of three great religious traditions (Hinduism, Buddhism, and Sikhism) and host to a fourth (Islam), nationalism was an idea that engaged only a tiny minority of Western-educated Indian elites at the start of the twentieth century; what mattered most to the subcontinent's 300 million people was the life of the village, family, and one's caste obligations.

At one level Indian independence was an enormous success: On August 15, 1947 the new state instantly became the world's most populous democracy, where citizens enjoyed full political rights irrespective of their social, economic, or educational status. And since the 1950s, as the population moved inexorably toward the one billion mark, the country has managed to avoid the tragic descent into military dictatorship that has become the lot of so many postcolonial states. As a multiethnic, multilingual country whose hundreds of distinct cultural and linguistic traditions might point toward political fragmentation, India has been a model of successful inclusion under civilian rule.

From another perspective, however, independence brought great sadness to South Asia, since it was achieved through a bloodstained partition of the subcontinent into two mutually hostile states, India and Pakistan. There have been three wars and innumerable border clashes between these nuclear-armed neighbors since 1947, and as precious financial resources have been dedicated to their respective military establishments, acute domestic-sector needs, especially in the social services, have been neglected. Pakistan in particular has betrayed the ideals of its founders, slipping into the turmoil of military rule in 1958 and remaining in that condition more or less since the 1950s. In 1971 a secession movement in East Pakistan led to civil war and the eventual formation of a fourth country on the subcontinent, Bangladesh (the island nation of Ceylon, or Sri Lanka since 1972, is the third).

Colonial legacies

English commercial interest in South Asia began at the same time that the first English settler colonies were established in North America. As the once powerful Mughal empire began to fracture in the 1700s, the East India Company assumed a large and unprecedented role in the political life of the subcontinent. By the start of the nineteenth century, what was ostensibly an international trading company was deriving most of its profits from the collection of taxes in the northwest province of Bengal. After a serious rebellion against the East India Company in 1857, the government of Queen Victoria assumed direct political control over the subcontinent. The crown encouraged the recruitment and training of high-caste Indians for employment at lower levels of imperial administration and undertook to enhance the transportation infrastructure of the country. The primary goal of these efforts was increased trade revenue. In the half-century beginning with the 1857 takeover, India provided key raw materials (especially cotton) for factories in Britain, absorbed British manufactured goods and investment capital, furnished inexpensive troops for the British military, and served as a strategic base for the projection of British power in Asia. By the start of World War I, British interests controlled all of India's principal economic activities, including tea and jute production, mining, banking, and shipping. So great was British control over the economic life of the subcontinent that Jawaharlal Nehru, the future first Prime Minister of independent India, wrote from his British jail cell in the 1940s that the metropolitan center had successfully "deindustrialized" India by imposing punitive tariff policies that prevented the growth of native manufactures.

Colonial government in India was conducted very much on the cheap. Across two-thirds of the subcontinent, a tiny number of highly trained Indian Civil Service officers (all of whom were British) supervised over half a million local Indian administrators at the provincial and village levels. In the remaining third of the country, regional Indian princes continued to rule as subordinates of the resident British Viceroy. The Indian military and law enforcement followed the same model – local recruits led at the highest levels by Britons. Collaboration, not coercion, was the key to imperial rule in South Asia, and later independence leaders like Mohandas Gandhi recognized that any change in the political status quo required a basic change in Indian consciousness, in particular a willingness to refuse further cooperation with British authorities.

The British had ample experience with colonial independence movements; the US secured its freedom from London in the late eighteenth century; Canada, Australia, and New Zealand followed in the nineteenth century; and South Africa won the right to selfgovernment in the early years of the twentieth century. But these were white settler colonies whose governing elite, educated into British habits of thought, could be viewed as safe alternatives to direct rule from London. Granting independence to colonies that had been under the control of a tiny minority of white administrators, in a land where few Britons chose to relocate, was another matter. There was a small Western-educated Indian elite centered in cities like Bombay, Calcutta, and Madras, and it was these men who, beginning in the late nineteenth century, assumed the mantle of leadership in the struggle to secure a greater voice in the government of their homeland. The establishment of the Indian National Congress in 1885, endorsed by the British, provided a platform for educated Indians from largely urban areas to voice their concerns in a peaceful manner. Although the doctors, lawyers, teachers, and journalists who were active in the Congress did not wish to forge a mass movement that would usher in sweeping social change, they did view themselves as the natural leaders of India's impoverished millions. Muslims were both welcome and active in the Congress during its early years, but in 1905 a separate Muslim League was established – again with British encouragement – to represent the interests of one-quarter of India's population.

India and the world wars

Most of India's indigenous leaders, including Gandhi, had supported the crown during World War I. Indian troops fought bravely in a number of theaters, including East Africa, the Middle East, and the Western Front, and in 1917 the crown indicated that it favored a move toward "responsible government," something akin to home rule. But a postwar crackdown against peaceful opponents of empire led to increasing calls for noncooperation with the imperial government. The leaders of the Congress Party recognized that they could not wrest power from the British without broad-based support, and it was at this juncture that Mohandas Gandhi provided that essential linkage between the indigenous political elite and the common people. Gandhi was from a merchant-caste family and had received a Western-style education in India. After studying law in London, he moved to South Africa and took up the cause of poor Indian laborers who faced discrimination under the entrenched white minority government. Returning to India in 1915, Gandhi adopted an ascetic lifestyle and advocated for change through *satyagraha*, or "soul force." In particular, Gandhi and his followers employed the tactic of nonviolent resistance combined with the use of boycotts, strikes, and noncooperation to effect change in British policies. In the early 1920s Gandhi became a leader in the Congress movement. The largely high-caste leadership of the Congress supported Gandhi's nonviolent tactics because it feared the sort of violent guerrilla resistance to British rule that, if successful, might also threaten India's traditional elite. A new Government of India Act was passed by Parliament in 1935, creating representative assemblies at the provincial and national levels, and limiting the Viceroy's authority to defense and foreign affairs. It appeared to some in the Congress Party that the peaceful, gradualist approach to independence was bearing fruit.

During World War II the British, who had unilaterally announced that India too was at war with Germany, promised full autonomy for India, but only after the end of the conflict. Fearing that no concessions might trigger mass revolt in India and a possible Japanese takeover, the British could ill afford a wartime crisis in their largest colony. Despite the fact that approximately two million Indians volunteered to serve in the war, the Congress Party leaders were furious that they had not been consulted on the decision to go to war and insisted that autonomy come before any pledge of Indian support for the military effort. When the government rejected this application in 1942, the Congress passed a "Quit India Resolution," demanding immediate independence. The imperial response was heavy-handed: The Congress Party was outlawed, its leadership (including Gandhi and Nehru) jailed for the duration of the war, and all forms of dissent stifled. Thousands of Indians living in Southeast Asia, including a former Congress Party leader, Subhas Chandra Bose, allied themselves with the Japanese and fought against the British "occupation" of India. The Muslim League under the leadership of Mohammad Ali Jinnah, on the other hand, offered to support the British war effort, and this decision would work to the League's advantage once the war was over and talks on the future status of the subcontinent resumed in 1945.

The tragedy of partition

The victory of Britain's Labour Party in the national elections of May 1945 elated the leaders of the Congress Party. Clement Attlee's government was committed to independence for India both on grounds of principle and economic self-interest. At the end of the war London owed India millions of pounds for services rendered during the struggle against Germany and Japan. The once favorable trade balance with India had been reversed, while the cost of maintaining Britain's administrative and military structure in South Asia placed an intolerable burden on the shattered postwar domestic economy. When captured officers of Bose's army were put on trial for treason in Delhi during the winter of 1945–6, defense attorneys (including Jawaharlal Nehru) skillfully portrayed the men as daring nationalists and patriots. Each of the accused was given a suspended sentence, but not before the Royal Indian navy mutinied in Bombay harbor and some members of the Royal Indian Air force refused to obey direct orders. The time to bring an end to empire in South Asia was clearly at hand, but Attlee's government was eager to withdraw from India knowing that a stable and democratic successor state was in control, that the country would not descend into anarchy.

It would not be an easy task. Hindus and Muslims had lived together in India for centuries. The Muslim population was concentrated in the northwest province of Punjab and in Bengal in the northeast, but no region of the country was entirely Hindu or Muslim. While clashes between the two communities had increased during the first half of the twentieth century, Gandhi, Nehru, and the other leaders of the Congress Party believed that the best solution to the problem of religious intolerance was the erection of a single, nonsectarian polity where all faith traditions would be respected. Since the 1930s Jinnah's Muslim League had been demanding the creation of either a loose federation of Muslim and Hindu states or two distinct countries on the subcontinent. The leaders of the League were convinced that despite the inclusive views of Nehru and Gandhi, Muslims would be discriminated against in a Hindu-dominated India.

Elections were held in 1946 to choose leaders to an assembly that would negotiate terms of independence from Britain, but after it became clear that Hindus had won a majority in every province, Jinnah called upon India's 95 million Muslims to engage in a day of "Direct Action" involving strikes and street demonstrations. It was a *de facto* call to violence, and frustrated elements of the Muslim community responded with vigor. Riots and atrocious killings took place across the country during the late summer and fall of 1946; in Calcutta alone communal violence led to the deaths of approximately 6000 civilians. British troops intervened in an effort to stem the violence, and Gandhi – at great personal risk – set out on foot in Bengal to appeal for calm.

Frustrated and alarmed by the escalating violence, Attlee's government set down an ultimatum: The British would withdraw from India by June 1948, and they would leave irrespective of the conditions on the ground. Neither the Congress leaders nor their Muslim League counterparts welcomed this statement because their own positions were at risk should anarchy prevail in the absence of British military assistance. The last British Viceroy, Lord Louis Mountbatten, arrived in New Delhi in March 1947 and quickly pushed up the British exit date to August of that same year. In difficult negotiations with both Jinnah and Nehru, partition was agreed, much to the sorrow of Gandhi, who viewed separation as a surrender to the forces of sectarianism and communal division.

Over the next two months, while negotiators worked frantically to divide up the material resources of a nation, communal violence skyrocketed. As Muslim refugees (sometimes whole villages) fled north across Punjab province into what would become Pakistan, panicked Hindus retreated south by train and on foot. The vulnerable refugees were attacked mercilessly by gangs of religious fanatics. It is estimated that more than a quarter of a million men, women, and children (some estimates are closer to one million) were massacred as they left their homes in despair. Another 17 million people became refugees, their status made more desperate by the fact that neither fledgling government was prepared to handle such an enormous humanitarian crisis. Gandhi again tried to staunch the killing, this time in Calcutta, by declaring a fast to the death in September 1947. In this sprawling city with a population equally divided between Muslims and Hindus, the Mahatma was able to diffuse tensions in the short term. But within four months he too was dead, gunned down by a Hindu fanatic in the capital city of Delhi.

Enduring conflict

The intensity of the communal violence that occurred during the lead up to independence served to embitter bilateral relations between the two countries from then on. And while a boundary commission under the direction of Sir Cyril Radcliffe attempted to be impartial, it was unavoidable that Sikhs and Hindus would find themselves an instant minority in Pakistan. The most serious boundary disagreement involved the Himalayan province of Jammu and Kashmir. Soon after independence on August 14–15, 1947, the two governments clashed over this territory. Although a majority Muslim province, the Maharaja was Hindu, and Nehru (who was from a prominent Kashmiri family) was not about to let this region fall into the hands of Pakistan. When the Maharaja opted to join India in October, Pakistani forces moved swiftly toward the capital of Srinagar. The Indian army was immediately dispatched to Kashmir, and armed clashes intensified into undeclared war. The fighting continued until January 1949, when the UN negotiated a ceasefire and called for a plebiscite in the disputed Himalayan province. India refused to allow the plebiscite to go forward, and the disputed territory has remained a source of acute tension between the two countries to this day.

Nonalignment

While a number of South and East Asian countries (including Pakistan) became members of the US-sponsored Southeast Asia Treaty Organization in 1954, Nehru was determined to remain neutral in the Cold War struggle. Serving as his own foreign minister, he encouraged other newly independent nations to join with India in rejecting the embryonic bipolar world order. Nehru skillfully negotiated trade agreements with the West and secured crucial development aid from the US, while simultaneously accepting Soviet technical assistance on a variety of state projects. Unfortunately, Pakistan did not share this neutralist perspective. In 1954 the Eisenhower administration began to provide military aid to Pakistan, an act that India interpreted as unfriendly. The Pakistanis willingly cooperated with the US in its policy of containment, while India sought to maintain cordial relations with both China and the Soviet Union. American Secretary of State Dulles characterized Nehru's nonaligned movement as immoral, while India's efforts at the UN to have the People's Republic of China recognized as the legitimate representative of the Chinese people further alienated American policymakers.

After 1958, when Pakistan's constitutional democracy broke down, the US found itself committed to an antidemocratic military government on the subcontinent while its bilateral relations with the world's largest democracy continued to deteriorate. The estrangement abated momentarily in 1962, after Chinese troops crossed the border in the northeast and northwest and routed Indian forces stationed there. The attack was a fatal blow to Nehru's earlier policy of peaceful coexistence with communist China. In the wake of this humiliation, India requested and received military assistance from Great Britain, the US, Canada, and the Soviet Union. The Congress Party now redoubled efforts to build a military establishment that would guarantee the inviolability of existing borders in the future. After Nehru's death the government tilted closer to the Soviet Union – now undergoing its own estrangement from China. American policymakers concluded that an incipient Moscow–Delhi alliance was underway and proceeded to strengthen its partnership with Pakistan. When India and Pakistan went to war in 1971, the Nixon administration threw its support behind its ally in Islamabad. Three years later India became a member of the nuclear club, and by the 1990s it had assembled the world's third largest army, totaling over one million men and absorbing 15 percent of the country's overall budget.

Strategic reversals

American support for the military government in Pakistan was driven by Cold War priorities; as arms, economic assistance, and political support were given to this Muslim ally in South Asia, little concern was expressed over the fact that the Islamic Republic of Pakistan had proven a signal failure as a postcolonial democracy. The government in Islamabad played a key intermediary role facilitating the diplomatic reconciliation between the US and China during the early 1970s, and in 1979 it joined with Washington and Beijing in opposition to the Soviet invasion of Afghanistan. Throughout the 1980s Pakistan served as an important conduit for the transfer of US arms and material to Islamic fundamentalist fighters in Afghanistan. Once the Soviets withdrew and the Cold War ended, however, the Americans undertook a reassessment of their unqualified support for the government in Islamabad. In the years since India first tested a nuclear weapon in 1974, their rival to the northwest secretly undertook to develop its own nuclear device. Only in the mid-1980s did the US Congress raise concerns over the prospect of nuclear weapons in the hands of an Islamic military government.

With the collapse of the Soviet Union, decades of American apprehension over possible communist aggression in South Asia evaporated, just as new worries over the growth of Islamic fundamentalism began to focus the attention of diplomats. By 1990 the free flow of US military and economic assistance to Pakistan had come to an end, only to be revived at the start of the twenty-first century as Pakistan again became of strategic importance to Washington. This time the opponent was the Frankenstein monster in Afghanistan, the fundamentalist Taliban regime, whose fighters had been on the receiving end of CIA military assistance and training in the 1980s. Again, the American administration found itself torn between cultivating a stronger economic partnership with democratic India and bankrolling the military government of General Pervez Musharraf, a government increasingly threatened by Islamic militants and one that allegedly proliferated nuclear weapons technology both to the paranoiac communist dictatorship in North Korea and to the fundamentalist anti-American regime in Iran.

Democracy and development

In a moving speech proclaiming India's independence on August 15, 1947, Nehru asserted that "the service of India means the service of the millions who suffer. It means the ending of poverty and ignorance and disease and inequality of opportunity." His words encapsulated the central social vision of nationalists in European colonies around the world. Their demand for independence was anchored in the claim that indigenous leaders of independent states, not imperial administrators, could best provide for the basic material needs of their fellow citizens. Once the yoke of colonialism was broken, the creative energies of self-governing peoples would transform each newly liberated state. In the South Asian states that secured their freedom from Britain after the war – India, Pakistan, and Ceylon – democratic institutions and written constitutions were in place soon after independence. And since both India and Pakistan possessed a large corps of trained civil servants, a sound transportation system, professional military forces, and modest experience in the practice of self-government at the local and provincial levels, the promise of a better life seemed to be within reach.

Serving as Prime Minister and leader of the Congress Party from 1947 until his death in 1964, Nehru struggled to create a nation-state that respected varied regional, linguistic, and religious interests. Although he enjoyed enormous popular support and did not recoil from using force when he believed that national unity was threatened, Nehru did not succumb to the temptation to rule in an authoritarian manner. All but two of the 550 independent princely kingdoms voluntarily ceded their autonomy in return for generous state pensions, and in 1950 a national constitution was adopted. It called for the establishment of a federal structure of government, with cabinet leadership and legislative assemblies at both the national and provincial levels. A supreme court was vested with the power of judicial review. The new central government was responsible for defense, foreign affairs, transportation, currency, and the postal service, while the states took charge of education, police protection, health and sanitation, and agriculture. Nehru reluctantly agreed to the formation of states along linguistic lines. The constitution guaranteed individual civil rights and equality of status and opportunity, and affirmed the principle of universal suffrage in local, provincial, and national elections. In March 1952, the country's first democratic elections took place. One hundred and seventy three million citizens (three-quarters of whom were illiterate) were eligible to vote, and turnout reached a surprising 45.7 percent. Congress emerged victorious in these inaugural elections and remained the most powerful political party in the country for the next 40 years.

As a socialist, Nehru wished to address the problem of massive poverty in India through effective state planning. Given the fact that key supporters of Congress were wealthy landowners, and that three-quarters of India's population lived in impoverished rural areas, the Prime Minister's agenda was daring and ambitious. No attempt was made to expropriate private land, but state control over key sectors of the economy such as steel, gas, electricity, irrigation projects, and transportation infrastructure allowed the government to set the broader economic agenda. In particular, Nehru adopted a set of five-year plans to improve the quality of life through industrialization and agricultural modernization. In a country where the average life expectancy was less than 40 years, improving nutrition was imperative, especially if diseases associated with malnutrition were to be brought under control. The early results of the First Five Year Plan were encouraging, as agricultural yields improved and industrial production rose, but a rapidly expanding population (from 300 million at independence to 700 million in 1970) frustrated government efforts to improve the quality of life through better nutrition and education. Nehru encouraged the adoption of village councils and cooperatives to improve cultivation, but since agricultural policy remained under regional state control, traditional landed elites continued to hamper innovation. Despite the best efforts at rural reconstruction, India continued to import grain, and the specter of famine did not disappear. And while the constitution abolished untouchability and affirmed the equality of persons, the *de facto* power of caste and tradition remained, especially in rural areas.

The government attempted to undermine the caste system by adopting an official policy of positive discrimination (what later became known as affirmative action in the US) that enabled members of the "scheduled castes," or untouchables, to win seats in state and national assemblies, to attend universities, and to compete for government posts at every level. But limited access to training frustrated these efforts. India's commitment to public education at the primary level remained lackluster, and this in turn compounded the problem of population control. As late as the mid-1980s only 3 percent of Gross Domestic Product (GDP) was spent on basic education, while just under 20 percent was dedicated to the military (in Pakistan nearly 40 percent of spending was dedicated to defense). As late as 1990 less than half of India's population was literate, with the vast majority of citizens still living in rural poverty. Not that relocation to the city provided enhanced opportunities; urban infrastructure was fragile at best and unprepared to address the housing and employment needs of new arrivals. Provision for education was a state matter, and while authorities at the central government understood the connection between basic education and population control, no national mandates could be created. A government-sponsored family-planning program was begun in 1952, and the age for legal marriage was raised to 15 in 1955, but funding for the first was modest and enforcement of the latter lax, especially in light of the fact that it clashed with centuries of Hindu child-marriage practice. During the 1960s inroads were made against a number of diseases such as cholera, malaria, and typhoid, but without effective birth-control education these important medical breakthroughs unintentionally served to exacerbate the population problem.

Nehru's daughter Indira Gandhi was elected prime minister in 1964 and served until 1977. She returned to the premiership in 1980 and ruled until her assassination in 1984. During her tenure in office, the government's emphasis on state planning and high protective tariffs led to an increased level of bureaucratization and administrative red tape – what critics referred to as the "permit raj" – and to growing corruption and complacency. A heavy-handed program of birth control alienated traditional Indian society. The dominant Congress Party evolved into a makeshift coalition whose leaders projected themselves as champions of national, as opposed to regional, religious or ethnic interests. By the 1980s, as a number of nations in the Pacific Rim began to deregulate their economies and attract foreign investment thanks to low (chiefly female) labor costs, India was losing its already tiny market share of total world trade, despite the fact that nearly one in every six people on earth was Indian. Only in the 1990s did India begin the process of deregulation and market reform. But while foreign investment, especially in the areas of technology and computer software, helped to strengthen the middle class in some regions of the country, the predicament of population growth continued to frustrate national efforts to improve the quality of life for the vast majority of the nation's population.

AFRICA'S HOPE AND MISFORTUNE

The success of the Indian independence struggle set a powerful precedent for nationalist movements in the rest of the colonial world, and perhaps no more so than in Africa. Despite its proximity to Europe, the vast African continent had remained largely outside of the territorial grip of the Western powers until the 1870s. This was especially true of black sub-Saharan Africa, where the advent of the transatlantic slave trade in the late fifteenth century had generated powerful economic incentives on three separate continents. But the slave trade had not entailed the political subjugation of indigenous kingdoms in West Africa. This occurred only after the end of the nefarious slave trade, when a frenetic "scramble" for Africa was launched by the major European powers. The carve-up was completed within a matter of years, and even after Germany was stripped of its colonial holdings at the end of World War I, the occupation of Africa under Western auspices continued. In 1945 only three African states remained outside of the European sphere of influence: South Africa, Liberia, and Ethiopia. Britain held sway over the largest African empire, followed by France, Germany, Italy, Portugal, and Belgium.

Direct political control, however, wrapped in the rhetoric of white superiority and the need to "assist" benighted Africans, did not translate into meaningful social and economic benefits for subordinated peoples in over 50 colonies. European taxpayers may have applauded the rapid spread of empire before World War I, but they were not prepared to support the use of government funds to improve the quality of life for overseas subjects, especially black Africans. Instead, millions of Africans were obliged to work for European employers in order to pay taxes that were assessed to fund white-dominated colonial administrations. Educational initiatives, where they existed at all, were led by a handful of Christian missionaries. In Britain's Gold Coast colony (Ghana), for example, there were fewer than 40 Western-trained physicians and 25000 secondary school graduates out of a population of over four million in the late 1940s. More telling still, at the start of World War II there were only 400 Africans from all of Britain's sub-Saharan colonies attending universities in the UK.

Similar neglect was evident in all of the European colonies. What mattered was cash-crop farming and the extraction of minerals, often under conditions of forced labor. In West Africa the production and export of peanuts, cocoa, palm oil (used as an industrial lubricant); in the Belgian Congo the export of rubber, copper, and uranium; in South Africa gold and diamonds – these and other products of value to a predominantly Western market became the focus of colonial economic initiatives in Africa – all to the neglect of diversified agriculture for domestic consumption. With respect to the number of urban centers, manufacturing base, transportation and communications infrastructure, levels of literacy, and agricultural productivity, the African continent secured its independence in a less developed condition than any other area under European imperial control. Clearly, each of the great powers developed their colonial relationship on the basis of what could be taken from Africa, with little regard for balanced internal economic development.

Nationalist leaders

Hundreds of thousands of Africans had fought in both world wars, and North Africa became a pivotal battle zone between the Allies and German forces from 1940 until 1943. In addition, Free French forces under Charles de Gaulle found refuge in West Africa during the Nazi occupation of France. While all the imperial powers were loath to let go of their holdings in 1945, during the following decade world opinion, and especially opinion in newly independent Asian and South Asian countries, turned sharply against the

European presence. Some Africans began to speak optimistically about the future of an independent continent that occupied one-fifth of the world's land mass, but nowhere has the postcolonial experience been more troubled; nowhere has the practice of democracy and constitutional government been more fragile.

During the late 1950s and 1960s, over 30 new nation-states were created out of former European holdings on the continent, and by the late 1980s the number had increased to 51 and no African state remained under the control of a foreign power. The Western-educated leaders of these new countries were committed territorial nationalists; they believed that the arbitrary boundaries of colonial states erected by Europeans, with all of their ethnic, religious, and linguistic differences, could be molded into nations where primary allegiance was to a larger territorial entity. However, the task of bridging historic differences and transcending local allegiances to forge a strong sense of national self-consciousness would require unsurpassed political and fiscal management skills, neither of which had been encouraged by imperialists during the colonial era. Whereas India's Western-educated elite had secured access to self-government at the local and provincial levels long before national independence was won, African leaders had been afforded few such opportunities. And whereas India's nationalists could at least claim a certain level of cultural cohesiveness on the basis of two predominant religious traditions, Africa's aspirant leaders could make no such claims. Finally, Africa's economic infrastructure was rudimentary at best, focused on export over domestic needs, and tied inexorably to the vicissitudes of Western capitalist markets.

The roots of instability

Like the members of India's Congress Party in the early twentieth century, Western-educated African elites who led the drive for independence often had more in common with their former colonial masters than with their own impoverished citizenry. They did not embrace nationalism as a vehicle for dramatic social change, as in communist China, but sought instead to enhance their elevated status in a traditional social order. Before 1945 they opposed imperialism because it prevented them from assuming leadership roles in their own countries, not because it failed to provide opportunities for the rural masses. Although they began to reach out to a mass audience as a tactical necessity after independence, they assumed power without any experience of self-rule, and when they were unable to deliver quickly on the promise of economic and social betterment under a democratic polity, constitutional governments gave way before authoritarian rulers and their military backers. Efforts to erect centralized planned economies failed miserably, as export-driven development made it increasingly difficult for agriculture to meet the needs of expanding populations.

In addition, some of the antidemocratic successor regimes were corrupt, their leaders intent on enforcing social order as a prerequisite to their own looting of the public treasury. Power changed hands frequently in these fragile states, with 40 successful insurrections during the 1960s alone in Africa's 30 independent countries. While the civil wars, ethnic conflicts, and military coups continued, the economies of these countries spiraled downwards. Meanwhile their populations burgeoned, civil order crumbled, and malnutrition and epidemics became commonplace. During the 1970s, as the oil shocks dampened Western economies and led to a fall in commodity prices worldwide, Africa's economic relationship with the rest of the developed world deteriorated even further, just as the population across the continent was exploding and as a new scourge, the Aids epidemic, was beginning. By the close of the twentieth century Africa had become a continent of the displaced, home to the largest number of international refugees in the world.

The failure of early efforts to create stable democracies is not surprising in light of the fact that the experience of self-government was denied throughout the colonial period. The majority of poor and uneducated Africans were not politically active above the level of lineage-based communities. The Western nation-state was a meaningless abstraction to traditional peoples, and political loyalties outside of the village setting typically accented the divine power of monarchs. This hierarchical thinking was deepened by decades of colonial rule in which foreigners insisted upon unquestioned obedience, both to indigenous surrogates and to white administrators. In addition, the heavy-handed approach to dissent employed by the imperial powers did not inculcate values associated with the give and take of pluralist democracy. Once in power, African political leaders eager to cultivate a strong sense of national identity found it hard to countenance political opposition that was rooted in ethnic or tribal identity. Authoritarian forms of rule were accepted, even applauded, as soon as it appeared that the parliamentary process could not assure domestic tranquility and economic progress.

Early prospects

In the British and French colonies of sub-Saharan Africa, the process of decolonization was both rapid and relatively peaceful. Especially in colonies that did not contain a significant white settler population, where the prospective leadership elite consisted of a small professional class, and where Western economic penetration was deep enough to ensure a favorable economic relationship after independence, the road to independence was comparatively smooth. In Britain's West African colonies of Gold Coast (1957), Nigeria (1960), Sierra Leone (1962), and Gambia (1965), and in French Morocco and Tunisia, all of these conditions were met. Gold Coast was only the second African colony (after Sudan in 1956) to achieve independence. Renamed Ghana in 1957, the country's charismatic, British- and American-educated leader, Kwame Nkrumah, was a skilled organizer whose Convention People's Party employed strikes and boycotts to win major concessions from the British government in the early 1950s. On independence day in 1957, Nkrumah was joined by many world leaders, including American Vice-President Richard Nixon, as the new nation took its place alongside the world's other sovereign states. There was a heightened sense of hope and excitement for all of Africa at this moment, especially since Ghana's cocoa, hardwood, and mineral-ore exports provided a good foundation for the creation of a diversified and sustainable economy. Postwar demand for African products was high, and Ghana was well positioned to take advantage of this robust trade environment. In addition, Nkrumah had earned a reputation as a leader who looked beyond artificial national boundaries to identify and encourage points of contact among all African peoples. "Freedom brings responsibilities," he noted in his 1959 autobiography, "and our experience can be enriched only by the acceptance of these responsibilities."

African commonalities?

Nkrumah's hope for Africa's future lay in the prospect of greater interstate cooperation. In the early twentieth century, the African-American intellectual W.E.B. Du Bois influenced black African thought with his emphasis on a common African culture. Pan-African conferences involving blacks from both sides of the Atlantic took place during the first half of the century. These meetings fostered belief in a common cultural tradition even when, in fact, historically Africa was a myriad of traditions, customs, and beliefs. In part the experience of imperialism itself was the common touchstone that all Africans could share, and resistance to colonial oppression became the bond that transcended colonial frontiers. The first post-World War II meeting of the Pan-African Congress, held in Manchester, England, proclaimed that Africans would redouble their efforts in the fight for "freedom, democracy and social betterment." In May 1963, after the process of liberation was well underway, a crucial meeting of independent African states was held in the city of Addis Ababa, Ethiopia. Its purpose was to inaugurate a new Pan-African enterprise, the Organization of African Unity. Led by Nkrumah and influenced by the ideas of Du Bois and by the example of Nehru's nonaligned movement, the delegates sought a common strategy that would enhance each new nation's chances for social, economic, and political success.

The territorial boundaries of the new states had been drawn by white colonial officials during the late nineteenth century with scant regard for ethnic and linguistic differences, guaranteeing that future political success could only be secured in a pluralist setting. At the Addis Ababa meeting, heads of state from each country pledged to respect the integrity of existing national frontiers, even though these boundaries had been created by Europeans with little regard for the needs of native cultures. Nkrumah was eager to set the groundwork for a broader African union that would eclipse arbitrary national boundaries and forge a continent-wide political union. Short of such an ambitious goal, he supported the establishment of a transnational military force that would be capable of rebuffing any future foreign aggression while also serving to assist established national governments during periods of civil unrest.

Unhappily, the ambitious ideals of Pan-Africanism, at least under the leadership of Nkrumah, were not to be realized. In Ghana itself, the promise of a better life under independence was shattered within three years. Nkrumah began to rule in an increasingly un-democratic manner, restricting press freedom and detaining critics and political opponents. When he became president for life in 1964, a cult of personality developed and the Congress People's Party wrested control of the country's unions and the civil service. On the economic front, Nkrumah was committed to the notion that modernization could only succeed under the direction of the sort of top-down state management that characterized the Soviet and Chinese economies. The president mismanaged foreign development aid and direct loans from the West in unsuccessful efforts to jump-start the process of industrialization. By the mid-1960s he had lost most of his earlier domestic support, and his acceptance of Soviet military trainers alarmed both American and Western European political leaders. While on a state visit to China and Vietnam in 1966, disgruntled military officers removed him from power. For the remainder of the century, Ghana lurched from one economic crisis to another, while military and civilian rulers alternated in power, each unable to place the country on a sound material footing.

Ugandan xenophobia

In the British East African colony of Uganda, a similar collapse of democratic institutions took place soon after independence. A multiparty parliamentary system was adopted in 1962, but efforts to build a sense of national identity among the nation's 19 million citizens and 40 different ethnic groups faltered by mid-decade. In 1966 Prime Minister Milton Obote suspended the constitution, proclaimed a one-party state, and suppressed all political opposition. Ousted by the former army officer Idi Amin Dada in 1971, the next eight years were to prove catastrophic for this lush agricultural country. The mercurial Amin lashed out at British expatriates living in Uganda, and he ordered the expulsion of approximately 30,000 settlers from South Asia. These enterprising Indian migrants constituted the core of Uganda's business and professional community, and with their forced departure the nation's economy went into a tailspin. Rampant inflation and a precipitous drop in production left the population in a desperate condition. Ignoring the ill effects of his senseless domestic policies, Amin's tirades against Israel and its American and British allies, together with his coddling of pro-Palestinian terrorists who landed a hijacked Air France plane in the Ugandan capital in 1976, earned him the contempt of the world community. Other African leaders began to distance themselves from this brutal dictator, and when Amin ordered Ugandan troops to attack neighboring Tanzania in 1978, the ensuing military debacle led to the dictator's flight. The country that he left behind, shattered by lawlessness and contempt for human life, has yet to recover fully.

Kenya, Rhodesia, and white settlement

In the East African colony of Kenya, where 30,000 white settlers controlled the most productive land in the country, British authorities faced increasing resistance from members of the Kikuyu, Kenya's largest tribe. Revolt broke out during the 1950s, and in response the British declared a state of emergency, banned all public meetings, and arrested the leading nationalists, including Jomo Kenyatta. By 1954 almost 80,000 (one in three adult male Kikuyu) were under some form of detention in Kenya, and in 1956 the rebel movement had been defeated. When he finally emerged from prison in 1961, Kenyatta did not seek retribution but instead called for the formation of a multiracial Kenya, a position that had been accepted in London one year earlier. Elected prime minister in 1963, he began a process of purchasing (with British aid) the choice lands held by white minority landowners. For the next 15 years, Kenya remained one of black Africa's more stable countries. Agricultural development wisely focused on domestic consumption, while Asian and European settlers were welcomed for their technical and entrepreneurial skills. Kenyatta avoided creating a large and costly military establishment, and in general he maintained good relations with the West. But while parliamentary procedure was observed and the judiciary remained largely independent, the country evolved into a one-party state under its authoritarian leader.

White settlement also frustrated black nationalists in British-controlled Southern Rhodesia. London was able to impose a constitutional government on Northern Rhodesia, which became the independent state of Zambia in 1964, but whites in the South declared their independence under the leadership of Ian Smith, a white supremacist who enjoyed the support of the apartheid regime in South Africa. The embarrassed British government immediately imposed economic sanctions against the country, but neither apartheid South Africa nor Portuguese-controlled Mozambique cooperated with the sanctions regime. For the next 15 years, white Rhodesia held out in the face of mounting international opposition and diplomatic isolation. Only in 1980, after years of black nationalist guerrilla warfare, the collapse of Portugal's African empire, and the waning of South African support, did free elections on the basis of universal suffrage take place. The new black majority government renamed the country Zimbabwe after the medieval African empire of that name. Elsewhere in neighboring Uganda and Tanganyika (Tanzania), where whites had not settled, British withdrawal in 1961 and 1962, respectively, was orderly and relatively peaceful.

French Algeria

Immediately after World War II, the French hoped to preserve their African empire by conferring metropolitan citizenship on their colonial peoples, encouraging them to think of their homelands as part of a wider French Union. They even called for the election of colonial representatives to the French assembly in Paris, but by the mid-1950s the call for total independence was incessant. Morocco and Tunisia broke away in 1956, and two years later the French government, under newly elected President Charles de Gaulle, offered all of the remaining colonies both independence and financial assistance under the umbrella of an association called the French Community. The alternative was independence without any French support, and only one colony, Algeria, chose this option.

French control over Algeria began in the 1830s, and by the end of World War II the politically dominant settler population had reached over one million (in a Muslim population of almost nine million). A bloody war of national liberation, led by the Algerian National Liberation Front, began soon after the French withdrew in defeat from Vietnam in 1954. It continued for eight long years, with Arab and Berber nationalist rebels terrorizing any Algerians who did not actively support them, and with the French army, backed by white settlers, responding to attacks with brutal reprisals. The protracted colonial conflict eventually led to the collapse of the Fourth French Republic in 1958, the return of Charles de Gaulle to national prominence as President of the Fifth Republic, and the withdrawal of French forces in July 1962. The multiracial Kenyan solution appeared to be impossible in Algeria owing to the cruelty of the struggle, and almost 1.5 million white settlers left Algeria in the wake of independence. Most returned to France, embittered and hostile toward the de Gaulle government. For its part, the new government of Algeria faced a daunting task of reconstruction in the wake of a war that had taken the lives of one million Algerians and led to the flight of an enterprising French business class.

Apartheid in South Africa

In February 1960, on a visit to the former colony of South Africa, British Prime Minister Harold Macmillan observed that "winds of change" were sweeping across the entire continent, bringing independence under democratic rule to millions of people in multi-ethnic settings. His audience was not impressed. A member state of the British Commonwealth, South Africa had been ruled by a white minority government since independence in 1910. Although governed under a parliamentary system with an autonomous judiciary, over one million white Afrikaners (descendants of Dutch settlers who had arrived as early as the seventeenth century) dominated the economic, political, and legal systems. They viewed themselves as the natural leaders of society, and they were prepared to use force in order to maintain their ascendancy.

The majority black population, together with indentured servants from India, Asian guest workers, and Coloreds (mixed race), were discriminated against in housing, employment opportunities, access to public services, and education. During the 1940s, just as the forces of black nationalism were stirring across the rest of Africa, the South African system of discrimination hardened into what the dominant Nationalist Party termed *apartheid*, or separateness. Nonwhites were restricted to identified "homelands" outside of the major cities and permitted access to urban areas only under special work passes. A large percentage of black South African men often lived in temporary residences located long distances from their families, toiling on commercial farms, in factories, and in the gold and diamond mines owned and operated by whites. The spouses of these migrant laborers were left to work in subsistence agriculture and raise the children while also serving as the *de facto* heads of household.

The majority black population was not docile in the face of this elaborate system of discrimination. Resistance took the form of peaceful protests under the direction of the African National Congress (ANC), established in the early years of the twentieth century by a handful of educated black South Africans. Like the Congress Party of Gandhi and Nehru (the former had spent nearly 20 years in South Africa fighting on behalf of Indian workers), the ANC was committed to reform through constitutional means. In 1955 the leadership issued a "Freedom Charter" calling for an end to apartheid and the formation of a pluralistic and democratic society. Their campaign of nonviolence attracted broad support among blacks and even a handful of liberal whites.

One of the organization's emerging leaders was Nelson Mandela, a lawyer by training, who had worked in the ANC's Youth League in an effort to build popular support for the ideal of a multiracial democratic state. In 1960 the ANC organized a series of protests against the hated pass system, and the government responded with a violent crackdown. In the black settlement of Sharpeville, just south of the city of Johannesburg, police opened fire on 10,000 unarmed civilians, killing 69 and wounding 200 others. Mass arrests followed and the ANC was outlawed as the apartheid regime moved to crush the protest movement. When the British condemned these actions, the government brusquely withdrew from the Commonwealth. At this juncture the underground ANC leadership diverged from the earlier tactics of the Congress Party in India and the current tactics of the black civil rights movement in the US.

A decision was made to undertake a campaign of sabotage against the unbending regime. Nelson Mandela accepted a key role in this resort to force. Arrested and convicted of treason in 1962, he would spend the next 28 years in prison.

Despite the persecution and imprisonment, the reputation of the ANC continued to grow. The deaths of nearly 700 civilians during a 1976 uprising in the black township of Soweto prompted widespread condemnation from the international community. Western states began to impose economic sanctions on the apartheid state, leading to economic recession and rising domestic tensions. Only in 1989 did a moderate prime minister, F. W. de Klerk, take steps to dismantle the onerous system. Political prisoners, including Mandela, were released from prison and in 1994 free elections led to an overwhelming ANC victory in parliament, securing over 60 percent of the popular vote. In May 1994 Nelson Mandela, having spent almost three decades behind bars, became the first democratically elected president of multiracial South Africa. The remarkable transformation was made possible in part by the ANC's commitment to respect existing property relations and to encourage trade with the West. South Africa's mature economic base enabled the new government to assume power with the sort of fiscal resources necessary to avoid the political instability that plagued other black African states.

From independence to chaos

Neither the Belgians nor the Portuguese had ever afforded their African subjects any role in the government of their colonies. The precipitous Belgian withdrawal in 1960 from Congo, the largest state in sub-Saharan Africa, occurred without any genuine preparation and with no clear leadership elite in place to assume power. Indeed as late as 1960 there were very few trained professionals or university graduates in the massive, mineral-rich colony. The ill-disciplined Congolese army turned on white settlers while at the same time a variety of ethnic groups fought for supremacy. Chaos dissolved into civil war and the UN was obliged to insert a multinational military force in order to restore a semblance of order; one of the casualties of the conflict was the UN Secretary-General, Dag Hammarskjold, killed in a plane crash during a mission to Congo.

By 1965 a seasoned military man who had served in the colonial army, Joseph Mobutu, seized power, renamed the country Zaire, and while promising the restoration of peace and order, began a 30-year tenure that was marked by a singular disregard for the public good and large-scale pilfering of development aid. The corrupt Mobutu regime, which nationalized the profitable mining industry, was supported by the West throughout the period of the Cold War since it was staunchly anticommunist. By the 1980s public services were moribund, the economy was a shambles, and most of the country ignored the dictates of the central government. Mobutu continued to transfer the wealth of Zaire into his various European bank accounts until he was forced to flee in 1996, by which time the neighboring states of Angola and Uganda were providing direct aid to the rebel leader Laurent Kabila. The successor government restored the original name of the independent state, but Congo at the start of the twenty-first century continued to be plagued by ethnic unrest.

Forced retreat: Portugal

Having inaugurated the age of European empire in the late fifteenth century, the reactionary Portuguese government fought doggedly until the mid-1970s to hold onto its colonial possessions in Africa, turning Guinea-Bissau, Mozambique, and Angola into battlegrounds with distinct Cold War components. As one of the poorest countries in Western Europe after World War II, Portugal's strongman, Antonio de Oliviera Salazar, clung to African empire as a sign of national prestige and as a source of products such as tea, coffee, and sugar that helped to balance the Portuguese national budget. The government encouraged white migration to Angola and Mozambique, and in 1951 Salazar declared that the colonies were "overseas provinces" of Portugal, but in fact only a tiny percentage of the indigenous black population in each "province" was granted full Portuguese citizenship. The first serious rebellion began in 1961, the same year that Nehru's government forced the Portuguese out of their last Indian stronghold at Goa. The rebellion started in northern Angola and soon spread to Mozambique. Forty thousand Portuguese troops were dispatched and harsh military repression followed, but effective guerrilla campaigns continued.

By the early 1970s, over 150,000 Portuguese soldiers were stationed in the colonies, and military spending in Portugal rose to almost 50 percent of total government expenditure. As a member of NATO, Portugal received assistance from its Western allies, and in response, Soviet military aid and Cuban troops flowed to the Marxist guerrillas who opposed the regime. In 1974, as the military campaigns in the colonies faltered and morale sank, a group of middle-rank officers seized control of Lisbon and installed a new military junta that was committed to withdrawal from Africa. Independence was secured in all three colonies by 1975, but as in so many other African states, factional fighting and ethnic rivalries continued; fighting in Mozambique between Marxist and Nationalist forces, for example, dragged on until 1992. In Angola, Marxist fighters were aided by Cuba's Fidel Castro, who sent troops and weapons; in response, South Africa's apartheid government lent its support to a noncommunist rebel movement. In the midst of the internal conflicts, death, malnutrition, and disease became the lot of civilian populations who had gained nothing from the end of empire.

Ethnicity and the nation-state

Whenever political disorder became the norm at the national level, many Africans turned to local sources of authority and protection – the lineage group, clan, ethnic alliance, or tribe. And at the core of many of these relationships was a disheartening history of rivalry, suspicion, and conflict. This pattern of provincialism was deeply rooted in African culture, and its deleterious side was magnified in the absence of effective civic identity. Two tragic examples of states descending into ethnic quasi-states involved Africa's most heavily populated countries, the former British colony of Nigeria in West Africa, and the former Belgian colony of Rwanda in East-Central Africa.

Belgium's hasty and irresponsible withdrawal from Congo was repeated in 1962 in neighboring Rwanda, a small landlocked and densely populated state. Ninety percent of Rwanda's people were ethnic Hutu, and immediately after independence the minority Tutsi population were removed from whatever minor positions of power they had secured under the imperial regime. More radical

Hutus sought to expel all the Tutsi from Rwanda, and periodic attacks against the latter group were carried out by roving bands. When the Hutu head of state died in an airplane crash in 1994, irregular Hutu militia forces set upon Tutsi civilians. Before the savage attacks ended, an estimated half-million Tutsi had been massacred, nearly one-half of the entire Tutsi population. At the same time in the tiny neighboring state of Burundi, Hutu attacks against the Tutsi minority compounded the genocide. Those who managed to flee found exile in neighboring Uganda, where they assembled a military force with the aid of their hosts. Reentering their homeland, the Tutsi handily defeated their Hutu enemies. A new refugee crisis resulted, this time situated in lawless Zaire, as upward of two million Hutus crossed the border in fear of their lives. Embedded amongst the homeless refugees in the makeshift camps were those Hutus who had instigated the original massacre. The central government of Zaire exercised little control in the country's eastern provinces, and a coalition of neighboring states, including Uganda and Angola, joined with the Rwandan authorities to root out the Hutu guerrilla fighters. They also sponsored an insurgency movement that ultimately drove Mobutu's corrupt government out of power. In Rwanda, the search for the perpetrators of the 1994 massacre continued, with the UN establishing a war crimes tribunal.

In Nigeria, Britain's most heavily populated African colony, three powerful ethnic groups (in a land of some 200 distinct ethnic groups) competed for ascendancy at the time of independence in 1962. The adoption of a federal system of government under the 1964 constitution recognized these divisions by creating a three-province country. The Muslim Hausa people of the north had resisted what few opportunities were available during the colonial period for Western-style education, confident that their Muslim heritage provided adequate preparation for the responsibilities of statehood. In the southeast and southwest of the country, the Ibo and Yoruba peoples had taken advantage of English education, and English became the official language after independence. Two years after the adoption of the constitution, however, a military coup toppled the civilian government. Political assassinations and ethnic massacres followed these events, and in 1967 the Ibo-dominated eastern provinces broke away and declared the formation of a new state called Biafra. Although successful in gaining recognition from a number of African states, and securing arms from France, Portugal, and South Africa, the Biafrans were unable to prevail in a bloody two-year civil war. By the time that the fighting was over in 1970, an estimated one million people had died as a direct result of war and attendant famine.

Despite its success in quashing this secession movement, and Nigeria's potential as an oil-exporting country, the central government has been plagued by instability, with military takeovers, and government by military surrogates, becoming the disturbing routine ever since. There was a momentary ray of hope for this resource-rich country in June 1993, when a peaceful and fair presidential election took place. But when an opposition leader from western Nigeria won at the polls, the northern military elite nullified the election results and, ignoring international protests, restored military rule. Declining oil revenues during the 1980s and 1990s, combined with political uncertainty, led the government to default on most of its foreign debt, becoming yet another African state of great potential losing its way in the postcolonial quest for peace and prosperity.

ANTICOLONIALISM AND NATIONALISM IN THE MIDDLE EAST

The historic Arab heartland and adjacent regions of the Muslim world also felt the impact of colonialism and modern nationalism in the postwar period. Recently part of three declining empires – the Moroccan, Ottoman, and Persian – most of the approximately 70 million inhabitants of these autocratic lands felt no particular affinity for a broader Muslim nation. During World War I, the French and British had encouraged the inhabitants of the Middle East to rise up against the Ottoman Turks, intimating that such action would lead to independence after the war. In fact, both European powers were eager to divide up the region, and in the postwar years the French secured League of Nations-approved mandates over Syria and Lebanon, while the British supervised Palestine, Transjordan, and Iraq. The mandate system was designed under the assumption that the lands in question would be prepared for self-government by the occupying powers. For British and

French authorities, a region composed of small, separate states was preferable to a united Muslim Middle East. In the mandate area of Palestine, the British permitted Jewish immigration in the belief that the new arrivals would contribute to the process of economic development. Hebrew, Arabic, and English were recognized as the official languages of the Palestine mandate, a tacit acknowledgment of the historic association of Jews to the region.

Israel

Regional Muslim leaders felt little comity when the question of leadership within a proposed pan-Arab nation was discussed. But the single most important galvanizing force for Arab nationalism in the Middle East was opposition to Jewish immigration, and, after 1948, to the creation and survival of the State of Israel. Jewish settlement in Palestine had begun in the wake of European, and in particular Russian, persecution during the late nineteenth century. The movement to reestablish a Jewish presence in Palestine was called Zionism, and it generated considerable support within the international Jewish community during the first three decades of the twentieth century. During the 1920s, only a small number of European Jews (approximately 10,000 per year) migrated to Palestine, but as Nazi persecution escalated in the 1930s, more Jews arrived and Arab residents began to fear that they would soon become a minority in their homeland.

In 1939, eager to cultivate Arab support – and access to Middle East oil reserves – and in a climate of impending war with Nazi Germany, the British government set limits on the number of Jews who would be permitted to settle in Palestine. Approximately 390,000 Jews had arrived by this date. Effective migration stopped during the course of the war, but in 1945 the leaders of the Zionist movement concluded that in the wake of the Holocaust, Jews needed a sovereign state of their own and could no longer count on British protection in a mandate territory where hostile Arabs constituted the majority population. Not unlike the members of the Muslim League in India before independence, Jews were convinced that they would suffer discrimination and possible persecution at the hands of the majority population should Palestine secure independence, just as Iraq, Jordan, Lebanon, and Syria had by the war's end. When it became clear that London was not about to change its policy on limiting Jewish immigration to Palestine after 1945, some Jews resorted to terror tactics against British targets and officials. Unable to settle the issue, Attlee's Labour government handed the Palestine question to the UN, and in late 1947 the international body decided to partition the territory into two separate states, one Jewish and the other Arab. When the last British troops left in May 1948, the Jews swiftly declared their independence as the state of Israel. Both the US and the Soviet Union immediately recognized the new country, a nation-state designed as a haven for the victims of anti-Semitism around the world.

The Arab perspective on these developments was, of course, much different. Jewish emigration to lands that had been occupied by Muslims for 1000 years represented merely another episode in the long saga of European imperialism, and the callous resolution of a centuries-old Western problem (anti-Semitism) through the expropriation of lands in the Muslim world. Immediately upon independence, Israel was attacked by Egypt, Jordan, Syria, Lebanon, and Iraq. The separate offensives were ill coordinated, however, and seasoned Israeli troops (many of whom had fought for the British during World War II) not only rebuffed the attacks but were able to extend the borders of the new state well beyond the partition plan outlined by the UN. An armistice was brokered by the UN in February 1949, leaving the Palestinians without a state of their own and creating a huge refugee problem for Jordan and Egypt, as almost three-quarters of a million people fled east and south from the new Jewish state. One hundred and fifty thousand Palestinians remained in Israel, a distinct minority in a country of approximately 600,000 Jews.

The aftermath of the military debacle in the Arab states was swift. In March 1949, Syria's civilian government was overthrown in a military coup. Jordan's King Abdullah was assassinated by a Muslim extremist in 1951, and the following year Egypt's Turkish-born King Farouk was ousted in a military coup led by Colonel Gamal Abdel Nasser. For this new generation of Muslim nationalists, parliamentary politicians and Western-appointed monarchs had failed to protect the Muslim population of the Middle East from the forces of imperialism. The new military regimes promised to rebuild national prestige, support Muslim liberation movements elsewhere in North Africa, and prepare for another strike against the hated Israeli state.

Egypt and the Arab leadership

As the region's most populous state with 19 million people, most of whom had a much stronger sense of national identity than Arabs elsewhere, Nasser's Egypt became the leader in the Arab struggle against Western imperialism. The main symbol of that imperialist presence in Egypt was British control over the strategically important, and economically profitable, Suez Canal. In 1955, one year after London had withdrawn the last British troops from the Canal Zone, Nasser announced that his country would receive shipments of military hardware from the Soviet Union as part of a long-term loan package. When the US and Britain subsequently withdrew their financial support for Nasser's centerpiece infrastructure project, the massive Aswan Dam, the Egyptian leader announced that the Suez Canal was being nationalized. However, Nasser maintained that foreign shareholders would be compensated and freedom of navigation preserved under Egyptian supervision.

Nationalizing the canal was a bold gamble by Nasser's military government. Almost two-thirds of Western Europe's oil imports passed through the Canal from Saudi Arabia and Kuwait, and whoever controlled this potential choke point could inflict serious damage on the economies of an increasingly oil-hungry Europe. But when the British and the French, in alliance with the Israelis, invaded Egypt at the end of October 1956, both superpowers condemned the action and called for a ceasefire resolution at the UN. Although the Israelis had rolled back Egyptian forces in the Sinai while the British and French forces landed at Port Said, the Americans pressured their NATO allies to withdraw, allowing Nasser to snatch an unlikely victory from the jaws of military disaster at the eleventh hour. Having unexpectedly chastened two of Europe's former imperial powers, Nasser instantly became the leading figure in Arab nationalist circles. The Soviets stepped in and agreed to provide funding for the Aswan Dam, designed to bolster irrigation and electric power production, and Nasser intensified his pan-Arab rhetoric. He now envisioned a future in which an economically potent Egypt led an expansive state that would stretch eastward to the Tigris and Euphrates and involve the removal of the Western-appointed Hashemite monarchs in Jordan and Iraq. These ambitions were shattered in 1967 during a disastrous six-day war with Israel. Once again the superior Israeli military made short work of Nasser's forces; when the Egyptian dictator died suddenly in 1970, his successor, Anwar Sadat, was forced to scale back state spending and costly public works projects.

After another failed attempt to destroy the state of Israel in 1973, the Egyptian government slowly came to terms with its archenemy, becoming the first Arab country to recognize the State of Israel in 1978. Sadat ended his predecessor's close ties with the Soviets and made Egypt heavily dependent upon American economic and military aid. Considered a traitor by fellow Arab states, Egypt was expelled from the Arab League. In 1980 the Egyptian president was assassinated by Islamic militants, but his successor, Hosni Mubarak, continued the fallen leader's pro-Western policies. Egypt became the world's second largest recipient of US aid (after Israel), but with an escalating population and rising unemployment, the country had failed to achieve lasting economic and political stability. The increasingly authoritarian Mubarak regime, accused of corruption by its many opponents, faced ongoing challenges from the forces of Islamic fundamentalism, whose ranks were filled by members of Egypt's impoverished youth.

SOUTHEAST ASIA

With the one exception of Thailand, all of Southeast Asia was under the control of foreign powers at the start of World War II. Burma (now Myanmar), Vietnam, Cambodia, Laos, Malaysia, Singapore, Brunei, Indonesia, and the Philippines would secure their autonomy after the war in a climate charged by the success of the Japanese in routing the occupying Western powers. Prior to the war, nationalist sentiment was restricted to a handful of Western-educated elites who, not unlike their African contemporaries, were denied access to political power within their respective colonial administrations. The Americans were the first to leave this region, granting full independence to the pro-Western government of the Philippines in July 1946. The British reached an agreement with Burma in early 1947 and the transfer of power took place in January 1948. In an equally bloodless manner, independence came to British-controlled Malaya in 1957, with Singapore remaining outside of the new country as a self-governing polity. In the Dutch colony of the East Indies (Indonesia), on the other hand, the road to independence was complicated by the presence of a significant settler population and the economic importance of the colony to the metropolitan economy.

Indonesia

First acquired in the seventeenth century and referred to initially as the "Spice Islands," Indonesia developed a colonial export economy centered on tea, coffee, sugar, coal, and subsequently rubber and oil for a mainly European market. During the late nineteenth-century scramble for colonies in Africa and Asia, the Dutch had remained on the sidelines, content with their lucrative island archipelago whose geographical and population heart was the island of Java. Ruling through local elites, taxes were paid to imperial authorities in the form of cash crops which helped to sustain the economy of the Netherlands. There was also a considerable settler population in the East Indies; by the start of World War II, almost a quarter of a million Dutch and their offspring were resident amid a total East Indian, and largely Muslim, population of 70 million. As in British India and French Indochina, a small nationalist movement had emerged in Indonesia during the early years of the twentieth century, but it was hampered by the fact that many islands featured distinct languages, cultures, and communities who felt little sense of identity with the Javanese majority.

In 1941, after the Dutch government rejected Japan's request to purchase unlimited quantities of oil from the East Indies, Tokyo resolved to expel all of the Western powers from Asia, and by the spring of 1942 this objective largely had been achieved. During the years of Japanese occupation (1942–5), Indonesian nationalist leaders were released from jail and the indigenous population enjoyed greater access to political and administrative power.

The Japanese even made vague promises of independence once the war was over, fostering a strong sense of nationalism that carried forward into the postwar era. Dutch efforts to reassert control over these profitable islands after 1945 were unsuccessful, not least due to the fact that the Americans and the British had encouraged the formation of an anti-Japanese resistance movement during the war which was subsequently turned against the Dutch. Under the leadership of the charismatic Achmed Sukarno, Indonesia asserted its independence as a republic in August 1945. Since the Indonesian Communist Party played only a marginal role in the struggle for independence, the US did not intervene to assist the Dutch in their effort to maintain hegemony over the islands. The UN attempted to mediate between the two sides, but to little effect; four years of difficult fighting ensued before the Netherlands agreed to terms in 1949.

The Republic of the United States of Indonesia, consisting of some 3000 islands, pledged to recognize the nominal authority of the Dutch crown, but in 1956 Sukarno's government nullified this final concession to the imperialist past. Sukarno became president of a majority Muslim state, and over the next 15 years political freedoms narrowed and parliamentary democracy faltered. In 1957 the elected national parliament was replaced by one appointed by Sukarno. Dutch-owned businesses were nationalized and Europeans (along with their investments) departed. Rapid inflation, food shortages, and general economic decline followed. Communist Party membership increased sharply during this period, as did Sukarno's recruitment of communists into his cabinet. In 1963 he declared himself president for life. These developments alarmed Washington, especially since the US was deeply embroiled in Vietnam at the time. In the fall of 1965 a brutal military crackdown against suspected communists (some estimates run as high as half a million murdered) resulted in the rise to power of the authoritarian General T. N. J. Suharto, who ruled the country as president from 1968 until 1998. The massive abuse of human rights that accompanied the rise to power of the military government received little notice in the West; what mattered at the time was that Indonesia was moving firmly into the Western camp during the height of the Cold War.

In an effort to improve the economy, the Suharto regime offered incentives for foreign investment, but charges of corruption emerged early and often. Close associates of the president frequently represented overseas firms seeking to do business in Indonesia, and allegations of kickbacks and bribes became more frequent. Although blessed with considerable mineral, oil, and natural gas reserves, Indonesia was unable to enter the ranks of the developed states. What growth did take place during the 1970s was offset by the enormous disparities in wealth. Across the thousands of islands which constituted the republic, popular dissatisfaction with the regime could find no political outlet. Government-supported coalitions dominated the People's Assembly, guaranteeing the reelection of Suharto. For the better part of three decades, the regime was characterized by rampant corruption, intermittent attacks against Indonesia's minority Chinese population, the arbitrary arrest and imprisonment of political dissidents, and the brutal invasion of East Timor, formerly a Portuguese island territory, in 1975.

THE OVERLOOKED EMPIRE: RUSSIA

Because it was not a great maritime power, tsarist and Soviet Russia escapes most discussions of colonialism. In particular, the anti-imperialist and transnational rhetoric of the early communist state under Lenin tends to obscure the fact that Russia's land-based Eurasian holdings constituted what was arguably the largest colonial empire in the modern age. The Baltic states of Estonia, Latvia, and Lithuania were first conquered during the eighteenth century, as were sections of Poland during the protracted carve-up of that beleaguered state before 1800. Also during the eighteenth century, Russia began a momentous eastward drive that was not unlike the American push westward on the North American continent during the nineteenth century. These two expansionist powers met in Alaska, where the Russians sold their claims to the Americans in 1867. In Central Asia the Russians acquired Kazakhstan in 1731, and Uzbekistan, Turkmenistan, and Kyrgystan during the nineteenth century. These latter moves alarmed the British, who feared that the Tsar's government had designs on Persia and, more particularly, on northern India. In addition, since the time of Catherine the Great, Russia had had strong ambitions in the south, absorbing Ukraine, eastern Armenia, northern Azerbaijan, and Georgia.

Many of these regions briefly reestablished their independence in the wake of the Bolshevik Revolution and subsequent civil war. The Baltic states and Poland were able to maintain their independence during the interwar period, but the former fell victim to the Hitler–Stalin Pact of 1939 while the latter was taken, along with the rest of Eastern Europe, by the advancing Red Army in 1944–5. Through the establishment in 1923 of the Union of Soviet Socialist Republics (USSR), the Russians maintained the charade of voluntarism – even to the extent of allowing the theoretical right to secession – but the absolutist nature of Stalin's regime was apparent to all. The rhetoric of nationalism was anathema to the post-1945 Soviet regime, inasmuch as it threatened to undermine the Communist Party's claim to transnational worker solidarity. And until the late 1980s, the Red Army served as the guarantor of the grand fiction.

Only when the Russian economy began its nosedive in the 1980s, aggravated by a final quasi-imperial lunge into Afghanistan, did the harsh reality of colonial overextension inform policy. Gorbachev refused to use force in 1989 as one Eastern Bloc state after another peacefully (with the exception of Romania) rejected communism. In 1991 the Baltic states, stripped of their independence in 1940 and home to large minorities of Russians who had been relocated during the Cold War, successfully reclaimed their autonomy. In rapid succession the remainder of the states of the old Soviet Union broke away from the center; when Kazakhstan declared its independence in December the principle of nationalism, long the bane of Soviet ideology, had triumphed as the successor states to the USSR secured seats in the UN. Remarkably, the breakup of the feared Soviet empire had outpaced the dissolution of the European empires in Africa, redefining the map of Eurasia in a few short years.

ASSESSING THE COLONIAL LEGACY

The spread of Western-style nationalist ideology; the emergence of a Western-educated elite who were denied full access to political power; the postwar economic weakness of Western colonial powers; and the opposition of the superpower states to old-style overseas empire – all of these factors contributed to the fairly rapid dismantling of territorial empire after World War II. European empire had stood for decades as the preeminent symbol of national greatness, racial superiority, and economic might. Clothed in the rhetoric of lifting benighted peoples out of their uncivilized habits, the spread of empire was in fact an extension of European power politics, militarism, and economic opportunism. The latter incentive rarely panned out; few of the colonies returned a profit to the metropolitan power, and fewer still became points of settlement for European migrants. But empire was largely about perceptions of power, about the formation of cultural values and habits of economic practice that complemented the worldview of the developed states. In this respect late nineteenth- and early twentieth-century imperialism clearly accelerated the process, begun around 1500, of "Westernizing" the global community.

At one level, the end of old-style territorial colonialism and the emergence of hundreds of new sovereign states since the 1950s has strengthened belief in the essential equality of peoples irrespective of skin color or level of scientific, technical, and industrial accomplishment. From 51 original members of the UN in 1945 to just under 200 at the end of the century, the principle of equality is embodied in the organization's General Assembly, where voting power has clearly shifted to non-Western developing countries. But as new nations have adopted the territorial boundaries established by their former colonial masters, a host of multiethnic states, many too small and too underdeveloped to meet the needs of expanding populations, have struggled against daunting odds to achieve political stability, economic prosperity, and national self-consciousness. These handicaps continue to burden the leaders of developing countries around the globe.

Many postcolonial states began as Western-style parliamentary democracies. Indeed, the Western-educated Asians and Africans who led the independence struggles utilized Western ideas to claim the moral high ground in their quest for autonomy. But lacking any substantive experience in political pluralism and constitutional procedure, many of these governments quickly succumbed, under the strain of economic hardship, to the more familiar paradigm of authoritarian and military rule. Lacking a viable political opposition, a neutral military, and an independent judiciary, these one-party states, military juntas, and dictatorships have been characterized by corruption, legal caprice, and fiscal incompetence. Venality and authoritarianism have been compounded by low levels of education, literacy, and technical competence, all essential prerequisites, along with investment capital, to balanced economic development. The Western powers did little to address the problem of illiteracy during the colonial period, and this in turn complicated the population crisis facing so many post-World War II nation-states. During the twentieth century, while population levels moderated and then became stagnant in the developed First World countries, those nations least able to provide for their citizenry experienced the highest levels of growth. Today most of the world's population lives outside of the enormously affluent West, is increasingly exposed to images of this affluence, yet finds itself locked out of any hope of attaining to the commonplaces of First World existence.

Postcolonial relationships

During the Cold War, Western involvement in and influence over the internal affairs of newly independent states was motivated by the desire to contain the spread of communism, while simultaneously creating conditions by which developing nations sought financial, military, and technological assistance from the First World. Most of the Western powers sought to retain economic, military, and cultural links with their former colonies. The sale of sophisticated military hardware to Cold War client states, for example, became a significant source of revenue for both the US and the Soviet Union. Such were the profits to be made that other states, including Britain, France, Israel, South Africa, Brazil, the two Koreas, and China joined the list of sales outlets. Placing advanced weapons in the hands of disreputable Cold War allies may have increased the West's political leverage temporarily, but at very high cost when these weapons were later used in regional conflicts. The Pakistan–India conflict, and the Iraq–Iran war of the 1980s, represent tragic cases in point.

Former colonial powers sought to retain linkages with former subject peoples through new associations. London encouraged newly independent states to join the British Commonwealth (today the Commonwealth of Nations), and most of them accepted the offer. The French Community was another effort on the part of a major European power to build a larger postcolonial political and economic union, but like similar Spanish and Portuguese efforts, it did not attract a large membership. Beyond these formal partnerships, diplomatic and economic relations continued to favor former imperial powers. Since the end of the Cold War, the unequal relationship has been extended as a result of the West's insistence upon the need for open markets and access to an inexpensive labor pool. Governments in the developed world crafted aid packages that privileged countries who supported the international priorities of the donor state, while private corporations sought to negotiate agreements that afforded stockholders the greatest return on investment. Often these agreements involved labor contracts and tax policies that undermined the host country's efforts to improve the lives of its citizens. Defenders of free trade in developed industrial nations applauded the virtues of open markets, unrestricted investment, and ready access to cheap labor, in the belief that all states and peoples ultimately benefit in a self-regulating marketplace. Skeptics claimed that what appeared to be a marketplace of equal opportunity was actually an unbalanced playing field where fully mature economies exploited developing countries while simultaneously ascribing economic inequalities to poor decision making on the part of Third World political leaders. We shall return to this topic in Chapter 4.

Nationalism and modernization since 1945

Perhaps the greatest challenge for postcolonial states has involved the adoption (critics would say imposition) of Western political and economic frames of reference. The transition from crown, clan, village, and regional loyalties to the broader abstraction called the nation-state began in late eighteenth-century Europe. During the era of the American and French Revolutions, nationalism was closely associated with the rise of the citizen, the promotion of natural rights, and the emergence of the secular state as the vehicle for advancing the goal of human freedom. Nation-states adopted an internationalist posture that recognized the basic equality of sovereign peoples, and political allegiance lost its centuries-old connection to the person and found a new home in the law and in formal constitutional procedure. By the second half of the nineteenth century, however, influenced by the popular misapplication of evolutionary theory, the nation-state took a decidedly insular turn, becoming the embodiment of unique culture, language, and race; it also emerged as the locus of material and spiritual value, and the rival of competitive and sometimes hostile neighbors. Nationalism shed its previous association with anti-monarchical and anti-authoritarian political movements and increasingly became the tool of traditional political elites who sought to maintain power in an increasingly democratic age.

This later, more exclusive form of nationalism became the model for most postcolonial states in the developing world. In this area more than anywhere else, the culture of the West has shaped the outlook of the non-Western world. The formation of states on the basis of territorial boundaries set by Europeans was comparatively straightforward, but the work of cultivating national consciousness among peoples of disparate backgrounds and experiences was extraordinarily difficult. India became the great success story here, even in the face of partition and the creation of Pakistan. Comparable in size to Western Europe, with greater linguistic and religious diversity, the territorial nation-state idea has prevailed despite enormous social and economic challenges. Most other states have been less fortunate. Nationalism was ingrained in the consciousness of the leadership elite long before it made any headway amongst the general population, and in some cases – Nigeria, for example – it exacerbated ethnic and religious tensions instead of ameliorating them. Tragically and too often in the modern world, nationalism has been reduced to ethnic, religious, and cultural identity. In the process it has become the occasion for provincialism and division, having completely lost its earlier association with the Enlightenment tradition of universal rights and human equality.

Perhaps the most troubling and intractable feature of the postcolonial world is the widespread espousal (again, critics would say imposition) of Western material values, and in particular the elusive panacea known as development. The First World countries industrialized in an environment with only a handful of competitors, and under manageable demographic conditions where citizens had the option of overseas migration. After World War II, newly independent states faced daunting competition in their quest to afford a reasonable quality of life for their citizens. Competition from affluent states in a global marketplace where the rules advantage developed economies placed enormous hurdles in the path of countries seeking more equitable growth. Choosing not to embrace the Western industrialized criterion for an acceptable lifestyle seems as unlikely today as it was in 1947, when Gandhi urged a different path for South Asia, one where the self-sufficient village took precedence over the vagaries of the international market. The end of old-style territorial empire and the proliferation of sovereign nation-states since 1945 has inaugurated a global quest to share in the Western culture of rising expectations. The long-term environmental consequences of this paradigm have already become apparent in the fully developed economies of the West, yet today, as we shall see in subsequent chapters, there is neither democrat nor dictator in the developing world who would dare question the appropriateness of the paradigm for themselves.

3

AN ELUSIVE NEW WORLD ORDER, 1991-2005

KEY TOPICS

Integration and fragmentation
in wider Europe
The resurgence of China

Ambiguity in the developing world
Terrorism and the drift toward
unilateralism

The abrupt end of the Cold War in the late 1980s inspired hope that the material resources of the two superpowers and their respective allies could be redirected to address common human problems in a climate of cooperation and mutual support. But with the dissolution of the Soviet empire into 15 sovereign countries in 1991, the US was left as the world's only power with a truly global reach. It quickly demonstrated that reach in the fall of 1991 by successfully leading a UN coalition of nations in a war to oust the Iraqi military from neighboring Kuwait. America's preponderant wealth, technological prowess, and military might ensured that future international efforts to assist less-favored countries would most likely rely on its support. In a self-confident mood after the humbling of communism and the dethroning of command economies, politicians and pundits in the US affirmed that democratic political institutions and marketplace capitalism represented the universal road forward for all countries hoping to penetrate the envied portals of material affluence. President George H. W. Bush spoke optimistically of a "new world order" anchored in the proven values of Western political and economic thought.

Not everyone was so sanguine. Environmental degradation; rapid population growth; health issues and disease prevention; access to nutritious food, clean water, and education – each of these trans-national challenges was closely related to the least tractable predica-ment of the late twentieth century: the yawning economic gap between a very few wealthy nations, mostly located in the Northern hemisphere, and the deepening poverty of the many who lived and died without hope in the states of the developing South. Building a peaceful world without a comprehensive solution to global economic inequality appeared unlikely at the end of the twentieth century. In Europe, Australia, North America, and parts of East Asia and Latin America, humans had achieved an extraordinary level of material comfort by the close of the century. But elsewhere the struggle for existence remained very much at a preindustrial level. By the early twenty-first century, the backlash against the North's privileged political, military, and economic position manifested itself in a vari-ety of troubling forms, in some cases even threatening the domestic security of the most powerful nation-states.

In particular, the spread of nonstate terrorist groups whose sole affiliation was to a distorted version of Islam posed a new type of security challenge to governments whose traditional understanding of national security involved preparing for state-to-state conflicts. Some of these groups rejected modernity out of hand, insisting that democracy and liberal capitalism were anything but universal para-digms for political and economic organization. With access to sophisticated weapons, attracting committed ideologues willing to engage in suicide attacks, and preferring civilian "soft targets" instead of direct confrontation with the enemy's military forces, ter-rorists sought to dislodge pro-Western regimes in the Islamic world and to expel all Westerners residing in these countries. Domestic safety in this changed environment involved not only a more sophisticated and better-coordinated process of information gather-ing around the world, but enhanced investigatory powers for police, border and transportation officials, and immigration agents. Leaders of democratic nations struggled to preserve the type of personal freedom consistent with a free and open society while at the same time providing a level of domestic security that would allow citizens to carry on with their lives without fear of attack.

Another unanticipated sequel to the end of the Cold War involved the growth of what we might term "parochial nationalism." The global trend toward economic integration (see Chapter 4) stood in stark juxtaposition to a form of nationalism characterized by ethnic and religious intolerance. The breakup of communist Yugoslavia in 1991, for example, triggered a protracted and bloody conflict involving six major groups whose centuries-old ethnic rivalries had been suppressed by the government of Marshal Josep Tito. The conflict in the Balkans seriously tested the European community's resolve, especially after Serbian forces began a policy of "ethnic cleansing" that was disturbingly reminiscent of the darkest experiences of World War II. And as we saw in Chapter 2, in the tiny central African state of Rwanda, long-standing tensions between the country's two major ethnic groups, the minority Tutsi and the majority Hutu, erupted into massive violence in 1994. Over half a million people were killed and another two million were driven from their homes in one of the worst instances of government-sponsored brutality since 1945, yet the international community failed to intervene militarily in what amounted to genocide. In the Horn of Africa, the Islamist government of Sudan attempted to impose Sharia (Islamic law) on the Christian and animist population of the south during the 1990s, prompting a vicious civil war that led to the deaths of over a million citizens. The malfeasance continued into the new century, with an additional humanitarian crisis erupting in the Darfur region as progovernment Arab gunmen terrorized blacks and destroyed homes and villages with impunity. By mid-2004, upwards of one million Sudanese had been displaced and approximately 50,000 killed.

These and many other ethnic and religious clashes around the globe demonstrated that state creation and nation building were two distinct enterprises, the first sometimes aggravating tensions between peoples whose mutual antipathies long predated modern territorial boundaries. During the final years of the century, the call of Western political leaders and educators to "celebrate diversity and difference" fell on deaf ears in many parts of the world, where too often difference meant error and prompted an immediate call to arms. Even in Europe and the US, shallow and insular views of national identity occasionally frustrated efforts to achieve greater inclusion. Whether the issue was an expanded European community and the adoption of a European constitution, or immigration policy in the US, the narrow view of national identity was ignored by politicians only at their peril. Wherever nationalism was intertwined with an explicit ethnic, linguistic, or religious identity, there the proponents of global markets, global communications, and global culture were sure to be dismayed. At the start of the third millennium, the affirmation of difference too often retained its historic alliance with enmity born of ignorance.

In this chapter we will look first at the remarkable reestablishment of sovereign states in Eastern Europe in 1989, and then at the more dramatic collapse of the Soviet empire in 1991. While most states made a peaceful transition to democratic government and market-based economies, the breakup of the former Yugoslavia severely tested Europe's commitment to joint security in the face of bitter ethnic and religious conflict. We then turn to China, where the years since 1990 have been marked by an unprecedented economic transformation. Other areas of East Asia experienced economic change during the 1980s and 1990s, and these will be addressed in Chapter 4. But China was different, both in terms of its demographics and its potential as a great military power. The leaders of the world's most populous communist state were determined not to go the way of Eastern Europe and the Soviet Union, irrespective of the cost in human life. The focus next shifts to states in Latin America and their recent relationships with the US, looking especially at the ongoing problem of economic dependency. The issue of international terrorism rounds out the discussion, bringing us back to some of the implications of emerging global culture and US global preeminence. The US invasion of Iraq in 2003 affirmed that preeminence, but also raised the specter of unilateralism propelled by faulty information-gathering, a combination that was deeply troubling to many of America's traditional allies. By 2005, the new world order that was envisioned in 1991 by many in the West, an order centered on democratic governments and market economies, remained both strangely elusive and deeply contested.

INTEGRATION AND FRAGMENTATION IN WIDER EUROPE

Demise of the Iron Curtain

The end of the Cold War and the restoration of political autonomy in the former Eastern Bloc countries signaled a new chapter in the decades-old process of greater European integration. In 1989 a series of bloodless revolutions, each taking place within the context of deepening economic woes and with the acquiescence of Mikhail Gorbachev, spelled the end of Soviet domination in Eastern Europe. Poland, Hungary, Czechoslovakia, East Germany, Romania, and Bulgaria all secured their autonomy after four decades of sub-servience to the Soviet empire. Global criticism of the Chinese communist crackdown on pro-democracy protesters in Tiananmen Square in May 1989 served as a somber backdrop to the events, but Gorbachev's unwillingness to intervene militarily was informed by his conviction that better relations with the West and market reforms at home were essential to the preservation of the Soviet Union. Thanks to television images and some travel opportunities, residents of Eastern Europe had already been exposed to the higher standards of living available in the West, and once the heavy hand of Soviet control was lifted, the demand for meaningful political reform could not be silenced.

Poland set the precedent for the reform agenda. Despite the government's crackdown on the Solidarity movement and the imposition of martial law during 1981–3, resistance to communist rule festered throughout the 1980s as the economy worsened and shortages of basic necessities became commonplace. Polish-born Pope John Paul II provided moral support for the anticommunist cause during these difficult times, and the citizenry continued to push for basic change. Finally, a series of massive strikes in the summer and fall of 1988 prompted General Jaruzelski's government to call nationwide elections in June 1989, but with the caveat that the majority of the seats in the lower house or *sejm* would be reserved for communists and their allies. The elections proved a stunning upset, with Solidarity candidates winning virtually all of the seats in the upper house or Senate, and all but one of the freely contested seats in the *sejm*. Jaruzelski reluctantly appointed a Solidarity leader as prime minister, and Poland's first noncommunist government since 1939 took office, charged with reversing the damage caused by an unresponsive command economy. The transition was eased by Solidarity's willingness to support Jaruzelski as president, while other communists were allowed to fill a small number of ministerial posts in the new government.

The collapse of the Polish satellite state was followed by parallel changes elsewhere. Without the support of Soviet troops to prop up their despised regimes, most of the Eastern Bloc's aging communist leaders resigned in the face of mammoth street demonstrations. In Hungary, reformers within the communist government allowed the formation of independent political parties during the spring of 1989. These reformers had earlier allowed some free-market reforms, and the positive results helped to spur political change. By the late 1980s middle-class Hungarians enjoyed Western-style shopping centers, second homes in the countryside, and a vibrant cultural life. Now the call was for political pluralism. The leader of the 1956 Hungarian rising against Soviet domination, Imre Nagy, was rehabilitated posthumously, and in the fall of 1989 a call for multi-party national elections was issued. In neighboring Czechoslovakia, communist rule imploded after a series of well-organized street demonstrations and mounting political opposition. At one demonstration in Prague, Alexander Dubček, leader of the failed 1968 uprising against Soviet overlordship, appeared on a balcony with Václav Havel, a dissident playwright who had spent years in a Czech prison for his defense of freedom, and who was now the coordinator of Civic Forum, an umbrella group for all opponents of the regime. A coalition government took office in early December 1989, and by the end of the month the political novice Havel was elected president.

The status of East Germany and the city of Berlin stood as the crucial test of Soviet policy toward greater Europe. In a land where frustration over the postwar division of the country was exacerbated by the lack of freedom and the type of economic prosperity found in the West, the demand for change came most dramatically in the form of massive human flight. Beginning in May 1989, thousands of East Germans fled across the newly opened border with Hungary. Some demanded asylum and camped out at the West German embassy in Budapest; others drove their automobiles to the border with Austria and eventually made their way to West Germany, where they were accorded instant citizenship. The exodus received full television news coverage, further discrediting the communist regime. Many of those who remained behind participated in pro-democracy demonstrations in cities and towns across the country, calling for the resignation of the elderly party leader Erich Honecker and ultimately forcing an embarrassed government to open the symbolic gates of the Berlin Wall in November 1989. The most depressing symbol of the Cold War had now been made irrelevant as hundreds of thousands crossed into West Berlin to celebrate, visit, shop, and consume. New communist leaders attempted desperately to push through a reform program that would placate a population eager to win additional freedoms, but it was too late. The entire East German Politburo resigned in early December, and subsequent free elections returned a government that was committed to reunification with the Federal Republic, a goal that was finally realized in October 1990. The Chancellor of reunited Germany, Helmut Kohl, reassured his Western allies that the new Germany would become a full participant in the ongoing process of European integration.

The swiftness of the fall, and the peaceful manner in which the communist leadership surrendered power to the opposition, would not have been possible without Soviet restraint. But success was also contingent upon both the depth of popular discontent and the willingness of millions of common people to take to the streets on behalf of democracy. Even in Bulgaria, where popular protest was minimal, younger communist party leaders acknowledged the need for reform. They ousted communist party secretary Todor Zhivkov, who had held power since the 1950s, and permitted multiparty elections in 1990. In every country where the Soviet Union had wielded its influence for more than four decades, the promise of communism appeared hollow to workers who lived in substandard housing, stood in long lines to purchase shoddy consumer goods, lacked meaningful opportunities for professional development, and saw little prospect of a better world for their children. The predictions of Marx, Lenin, and Stalin about the inevitable collapse of capitalist society seemed hopelessly in error; and while Marx's analysis of the oppression of the working class was still valid, ironically the bulk of the hardship seemed localized in the very communist states where the well-being of the proletariat was ostensibly the main concern of the government.

In one country only did the old order refuse to concede defeat. Romania's Nicolae Ceauşescu had ruled the country as a virtual dictator since the mid-1960s. Like Yugoslavia, Romania had broken with Moscow but remained committed to the rhetoric of the Marxist utopia. The reality, of course, was much different, and by the 1980s the country was saddled with enormous debt, food shortages, and some of the worst industrial pollution on the continent. Although access to television was restricted by the dictator, news of the revolutions elsewhere in Eastern Europe prompted a series of protests against the repressive policies of the government during December 1989. After ordering troops to open fire on demonstrators in the city of Timisoara on December 17, 1989, the demonstrations spread to the capital of Bucharest. Ceauşescu attempted to shore up his control with a televised outdoor speech to a hand-picked audience in Bucharest. When the speech was interrupted by shouts of derision from the crowd, the dictator appeared shaken and irresolute. In the face of mounting protests over the next few days, Ceauşescu and his wife Elena attempted to flee the country, but they were apprehended by a militia force, subjected to a military show trial, and executed by firing squad.

Soviet demise

The emancipation of the Eastern Bloc countries, together with the withdrawal of Soviet troops from Afghanistan, confirmed that the new leadership in the Kremlin was serious about domestic reform. Forging better relations with the West and focusing resources on domestic priorities were designed to reinvigorate the Marxist promise of a better quality of life for all. Most Soviet citizens welcomed the political liberties introduced under glasnost during the late 1980s, but Gorbachev's decision to dismantle the Soviet command economy and allow limited market-based reforms created enormous hardships for people who for decades had relied on state-subsidized consumer goods. When coupled with higher prices for basic necessities, the closure of inefficient state factories and the loss of job security that accompanied privatization raised the specter of widespread social unrest. Levels of frustration were especially high in the non-Russian Soviet Republics, where aging and often corrupt communist leaders were replaced by younger nationalists eager to sever all connections with Moscow. In the Baltic states of Latvia, Lithuania, and Estonia, popular calls for the restoration of sovereignty and the expulsion of Russian nationals, fueled by memories of the aggressive 1939 Hitler–Stalin Pact, inspired similar drives for independence across the empire. Nationalism was poised to triumph over the Leninist ideal of Soviet Socialist republics.

These dramatic convulsions were too much for hard-line communists and some military commanders to abide, and a plot to overthrow Gorbachev was carried out in August 1991 as the Soviet leader was vacationing at a Black Sea resort. Into this crisis stepped the newly elected president of the Russian Soviet Republic, Boris Yeltsin. A former communist who had joined the reformers in 1988, Yeltsin championed the ideals of democratic government, market economics, and Russian nationalism. Backed by thousands of protesters in each of Russia's major cities, the president was able to win the support of the military against the conspirators. Gorbachev returned to Moscow, but his power, and the credibility of the Soviet Communist Party, were irrevocably compromised. Yeltsin became an instant hero and the locus of real leadership, and when Ukranians voted for independence in the fall of 1991, the Russian leader declined to intervene. The remaining 14 Soviet republics wasted little time in following the Ukranian precedent, and by the end of the year the once powerful Marxian experiment that began in November 1917 was brought to an inglorious conclusion as the Soviet flag was removed from the Kremlin.

Yeltsin and Putin

During Yeltsin's tenure as president of Russia (1991–9), arms reduction talks with the US initiated under Gorbachev led to agreements that reduced the number of intercontinental ballistic missiles and eliminated an entire class of intermediate and short-range weapons.

The four former Soviet Republics that possessed ICBMs agreed to transfer these weapons to Russia, and the US provided financial assistance for the dismantling process. The threat of a superpower nuclear exchange that everyone understood would leave the earth uninhabitable was suddenly and thankfully removed. The Warsaw Pact was dissolved, and the former Eastern Bloc countries, keen to improve living conditions after four decades of subservience to the Soviet command economy, vied for membership in the dynamic and prosperous European Union.

Yeltsin moved quickly to accelerate the pace of market reforms, but he was opposed by conservatives in the Congress of People's Deputies. The conflict came to a head in 1993 when the president dissolved the Congress and ordered the delegates to vacate the parliament building, known as the White House. After anti-Yeltsin forces attacked the state television station, the president ordered the use of military force against the White House, compelling his opponents to capitulate. Elections in December 1993 allowed Yeltsin to retain a slim majority of support in parliament, but while he was reelected to the presidency in 1996, the increasingly mercurial leader was unable to lift the country out of its economic woes. Often in poor health, Yeltsin was accused by critics of being the unwitting tool of urban oligarchs who enriched themselves in the new market economy through their political connections. The conspicuous consumption of the few in Russia's major cities bred much popular resentment and disaffection. During the period 1989–97 GDP decreased by nearly half, wages were depressed, and crime statistics reached record highs.

By the time that prime minister Vladimir Putin, a Yeltsin protégé and career KGB officer, was elected president in March 2000, many Russians had lost confidence in the government's ability to improve their lives through market-based reforms. Across the country there was a growing mood of nostalgia for the securities of the old Soviet system, with its guaranteed employment and provision of basic goods and services. Putin, who at age 47 was both an uncharacteristically youthful national leader and a practicing Russian Orthodox Christian, pledged to crack down on official corruption, put an end to the illicit black market in goods and services, and resolve the ongoing military crisis in the province of Chechnya. He began a concerted effort to accrue more power at the center by removing the governors of Russia's 89 regions from the upper chamber of parliament, and by increasing state control over the television networks. But while he was elected to a second term in 2004, the rise of terror attacks by Chechnyan separatists forced the president to turn most of his attention to domestic security issues, neglecting more basic economic reforms.

Europe's economic integration

First established in 1958 and designed to give small states the type of bargaining influence in the world economy normally reserved for great powers, the European Economic Community (EEC) swiftly became an enviable free-trade zone by the mid-1960s. The EEC also served to undo some of the more belligerent forms of nationalism that had divided Europeans and contributed to two world wars. Membership expanded during the 1970s and 1980s, to the delight of those who were convinced that common economic ties would lessen the likelihood of future political and military conflict in Europe. In 1992 the 15 member states of the renamed European Union (EU) signed the Maastricht Treaty, a landmark agreement designed to achieve full economic and monetary union across multiple borders. By that date the EU had become the single largest market in the world, producing over 20 percent of world exports. EU residents enjoyed the right to work in any member state, and a European parliament and court of justice, although occasionally disparaged by individual heads of state, made incremental progress in the work of building a common political culture. In 1999 most EU states adopted a common currency, making trade across borders even more seamless. By every economic measure, the once-shattered continent had transformed itself into economic superpower. The post-World War II American dream of a peaceful and prosperous Europe was now a reality, with cross-border travel, trade, and employment tempering old national rivalries and setting new standards for regional development.

Not surprisingly, most of the former communist countries in Eastern Europe applied for membership in the EU, and in the North Atlantic Treaty Organization (NATO), by the end of the twentieth century. The original Cold War mandate of NATO was to prevent Soviet expansion into Western Europe, and with the demise of the Warsaw Pact some observers questioned the purpose of the NATO alliance. But the US pressed for a reconceptualized NATO as a regional security organization. This was little comfort to officials in Moscow, especially when membership was extended to Poland, Hungary, and the Czech Republic in 1997. Yet despite their public upset, neither Yeltsin nor Putin allowed the issue to compromise US–Russian diplomatic relations. The bid for EU membership was much more significant for the future of Europe in terms of economic integration and parity across borders. Most of the newly democratic states in Eastern Europe did not experience any significant improvement in living conditions during the 1990s. Saddled with debt to the West (much of it contracted by their spendthrift communist predecessors), lacking the modern industrial and technological infrastructure enjoyed by the West, struggling with high levels of unemployment, and facing trade barriers that frustrated efforts to penetrate the EU market, securing membership in the EU became a top priority for political leaders of all parties. By 2004 Hungary and Poland had been admitted, while Turkey's candidacy (a NATO member) had become embroiled in a wider debate over the place of a predominantly Muslim country in the organization.

Southeastern Europe and the NATO consensus

The American vision for a new NATO was put to the test in the lands of the former Yugoslavia during the mid-1990s. Beginning in the 1970s, the Tito regime had liberalized its economic policies, allowing the development of small private-enterprise sectors and introducing profit-sharing schemes for workers in state-owned factories. Trade links with the noncommunist world were strong, and the government ensured that Yugoslavia's multiethnic population, which included an Orthodox and Catholic majority in Serbia and Croatia, and a large Muslim population in Bosnia, lived and worked together in relative harmony. After Tito's death in 1980 no one political figure ascended as the symbol of unity within the existing federal system, and with the fall of communism elsewhere in 1989 the call for national self-determination along ethnic lines reached a crescendo. In 1991 the leaders of Slovenia and Croatia declared independence for their respective republics. The ex-communist Serbian leader, Slobodan Milošević, immediately raised the banner of ethnic nationalism, demanding that all ethnic Serbs – irrespective of where they may have migrated over the previous 40 years under Tito's government – were in fact part of a greater Serbian state.

Convinced that the nationalist card offered him the best opportunity to remain in power, Milošević sent Serbian troops first into neighboring Croatia, and then into Bosnia, to secure those regions where Serbs constituted a majority of the population. Not content with their territorial aggression, the Serbs instituted a policy of "ethnic cleansing" in Bosnia, terrorizing the Muslim inhabitants with the goal of expelling them from their homes. The Bosnian capital of Sarajevo was bombed, reducing portions of the central city, host of the 1984 Winter Olympics, to rubble. In the meantime, the Croatian government began expelling ethnic Serbs from its sovereign territory, and joined the cynical assault on Bosnia in an effort to seize lands where ethnic Croats constituted a majority of the population.

The resurgence of ethnic nationalism in Southeastern Europe, with neighbor distrusting neighbor; private armies pillaging and raping with impunity; cities, towns, and villages destroyed; and political leaders fueling the culture of hate, all served to put a prosperous European community on notice that the politics of division remained very much alive on the continent. Former British Prime Minister Margaret Thatcher equated ethnic cleansing with the worst horrors of the Nazi regime. By 1994 over one million people had become refugees in the Balkans, thousands of civilians had been killed, and prospects for a peaceful resolution to the fighting were dim. Bosnia appealed to the UN for help, and in 1995 NATO aircraft began bombing Serbian-held positions in the country. The air attacks seemed to have the desired effect, and in 1995 an agreement was brokered in Dayton, Ohio, giving Bosnia independence and inserting NATO ground forces to guarantee the peace.

Milošević quickly identified alternative targets for Serbian nationalist rage. Beginning in 1997, Serb troops moved against ethnic Albanians who lived in the province of Kosovo. Once again stories of ethnic cleansing dominated the Western media; once again NATO air strikes were ordered against the Serbs. Facing strong international sanctions and a crippled economy, Milošević was voted out of power in 2000. Arrested the following year and extradited to the UN War Crimes Tribunal in the Hague in 2002, the Serbian leader was charged with crimes against humanity and genocide for his role in three wars that claimed the lives of more than 200,000 people during the 1990s. Nonplussed by the accusations against him, the defiant former president of Yugoslavia insisted on serving as his own attorney and claimed that the prosecution's case amounted to "an unscrupulous lie and a treacherous distortion of history." Whatever Milošević's reading of the past, Southeastern Europe remained under the watchful eye of NATO peacekeepers at the start of the twenty-first century, a fractured land where the poison of ethnic nationalism stood as a dark counterpoint to the promise of European union.

THE RESURGENCE OF CHINA

Viewed within the context of the entire sweep of world history, the economic, political, and military dominance of the West has been in place for but a moment. Indeed less than 200 years ago, two non-Western agrarian empires – India and China – were responsible for two-thirds of the world's total economic output. Only with the formation of the modern nation-state, born of the French and American Revolutions, together with the rise of industrial capitalism in the nineteenth century, did Western Europe, and subsequently the US, attain levels of global influence that dwarfed all earlier efforts. This influence continued throughout the period covered by this book, but toward the end of the century East Asia began to reassert its historic dynamism. Japan's postwar economic growth was astounding; by the year 2000 this resource-poor democracy had become the world's second largest economy. The four Asian "Tigers" – Singapore, Hong Kong, South Korea, and Taiwan, raced ahead of their neighbors to create mature industrial economies. And China, with over 1.2 billion inhabitants in 2000, was projected to surpass both the US and Japan in total economic output by the third decade of the twenty-first century.

The great anomaly

China's rapid economic development under the leadership of Deng Xiaoping during the 1980s and 1990s enabled the country to re-assume its leading role in international affairs after almost two cen-turies of humiliating neocolonial status. Deng's accomplishment was all the more striking in light of the very long shadow cast by China's "Great Helmsman," Mao Zedong. From the moment of victory in 1949 until his death in 1976, Mao's unwavering vision of China's economic future was guided by the promise of Marxist–Leninist eco-nomic theory. For nearly three decades, Deng stood as a rival to Mao within the leadership of the Chinese Communist Party, and at most critical junctures Mao emerged triumphant. Although both men rep-resented the first generation of communist leaders (Deng was 11 years younger than Mao), they disagreed over the appropriate role of the state in the economy, with Mao emphasizing heavy controls and a focus on China's self-reliance, while Deng adopted a more market-oriented, internationalist stance. Unlike Mao, Deng had spent time overseas as a young man, and this experience impressed upon him the need for China to engage with, and learn from, the Western powers. A brief look back at China's political and economic development under communism will better define the significance of the economic reforms undertaken by China's leaders since the mid-1990s.

In 1953, both Mao and Deng supported a Soviet-style Five Year Plan for China, and it was a success in terms of increasing the country's industrial output. Soviet advisors provided much-needed technical support, while loans from Moscow and direct taxes on the Chinese peasantry allowed the government to build and maintain hundreds of state-run factories. The collectivization of Chinese farms was nearly complete by the end of 1956, giving the govern-ment greater control over the revenues generated in the agricultural sector, and facilitating the transfer of wealth from the countryside to the industrial cities. Despite government ownership of major enterprises, however, China's industrialization tended to exacerbate the gap between rich and poor. This was most apparent in the cities, where a new managerial and technocratic class emerged. Together with growing numbers of engineers and scientists, by the late 1950s the educated elite lived a quality of life that was unavailable to most industrial workers and their rural counterparts.

Under the Five Year Plan, the percentage of government funds dedicated to agricultural improvements was minor. Mao, whose strongest base of support had always been in the countryside, began to fear that industrialization, instead of accelerating China's passage into the socialist utopia, was merely enriching those fortunate urbanites with the appropriate educational background or political connections. His principal rivals within the party leadership at this time, Liu Shaoqi and Deng, remained adamant in their support for urban industrial development, convinced that China's return to great power status could not be achieved without it. The resulting social and economic disparities were, in their view, a regrettable but necessary by-product of rapid modernization. In 1957, believing that socialist reforms were taking hold, the government relaxed controls over speech and artistic expression, inaugurating the so-called "Hundred Flowers" movement. Almost immediately, a torrent of criticism was directed against the Communist Party. It shocked and worried the leadership, and after the government hastily crushed the dissent, Mao moved to upstage his rivals by pressing for a radically different social and economic plan of action for China, one that he believed would ensure socialist equality.

The plan, known as Great Leap Forward, was designed to balance urban and rural development while taking better advantage of the vast pool of labor located in the countryside. Centralized bureaucracies were scaled back, and more power was placed in the hands of local party officials, most of whom were Maoists. In addition, Mao called for the creation of "people's communes" where industrial and agricultural pursuits would be undertaken without the corrupting influence of material rewards. Begun in 1958, some communes were affiliated with large factories, but the vast majority were located in the countryside. Each rural commune contained an average of 30,000 people and involved the construction of millions of small rural factories where peasants would learn basic industrial skills. In this way the distinctions between city and village would be eliminated, while the imposition of communal dining halls, child-care centers, and facilities for the aged would inculcate the values of socialist cooperation.

The progam affected every part of the country, but the vision of a new classless paradise fell tragically short. Steel production did reach record highs, but as thousands of peasants were diverted to mines and factories, agriculture was neglected. By 1959 grain reserves were exhausted, and when drought struck the interior and floods lashed the coastal areas that same year, disaster followed. More than 15 million (mostly rural) Chinese died from hunger between 1959 and 1961, and some estimates (no reliable statistics are available) place the death toll at double that chilling figure. This human catastrophe occurred just as China's estrangement from the Soviet Union was reaching a crisis point. In June 1959 Khrushchev informed Mao that the Soviet Union would no longer aid China with its nuclear development program; one year later the Soviets withdrew all of their technical advisors. Working-class solidarity across national boundaries, a central feature of Marxian thought for more than a century, was in tatters.

The Great Leap Forward was, in the short term, a political debacle for Mao. Although he remained as head of the Chinese Communist Party, his opponents on the Central Committee obliged him to resign as Chairman of the Republic. He was succeeded as head of state by Liu Shaoqi, while Liu's ally Deng remained in office as Secretary-General. During the early 1960s Mao and his political allies were in eclipse, yet they continued to criticize the government's failure to tackle the problem of growing economic inequalities. By 1965 Mao was convinced that a new appeal to China's youth was in order; he returned to Beijing from Shanghai, where he had been living for the previous year, and immediately called a meeting of the Central Committee of the Communist Party – the first such meeting since 1962. At that meeting Mao convinced the party plenum to approve a sweeping program dedicated to a great Cultural Revolution. If successful, it would put an end, once and for all, to the remains of capitalism – the private plots, the wage differentials, the production incentives, and the alleged lethargy and corruption at the highest levels of government.

The Cultural Revolution

During his years of diminished power, Mao had retained the support of the People's Liberation Army, and it was here that the handbook *Quotations from Chairman Mao* made its debut in 1964. Mao's "little red book" became the essential text of the unfolding Great Proletarian Cultural Revolution, a carefully orchestrated drive to discredit the policies of Liu Shaoqi and Deng Xiaoping and to restore Mao to political primacy in China. At the head of the People's Liberation Army was Lin Biao, a staunch supporter of Mao, and during 1966 the military allowed the formation of the "Red Guards," cadres of university and secondary students who took the lead in the ideological assault against the government of Liu Shaoqi. By the summer of 1966 the Red Guards had succeeded in closing most schools and universities pending the implementation of the Cultural Revolution; the universities would remain closed for the next four years. With Mao's tacit support, the Red Guards inaugurated a campaign of intimidation against government officials, assaulting and publicly humiliating local functionaries, teachers, and university administrators. All remnants of Western and capitalist influence in the arts, literature, and museums were targeted for destruction, and those who appeared to be lukewarm about the agenda were branded as unreconstructed capitalists.

By the end of the year the law and order functions of government were being severely tested by a movement that was now operating outside the normal confines of the Chinese Communist Party. Indeed the Red Guards were convinced, along with Mao, that the Party itself had become indifferent to the plight of the country's peasant majority. In Shanghai, the Cultural Revolution was spearheaded by the city's industrial proletariat. The workers wrested control of city government and in early 1967 established a semiautonomous commune. Elsewhere in China, confrontations between Maoists and pro-Liu and Deng factions became more numerous, inviting the specter of civil war. In the fall of 1967 Mao turned his reforming zeal against his opponents in the Party, exiling unreconstructed bureaucrats to "reeducation" labor camps in the countryside. Liu Shaoqi died in confinement in 1969, while Deng was discredited and removed from his leadership role. By the early 1970s the party organization had been remolded in Mao's image, and his closest ally during the height of the Cultural Revolution, army chief Lin Biao, was elevated to vice-chair of the Communist Party and designated as successor.

The excesses of the Cultural Revolution coincided with a further deterioration of Sino-Soviet relations. By 1970 there were almost one million Soviet troops facing an equal number of Chinese soldiers along their joint border. Mao's commitment to a policy of self-reliance, coupled with a deep suspicion of Soviet intentions (especially after the 1968 Soviet invasion of Czechoslovakia) worldwide, led him to embark upon another radical initiative: Negotiations with the US, a prospect that was anathema to Maoists just a few years earlier, now became the centerpiece of the Great Helmsman's foreign policy. Engagement with the US, Mao believed, would advantage China since it had successfully tested its own nuclear bomb in 1966, placing both superpowers on notice that China expected to be treated as an equal.

The return of Deng Xiaoping

Mao's designated heir apparent, Lin Biao, was unenthusiastic about the rapprochement with the Americans. His death in 1971, under circumstances still shrouded by mystery, cleared the way for President Nixon's visit to Beijing in February 1972. Zhoi En-lai had succeeded Lin as China's top administrator during the early 1970s, but when he was diagnosed with cancer in 1972, an ailing Mao reluctantly turned to Deng Xiaoping. It was an unlikely restoration. Detailed under house arrest during the early stages of the Cultural Revolution, Deng relocated to Jiangxi province in the southeast of the country in 1969. There he and his wife lived in modest retirement, no doubt assuming that political events had passed them by. Returning to Beijing in 1973, Deng assumed a number of high-level duties as vice-chairman of the party. After Mao's death in 1976 and the subsequent power struggle between the so-called "gang of four" (led by Mao's widow Jiang Qing) and premier Hua Guofeng, Deng methodically consolidated his support within the Party. By the end of January 1979 he undertook an official state visit to the US and approved the establishment of full diplomatic relations with Washington.

The death of Mao signaled the beginning of the end of China's command economy. As soon as he solidified his power at the

Eleventh Central Committee of the Communist Party in December 1978, Deng launched an ambitious economic program designed to upgrade agriculture, industry, national defense, and science and technology. Called the "Four Modernizations," the development goals were to be reached by adopting market-based reforms, what the Party leadership euphemistically referred to as "socialism with Chinese characteristics." In the agricultural sector, people's communes were abandoned and family farms were restored. While denied full ownership rights, farmers were permitted to lease land from the state for 50 years and retain all profits earned after paying an annual percentage to the government. The result of this "household responsibility" system was an immediate surge in agricultural productivity. Enterprising farmers hired their own laborers and began focusing on cash crops for distant markets, a strategy which in turn led the development of more efficient transportation networks and additional job opportunities.

Deng's government also encouraged the establishment of profit-driven private business and industrial enterprises. State-mandated price controls over industrial products and foodstuffs were lifted, and the so-called "iron rice bowl" – the guarantee of permanent employment for state-sector workers – was withdrawn. Managers were provided greater flexibility in the hiring and dismissal of workers, and state enterprises were expected to turn a profit. Four special economic zones were established along the southeast coast in Guangdong and Fujian provinces in 1979 and additional areas of market-based development – all open to foreign investment – were designated during the 1980s. Membership in the World Bank and the International Monetary Fund provided opportunities for China to secure valuable economic and technical advice. Thousands of Chinese college-age students were permitted to study in the US and Europe for advanced business, technical, and scientific training. By the late 1980s China's major cities were dotted with nonstate, for-profit enterprises, many of them owned by Western capitalists. The Maoist vision of self-reliance was cast off as foreign loans, investment, and manufacturing plants returned to the mainland. Living standards improved for skilled urban dwellers who now enjoyed higher wages and access to a wider range of consumer goods, while millions of rural laborers flooded into towns and cities seeking employment in the new private companies.

Deng's efforts to combine a pragmatic economic program with a repressive political system fostered acute tension within the leadership elite, with conservatives denouncing the corrupting influences of bourgeois economic values. University students, teachers, and state-sector workers were especially upset by allegations of widespread corruption and nepotism within the Party during the 1980s. In 1988, the official Chinese media reported that between 1983 and 1988 there were almost 300,000 cases of serious economic crimes involving such activities as theft of public property and bribery. The experiences of Chinese students who had trained in the West, the interactions with foreign visitors and businesspeople, and the increased access to foreign publications and electronic news outlets all contributed to a mood of growing discontent with the political status quo. By the late 1980s student protesters were joined by industrial workers who were threatened with unemployment as inefficient state enterprises were shut down, or whose real wages fell when inflation struck after the removal of traditional price controls.

Tiananmen and beyond

Reformers within the government recognized that they were navigating uncharted waters in their efforts to modernize the economy while refusing to permit challenges to the communist political order. They viewed with increasing alarm developments in Gorbachev's Soviet Union under glasnost, where new political freedoms after 1985 appeared to threaten the stability of the regime. Protests and work slowdowns in China became more common after 1986; in 1987 alone there were 129 strikes nationwide. When over a million students converged on Tiananmen Square in Beijing in the spring of 1989, shouting democratic slogans and erecting a mock-up of the Statue of Liberty, Party hard-liners led by Premier Li Peng urged a decisive crackdown lest the Chinese Communist Party lose its monopoly grip on power. The demonstrations were at their height in mid-May 1989 as Gorbachev arrived in Beijing to normalize diplomatic relations with the People's Republic. The visit, which should have been a moment of triumph for Deng's government, proved to be a huge embarrassment. Two days after Gorbachev's departure, the government imposed martial law, declaring that the safety and well-being of the country hung in the balance. On June 4 the tanks rolled into the center of the city. Estimates of the number of people killed by the People's Liberation Army vary widely, but the government's heavy-handed actions triggered protests and violence in other cities. Mass arrests followed the military assault; protest leaders were hunted down and in some cases executed, while most received extended prison terms. Intellectuals and supporters of press freedoms within the Party were expelled, and university students were forbidden to engage in further political activities. Despite widespread international condemnation, China's leaders defended their actions; the People's Republic was not about to suffer the fate of its communist counterparts in Eastern Europe.

The anomaly of political repression and capitalist economics continued during the1990s. Loath to forgo China's enormous potential as a trading partner, most of the international sanctions that had been imposed after Tiananmen were lifted by 1992. It was a decade of exceptional economic growth for China as GDP rose at an annual rate of 11 percent. Deng's economic strategy was reaffirmed by the Fourteenth Party Congress in 1992, and after his death in 1997 the reformers, led by Jiang Zemin, continued the push toward greater privatization and internationalization. Ethnic Chinese living overseas were encouraged by the government to invest in a wide variety of development schemes, and the response was vigorous. Successful ethnic Chinese living in Southeast Asian countries contributed 8 percent of the total foreign direct investment in China in 1997, suggesting that many members of the diaspora community felt a strong obligation to assist in the process of restoring China to great-power status. By the end of the decade, Japanese and American corporations, lured by attractive wage levels, represented the most important source of foreign investment in the country. For thousands of Chinese citizens, employment in one of the foreign-owned factories that produced virtually every type of product for a global market represented a unprecedented opportunity for economic betterment. A variety of consumer goods, previously unavailable in the domestic market, now lined the shelves of department stores. In China's major cities, a Western-style consumer culture supplanted the values of socialism as articulated by the Party under Mao's leadership. The most successful entrepreneurs embraced the philosophy of conspicuous consumption in a manner that highlighted the radical departure in the government's definition of progress.

As in other parts of the developed world, the new economic order in China created both winners and losers. Despite Deng's claims that there was a fundamental distinction between Western-style capitalism and a socialist "market economy," the social problems that troubled capitalist countries were very much in evidence in 1990s China. Most disturbing for those who remained wedded to, or nostalgic for, the Maoist state was the degree of economic inequality fostered by the market economy. Millions of unemployed – mostly recent arrivals to the cities – demanded assistance in the search for jobs and housing. Between 1997 and 2000, there were over 100,000 worker demonstrations nationwide, each involving several hundred persons protesting the closure of state factories. Cities faced rising rates of crime, prostitution, and drug use. Rural inhabitants begrudged the lower taxes and higher incomes enjoyed by city dwellers; residents in the interior of the country disapproved of the investment funds targeted at coastal areas; employees in government-owned industries resented the newfound affluence of their private-sector counterparts; teachers and university lecturers complained bitterly about their meager salaries and low social status; and everyone castigated political elites who appeared to use their official status and personal connections to enhance their wealth at public expense. When the mayor of Beijing, Chen Xitong, was sentenced to 16 years in prison in 1995 for taking bribes in a construction-licensing scandal, many believed that Chen was made the scapegoat for what in reality was a much larger pattern of official malfeasance across China. The unprecedented passage to a capitalist economic model in a communist country, where political power had for decades been restricted to a tiny elite, provided ample opportunity for the abuse of power, and despite a barrage of new regulations, the culture of official jobbery continued into the new century.

When Deng died in 1997 at the age of 88, the country was well on its way to becoming an economic powerhouse, although the party's leaders – Deng included – continued to insist that theirs was a uniquely socialist society. Whether Marx or Mao would recognize it as such was another matter; certainly the prospect of rising social tensions between the urban haves and the mostly rural have-nots threatened domestic order. Deng had opted for the course that would ensure rapid development; in the process the old communist revolutionary had deftly positioned China to take its place alongside the great capitalist countries of the globe. Whether this rising affluence (perhaps best symbolized by China's recent entry into the World Trade Organization) would prompt calls for greater openness and political liberalization remained, in 2005, very much an open question.

China and its borders

At the start of the twenty-first century China stood as the last great world empire, ruling over non-Han ethnic groups – all with distinct, ancient cultures – in Tibet, Xinjiang, Inner Mongolia, and Yunnan, and determined to restore the "renegade" province of Taiwan, and the islands of the South China Sea. China's grip over Tibet caused the greatest international friction; large anti-Chinese demonstrations in 1989 led to a harsh crackdown and the imposition of martial law. That same year Tibet's exiled spiritual leader, the Dalai Lama, was awarded the Nobel Peace Prize, but Deng's government continued to insist that Tibet was an integral part of the Chinese nation. When the Panchen Lama, traditionally second in command after the Dalai Lama, died unexpectedly in 1989, Beiing refused to accept the Dalai Lama's choice of a successor, naming their own more pliable candidate for the post. In the mineral-rich and majority Muslim province of Xinjiang, site of China's nuclear weapons installations, separatist tendencies were labeled as Islamic fundamentalism by the central government in Beijing. Clashes, bombings, and assassinations during the 1990s only hardened the resolve of the state; according to Amnesty International, Chinese authorities carried out almost 200 executions in the region between 1997 and April 1999. In 2002 the government's hard-line position was strengthened immensely when the Bush administration identified a Xinjiang Muslim group as a terrorist organization, thus effectively equating China's repressive policies in the region with the global war on terror.

The return of Hong Kong in 1997 marked an important milestone in the reconstruction of a country that had suffered repeated humiliation at the hands of Western imperialists during the nineteenth century. The agreement detailing the transfer from British to

Chinese control had been negotiated in 1984 by Margaret Thatcher's government, and it called for a 50-year period during which Hong Kong's capitalist economy would remain unhindered. Since the largest percentage of foreign investment in China during the early 1990s originated in Hong Kong, Beijing had a strategic interest in honoring the 1984 agreement, and the "one country, two systems" model paid important dividends for all interested parties at the beginning of the new century. And two years after the momentous transfer of Hong Kong to Chinese sovereignty, Portugal's 400-year-old colony at Macao was returned to China, thereby completing the exit of Western powers from the mainland.

Taiwan remained the most intractable and highly divisive of the territorial issues facing the market-oriented Chinese communist government during the 1990s. Both Deng Xiaoping and his successor Jiang Zemin echoed Mao's claim that Taiwan was a renegade province lacking international legitimacy. During Chiang Kai-shek's long tenure as president of Taiwan (1949–75), the island stood as a symbol of the global sweep of the Cold War. Even after the US recognized the People's Republic as the sole government of China in 1979, American pledges to defend Taiwan against a forcible takeover served to complicate every bilateral interaction. The prosperous Taiwanese economy, and greater democratization during the 1980s and 1990s, encouraged many native Taiwanese to push for a declaration of independence. All such soundings infuriated the government in Beijing and led to a number of provocative naval exercises and missile tests in the Straits of Taiwan.

While Taiwan's President Lee Teng-hui (1988–2000) worked assiduously to improve trade and travel connections with mainland China, the election of Chen Shui-bian as president in 2000 ushered in a new round of heightened tensions. The president had previously supported calls for independence, and although once in office he softened his position, his Democratic Progressive Party was viewed with deep suspicion in Beijing. The American administration of George W. Bush continued to sell sophisticated weapons systems to Taiwan, and the US president spoke repeatedly of honoring commitments to Taiwan in the event of a Chinese attack. Since political reunification would further boost mainland China's modernization program, and as China was nominally a participant in the wider war on terrorism after 2001, the Bush position on Taiwan appeared to some observers as unduly provocative. At the very least it contributed to Beijing's perception that the US remained committed to denying China its rightful place as the major power in East Asia.

Within this larger domestic and international context, the prospect that any independent political activity would be tolerated by the state remained weak. Even a popular religious movement that promoted traditional Buddhist and Taoist beliefs and practices, the Falungong, was banned in 1999 after 10,000 of its adherents demonstrated peacefully in Beijing. By the early twenty-first century, the Party leadership continued to perform its unprecedented high-wire act, claiming the mantle of Mao's revolutionary idealism and patriotism, while simultaneously rejecting the economic underpinnings of the Marxist worldview that Mao took with him to the grave. But as the communications revolution spurred by the Internet continued to sweep across China, and as the private-sector economy took its place as the most dynamic force in material culture, the future of political absolutism under the guise of communist solidarity appeared increasingly uncertain.

North Korea: The last Stalinist state

China's embrace of Western-style capitalism in the 1980s left North Korea as the remaining Marxist command economy in the region. And when its chief fiscal patron, the Soviet Union, disappeared from the international scene in 1991, North Korea's long-serving dictator, Kim Il Sung, sought to prevent the collapse of the secretive regime and to leverage much needed economic assistance by pursuing a nuclear weapons development program. China's establishment of diplomatic relations with South Korea in 1992, and the robust trade relationship that emerged between the two states, further isolated the dictatorship in Pyongyang. In 1994 the International Atomic Energy Agency, frustrated by North Korea's refusal to allow inspectors open access to suspected weapons sites, declared that the country was in noncompliance with the 1985 Nuclear Non-Proliferation Treaty. When Kim Il Sung died in 1994, he was succeeded by his equally paranoid and dictatorial son, Kim

Jong Il. While at first willing to freeze its weapons development program and dismantle existing nuclear energy plants in return for US and Japanese economic and energy assistance, the North Koreans continued to avoid full disclosure. Allegations of secret nuclear weapons sites persisted, and in1998 the government again refused to permit unrestricted access at suspected locations. By this point reports of widespread crop failures, malnutrition, and even starvation of upwards of two million people signaled the frightening prospect of a failed state capable of lashing out against its neighbors with weapons of mass destruction at a moment's notice.

As North Korea's internal economic crisis escalated, the prospect of a German-style reunification, where the Korean people might work out the problems afflicting the North, prompted the irredentist regime to rely more heavily on nuclear blackmail in order to survive. George W. Bush named the isolated Marxist state part of the "Axis of Evil" in 2002, and in predictable fashion Kim Jong Il withdrew from the International Non-Proliferation Treaty. The following year Pyongyang announced that it was developing a "nuclear deterrent" against hostile powers, and in February 2005 declared that it had nuclear weapons. Two months later the head of the US Defense Intelligence Agency stated that North Korea now had the technology to arm its missiles with nuclear warheads, making both Japan and the West coast of the US vulnerable to attack. Earlier six-party talks involving North Korea, South Korea, Japan, Russia, China, and the US failed to produce a meaningful agreement on the nuclear issue, and fresh approaches to resolving the decade-long stalemate seemed elusive.

AMBIGUITY IN THE DEVELOPING WORLD
Latin America and El Norte

The collapse of the Soviet Union and the discrediting of the collectivized command economy had important repercussions in Central and South America. Fidel Castro's Cuba became a relic of the Cold War, and while the rhetorical sparring between the old leader and successive American administrations continued after 1990, the island nation lost much of its relevance on the larger geopolitical stage. With a failing economy and disintegrating health and social services, Cuba's future under the Castro dictatorship looked grim, but without any meaningful political opposition, the government's adherence to failed economic policies continued.

With Cuba as the anomaly, the trend across much of Latin America during the 1990s was toward greater political pluralism and market-driven economic reform. The 1980s had been a "lost decade" for much of South America, as oil and commodity revenues decreased and debt to the North spiraled. Harsh military rule had been discredited in Argentina after the disastrous 1983 Falklands/ Malvinas War, while in Brazil, the continent's largest and most populous country, the 20-year ascendancy of the generals ended in 1985, setting the stage for political reform elsewhere. When José Sarney took the oath of office as Brazil's first civilian president in over two decades, he presided over the world's eighth largest market economy and the fourth biggest food exporter. Two-thirds of Brazil's 125 million citizens lived in urban areas, and all hoped that the return to democracy would translate into greater opportunity for the two out of three Brazilians who earned less than $115 per year. In order to address the mounting debt crisis, the new democratic governments were obliged to cut domestic spending and scale back popular social programs.

In the Central American states of Guatemala, Nicaragua, and El Salvador, bloody civil wars ended when leftist insurgents lost Soviet financial support. During the 1980s the Reagan administration provided covert military support and training for opponents of the Marxist Sandinista government in Nicaragua. The result was a bloody civil war in which thousands of civilians were made homeless or killed by anti-Sandinista guerrillas, or "freedom fighters," as they were referred to by the American president. Leftist insurgency in El Salvador sparked another brutal war in the region. Among the victims of right-wing death squads in the latter country was the archbishop of San Salvador and champion of the poor, Oscar Romero, who was gunned down while celebrating mass in 1980. In Guatemala, approximately half a million citizens had fled their homes in the early 1980s, fearful that the military junta would target them as opponents. A regional peace plan sponsored by President Oscar Arias of Costa Rica, calling for reconciliation and democratization, was signed in 1987, and this provided the framework for regional elections. The leftist Sandinista regime in Nicaragua was dislodged by voters in 1990, and two years later a UN-brokered peace agreement was reached in El Salvador. The conflict in Guatemala finally came to an end in 1996.

Across the continent during the 1990s state-owned businesses were privatized, tariff protections and official subsidies for favored enterprises were dropped, and in their place privatization schemes and incentives for foreign investors were adopted. In Peru, for example, President Alberto Fujimori began selling state enterprises to private investors soon after his election to office in 1990. For most of the decade Fujimori's authoritarian style was tolerated by the population as long as the economy continued to improve. Other right-wing leaders, like General Pinochet of Chile, similarly embraced the banner of free trade and private ownership. Following the advice of economists who were heavily influenced by the American model, inflation was brought under control and growth rates of 6 percent were realized by the early 1990s. Pinochet's civilian successors maintained his economic policies throughout the 1990s, winning the confidence of the Chilean financial community and fostering greater international investment.

The biggest sign of the changing political and economic climate in Central and South America involved plans for a multistate free-trade zone. In 1992 President George H. W. Bush called for the creation of a hemispheric trading partnership. This overly ambitious project did not come to fruition, but it did spur discussions on multilateral partnerships. After years of negotiation, in 1992 the US, Mexico, and Canada signed the North American Free Trade Agreement (NAFTA), eliminating trade barriers and encouraging the movement of goods and production facilities across borders. When the pact was implemented in 1994, a number of US manufacturing plants relocated just across the Rio Grande River in Mexico, drawn there by an abundant low-wage work force. In 2000 Mexican voters put an end to the monopoly on political power held by the Institutional Revolutionary Party since 1917, electing a president who pledged to further the market-based economic reforms. NAFTA-like multilateral agreements were worked out among other states in South America: Argentina, Brazil, Paraguay, and Uruguay created a giant free-trade zone, while Venezuela, Peru, Ecuador, and

Bolivia revived a regional Andean Pact that had first been adopted in the 1970s. The new emphasis on regional trade did not free Latin American economies from a heavy reliance on cash-crop exports, but it did foster a greater sense of regional integration and cooperation.

Lingering dependency

Despite the policies of economic liberalization, social and economic divisions remained great throughout the continent. According to historian Peter Winn, in 2000 Latin America had "the most unequal distribution of income, land, and wealth in the world." Approximately 40 percent of the population received less than 10 percent of the total income, at a time when spending on social programs was scaled back as part of the effort to reduce the size and cost of government. Rural-to-urban migration intensified during the 1990s, but most of those who crowded into urban shantytowns were unsuccessful in their quest for meaningful employment. Mexico City's population, for example, exploded from three million in 1950 to almost 20 million in 2000. Efforts to diversify national economies met with mixed success. In 2004 most countries in Latin America continued to rely heavily on the North for new technologies, while the information economy remained in its infancy.

The bulk of the Latin American export market remained tied to the agricultural sector, with products like coffee, sugar, and bananas serving as the key commodities in global trade. Only one cash crop managed to maintain its value in an increasingly volatile global market, and that crop happened to be illegal. Coca leaves cultivated by poor farmers in the Andean countries of Bolivia and Peru were transported to Colombia where clandestine factories refined them into pure cocaine. By the mid-1980s Colombia's leading narco-traffickers wielded enormous power and used a portion of their illicit profits to intimidate and bribe law-enforcement officers and politicians alike, thereby undercutting the very fabric of civil society. The US spent millions to support the Colombian government in its efforts to combat the drug cartels and their hired killers, but the lavish support did nothing to address the deeper problem of consumer demand. In November 1998 a Colombian air-force plane was seized at the airport in Fort Lauderdale, Florida. The plane had never been outside of the military's control, yet 600 lb of cocaine were discovered on board. The payoff for a successful smuggling operation was still worth the risks involved.

Thus the late twentieth-century transition to political democracy – to the point where nearly every Latin American country at the start of the new century had leaders elected through the democratic process – seemed to matter little in terms of broad-based human betterment. Delegates to a 1993 "Summit of the Americas" in Miami had spoken optimistically of hemispheric unity, the strengthening of democratic institutions, and the eradication of poverty. But four years later, when a second summit was convened in Santiago, Chile, the rhetoric was more restrained. A mood of ambivalence, a sense that the promise of democratic politics had not been met, and the suspicion that the market revolution and globalization were only exacerbating the economic and social ills of the long-suffering continent, led critics to question the value of the ballot box to fundamental reform. In 2002 the World Bank estimated that one-third of Latin America's 502 million people lived in poverty. The advent of political democracy in Latin America had been warmly applauded by the wealthy democracies of the North, but the messages of congratulations in a post-Cold War environment did not lead to increases in crucial development aid. "Trade, not aid" became the complacent maxim of the former. Unable to catch up with their affluent – and apparently indifferent – neighbors, but dependent on them as trading partners, the peoples of Central and South America faced the new century with growing uncertainty.

TERRORISM AND THE DRIFT TOWARD UNILATERALISM

Immediately after the terrorist attacks of September 11, 2001, a somber President George W. Bush addressed the American people and declared that the nation was at war. But it was not to be a conventional conflict, for the enemy served no state, defended no capital or territorial boundaries, and led no formal military establishment. The opponent transcended national frontiers, recruited its rank and file from an abundant pool of young persons, male and female, rich and poor alike, who shared a common disaffection for the US in particular, and for modernity in general. While the Bush administration scrupulously avoided making explicit linkages between the barbarity of 9/11 and Islam, and while most Muslim leaders in the US and overseas condemned the mass murder, it was obvious that the hijackers and their supporters viewed themselves as acting very much in the service of authentic Islam.

The mastermind of the attacks, a wealthy Saudi exile named Osama bin Laden, had established terrorist training camps during the early 1990s in the quasi-state of Afghanistan, a mountainous region long home to competing warlords, local conflict, and chronic lawlessness. After the Soviet withdrawal in 1989, a fanatical group of young fighters known as the Taliban managed to win military control over large parts of the country, including the capital city of Kabul. This radical Islamist regime proceeded to build a theocratic state where its own disturbed reading of the Quran informed all aspects of public policy. Men were obliged to adopt traditional robes and beards, while women were forced to cover themselves completely, absent themselves from public life unless accompanied by a male relative, and abandon all hope of formal education. Non-Islamic art was a particular focus of condemnation, and in one especially egregious act (ignoring multiple appeals from the international community), the Taliban government dynamited and destroyed a set of 1500-year-old giant statues of the Buddha located at Bamiyan.

When the Taliban rejected a post-9/11 ultimatum from the US to hand over bin Laden, American and British forces, in collaboration with anti-Taliban Afghan fighters and with full UN support, attacked and overthrew the Islamist regime. An interim Afghan government was put in place by the victors, and Taliban sympathizers (including bin Laden) retreated into the mountainous countryside and across the border into northwest Pakistan. Under intense pressure from the US, the military leader of Pakistan, General Pervez Musharraf, disassociated himself from the Taliban and cast his lot with the Americans in the war on terror. But Pakistani troops, many of whom were sympathetic to the radical brand of Islam propagated by the Taliban, proved singularly unsuccessful in stopping the cross-border migrations of Taliban fighters. It was widely suspected that bin Laden, who remained at large years after the 9/11 attacks, received support from sympathizers within Pakistan. Meanwhile, reconstruction efforts in Afghanistan were hampered by rivalries among regional warlords, difficult terrain, and the absence of any precedents for the creation of a democratic society. Free elections at the national level took place in 2004, but the president, Hamid Karzai, remained heavily dependent upon American support. Unfortunately for the reconstruction effort, the Bush administration quickly turned its attention elsewhere after the fall of the Taliban, claiming linkages (still unsubstantiated) between the Iraqi dictatorship of Saddam Hussein and al-Quaeda terrorist organization.

Terror states?

Although the main focus of the early war on terror involved groups and individuals who operated outside the confines of state structures, in his 2002 State of the Union address, President Bush pointed to a territorial "axis of evil" consisting of Iraq, Iran, and North Korea. These alleged sponsors of terror were put on notice that the US would no longer merely respond to acts of terrorism, but instead take preemptive military action if information-gathering agencies provided overwhelming evidence of malfeasance. The president outlined this momentous departure in American military policy in a commencement address at West Point in June 2002. He told the graduates that "Containment is not possible when unbalanced dictators with weapons of mass destruction can deliver those weapons on missiles or secretly provide them to terrorist allies." If the US were to wait for threats "to fully materialize," the security of the nation would be placed in jeopardy.

Historically islolationist, after 1945 America had committed its vast material resources to an international struggle against communism. As we saw in Chapter 1, the Truman Doctrine provided the intellectual underpinnings for that broader commitment. When the ideological conflict turned "hot," as it did in Korea in 1950 and in Vietnam during the early 1960s, US forces were deployed after regional surrogates had failed to defeat the communist opponent on the battlefield. Even in Afghanistan, the US acted only after the international community endorsed the use of force against the Taliban regime. Now the Bush administration was threatening military action *before* a potential opponent could strike at American interests at home or abroad. But sending young men and women into harm's way under the new doctrine of preemption placed additional burdens on information-gathering agencies, whose covert and electronic surveillance systems required constant upgrading and fine tuning. Confident that information sources had proven the existence of weapons of mass destruction in Iraq, the administration geared up for a war to remove Saddam Hussein from power. Bush won Congressional authorization for military action in October 2002, and despite opposition from the UN, the invasion took place in March 2003. British and American troops, with token representation from a handful of other allies, quickly toppled the brutal Hussein regime, but no weapons of mass destruction – the ostensible reason for the war – were ever discovered by the victors.

Critics of the invasion argued that US military action in Iraq sidetracked the war on terrorism as resources were diverted away from Afghanistan. The enormous sympathy and support that the Americans received from the international community in the months after 9/11 were dissipated in the wake of what was widely interpreted as American unilateralism in Iraq. In Britain, Prime Minister Tony Blair's popularity plummeted, while in Spain the conservative government which had supported the war was voted out of office in 2003. The first years of occupation in post-Saddam Iraq proved costly in terms of lives lost and goodwill squandered. Insisting that sovereignty be returned by the end of June 2004, the Americans struggled to identify a recognized Iraqi leader who could unite the country's Shiite, Sunni, and Kurdish populations. Increasing acts of terrorism, including the bombing of UN facilities, police stations, and other civilian targets all prompted rising disaffection for the occupying troops who seemed unable to protect Iraqi citizens as they struggled to rebuild their lives. By the start of 2005, the possibility of building a peaceful and democratic country that would serve as a shining beacon for the Muslim Middle East appeared uncertain. National elections were held in late January 2005, and despite the threat of suicide attacks and bombings, over 60 percent of eligible Iraqi voters turned out at the polls. But the American-trained Iraqi military remained woefully unprepared to assume the job of defending its own citizens from insurgents; without the massive presence of

US forces, the newly elected government was powerless to maintain law and order.

As the Bush administration ran up record deficits while dedicating billions to the Iraq operation, the "Axis of Evil" rhetoric dissipated even as evidence mounted that both North Korea and Iran were moving forward with plans to develop nuclear weapons. As we have seen, in December 2002 the North Koreans reactivated a nuclear-processing plant that had been closed in 1994, expelled inspectors from the International Atomic Energy Agency, and withdrew from the Nuclear Non-Proliferation Treaty. During the same period, opposition groups within Iran revealed the existence of two previously unidentified nuclear facilities, and work continued apace on uranium enrichment and heavy water production, the latter a step toward producing plutonium. As the theocratic Iranian government vehemently rejected charges that it was seeking to develop nuclear weapons, the mounting evidence contradicted the public statements. By the end of 2004, European diplomatic efforts to convince the Iranians to end their work had mixed results, and the Bush administration began to toughen its public statements regarding the emerging threat. The Iranian program was particularly worrisome to Israel, since elements of the Iranian leadership continued to declare their animus for the Jewish state.

A problematic ally

Significantly, the Bush administration's "Axis of Evil" did not include the Muslim state of Pakistan, even though it was widely known that Pakistani nuclear scientists had made secret trips to North Korea during the late 1990s, trading information on nuclear weapons development in return for assistance in building long-range missile systems. And in February 2004, a full two years after President Pervez Musharraf allied his country with the US in the global war on terrorism, the founder of Pakistan's nuclear weapons program, Abdul Qadeer Khan, admitted that he had been selling nuclear weapons technology on the black market for years. The revelation hardly surprised the International Atomic Energy Agency, whose head called Pakistan "the Wal-Mart of private-sector proliferation." Fearing for the stability of his regime should the popular Khan face prosecution and imprisonment, Musharraf granted him a full presidential pardon, while the government staunchly (and implausibly) denied that it had any knowledge of the illegal transfers.

Needing Musharraf's support to root out remnants of the Taliban (and to catch bin Laden) in the mountainous tribal regions bordering Afghanistan, the Bush administration chose to downplay the whole messy business. It was a high-stakes gamble on the part of the US, especially in light of Islamic fundamentalism's undeniable appeal in Pakistan. Musharraf narrowly avoided assassination on two occasions in the year after the 9/11 attacks, and polls indicated that the majority of Pakistanis opposed the alliance with the US and supported the objectives of al-Qaeda. By 2005 the security of Pakistan's nuclear weapons arsenal, originally developed within the context of a bitter rivalry with neighboring India, rested largely on the shoulders of a leader whose political priorities were at odds with the wishes of an increasingly radicalized minority of his own population.

The prospect of a nuclear-armed Pakistan under the control of Islamist radicals represented a nightmare scenario not only for the Americans, but also for the government of India, whose long-simmering disagreement with Pakistan over Indian-controlled Kashmir had soured bilateral relations for half a century. When the parliament building in New Delhi was attacked by gun-wielding terrorists in the late fall of 2001, Indian Prime Minister Vajpaih placed the blame squarely on the military government in Islamabad. America's key ally in the war on terror was now being accused by the world's most populous democracy of being a state sponsor of terror. US diplomats worked frantically to defuse the crisis in the weeks and months after the incident. While dialogue between India and Pakistan resumed the following year, it was clear that the global war on terror, like the earlier Cold War, would involve the US in a number of dangerous compromises with problematic allies.

Israel, Palestine, and the war on terror

The roots of Islamist terrorism were indeed varied. In the aftermath of the 9/11 attacks, President Bush attributed the acts of violence to a deep-seated disdain for the principles of a free and open society.

Others insisted that the suicide hijackers and bombers were nihilists and sociopaths, deranged men and women who killed for the sake of killing, and whose only core value was contempt for all values. But in their own statements, the terrorists and their supporters repeatedly referenced Western, and especially American, support for Israel in its conflict with the Palestinians, and for Western presence in, and influence over, established Arab countries like Saudi Arabia. By all accounts the Islamists did feel threatened by the spread of Western political and cultural values and by the larger forces of globalization, but the ongoing Israeli–Palestinian conflict served to concretize the animus against key features of modernity.

The Palestinian Liberation Organization's (PLO's) public support for Iraq during the first Gulf War infuriated its largest financial backers in Saudi Arabia, Kuwait, and the Gulf sheikdoms. After the war, the US worked to bring the Israelis and Palestinians into some form of dialog, and when the Labour Party under Yitzhak Rabin came to power in 1992, secret talks in Oslo led to a Declaration of Principles whereby the PLO renounced violence and recognized Israel's right to exist, in return for Israel's acknowledgment of the PLO as the official representative of the Palestinian people. The Declaration, known as the Oslo I accord, was signed by both parties on the White House lawn in September 1993. Oslo also called for Israel's withdrawal from Gaza and the West Bank city of Jericho, and approved the formation of a Palestinian governing authority. Forty donor countries stepped forward to help pay the administrative costs in the Palestinian zones, and when Arafat, Rabin, and Israeli Foreign Minister Shimon Peres were awarded the 1994 Nobel Peace Prize, the prospects for a permanent settlement seemed within reach.

The optimism was short-lived. Soon after Israeli troops began to withdraw from a number of West Bank towns in accordance with the principles of Oslo II (signed in Washington in September 1995), a Jewish extremist, alleging that the Israeli leader was undermining the security of the state, assassinated Prime Minister Rabin. Still the peace process moved forward, despite a series of terrorist attacks against civilian targets in Israel by the Iranian-funded radical Islamist group Hamas. But when the final status talks began in the spring of 1996, agreement on the creation of an independent Palestinian state was derailed by differences over two issues: the future status of Jerusalem, which both sides claimed as their historic capital; and the more intractable problem of the status of Palestinian refugees. Arafat again demanded that the three million Palestinian refugees living in neighboring Arab countries be accorded the right of return to their ancestral homeland. It was in this climate that another Israeli general election took place. The Labour government of Shimon Peres was turned out and a conservative Likud coalition led by Benjamin Netanyahu took power. The new Israeli government refused to accept the creation of a Palestinian state, rejected the right of return, and claimed Jerusalem as the undivided capital of the Jewish state. Jewish settlements in the occupied West Bank were expanded, and in the wake of Palestinian suicide bombings and protests, Israel's borders with the West Bank and Gaza were sealed off, creating enormous hardship for more than 150,000 Palestinians whose jobs were in Israel.

As attacks on Israeli citizens continued, Netanyahu's government accused Arafat and the PLO of failing to crack down on Hamas. Bilateral relations seemed on the verge of collapse when new elections returned Labour to power in May 1999. Sensing an opportunity, President Clinton invited the new Israeli Prime Minister, Ehud Barak, and Palestinian leader Yasser Arafat, to his retreat at Camp David in a final effort to break the impasse. After protracted negotiations, Barak agreed to withdraw Israeli forces from 90 percent of the West Bank and Gaza in preparation for the creation of a Palestinian state. Barak also pledged to hand over the non-Jewish sections of Jerusalem, together with the city's Muslim holy sites, to the Palestinian authority. It was a remarkable offer given the earlier stand of Netanyahu, but Arafat demanded more, specifically the contentious "right of return." The Israeli leader refused to go this far, fearful that the State of Israel would be overrun with Palestinian returnees who would outnumber the Jewish citizenry of the country. The meeting ended in failure, and in February 2001 the Israeli political pendulum swung again: Barak was voted out of office and a hard-line Likud government led by Ariel Sharon took power.

Unlike President Bill Clinton, George W. Bush did not take an active role during his first term in office to advance a settlement of the Israeli–Palestinian conflict. After 9/11 the Sharon government declared that escalating suicide attacks against Israeli civilians, in which 200 Israelis were killed and 1500 wounded in 2001 alone, constituted another front in the larger war on terrorism. Unlike his predecessor, the new prime minister did not believe that peace with the Palestinians was attainable in the immediate future, and he resigned himself to a policy of containment so long as Arafat was alive. Israeli forces responded to suicide bombings with air strikes in the West Bank and Gaza Strip, an assassination campaign against Palestinian activists, and the construction of a massive wall to prevent potential terrorists from entering Israel. Further negotiations with the Palestinian Authority, still headed by an increasingly isolated Arafat, were ruled out, and by 2003 the leader of the Palestinians had become a virtual prisoner in his own West Bank Ramallah compound, unwilling or unable to curb the gunmen and suicide bombers who continued their attacks. His death in November 2004 awakened some hope that a new Palestinian leadership would reengage with the Israelis, but in the midst of all the killing, public opinion on both sides grew more pessimistic about the possibility of ever living together in peace.

States, peoples, and discord

The terrible events of 9/11 put the world on notice that even the people of the richest, most powerful state in history were vulnerable when targeted by an ideologically committed and well-financed enemy. For the developed states of the industrialized North, and especially for the United States, the optimism of the post-Cold War era was short-lived. During a decade of increased ethnic tension and religious intolerance, the world of sovereign states that was embedded in the UN charter appeared to be an increasingly abstract and fragile model for the peaceful organization of peoples. By the start of the twenty-first century, the work of transforming states into nations, where diverse peoples shared a common allegiance despite their varied histories and cultural traditions, was undertaken against enormous odds. Indeed the prerogatives of peoples, not states, seemed to be the ascendant motif of the decade, with religious identity and cultural exclusivity trumping the claims of the sovereign state. The fragmentation of states into smaller ethnoreligious enclaves, the reassertion of theocratic rule where religious ortho-doxies were imposed on citizens, and the recrudescence of a form of nationalism that was restrictive rather than inclusive, all severely tested liberal democracy in ways that were largely unanticipated by those who had celebrated the fall of communism in the early 1990s.

Perhaps most importantly, the term "liberal democracy" itself was called into question by peoples who did not share in the unpreced-ented affluence of the West. What, after all, were the advantages of voting rights, political parties, and written constitutions when a bal-anced diet, adequate housing, educational opportunities, and basic health care were beyond the reach of billions? Under such condi-tions, the spread of Western material culture to the fortunate few in the developing world struck many as corrupting and dangerous, as a threat that must be countered by whatever means seemed effica-cious. As we turn now to survey developments on the postwar eco-nomic front, the movement of peoples across international borders, breakthroughs and advances in science and technology, and changes in the historic religious traditions, it is important to keep in mind the larger tension between the forces of globalization – more often than not Western forces – and the determination of peoples to improve their material condition while simultaneously affirming their culture's difference and singularity. Whether or not the latter aspiration can withstand the dynamic forces that regularly overstep the more parochial interests of sovereign states is uncertain. What is certain, however, is that neither states nor peoples can afford to ignore the pressures of global integration, at least not if they wish to preserve a modicum of identity not dictated from afar.

Part II
Globalization and its discontents

4

WHEN BORDERS DON'T MATTER: DEVELOPMENT AND GLOBAL CULTURE

KEY TOPICS

Classical liberalism in crisis
The Keynesian consensus
North and South, rich and poor

Neoliberal economics
Globalization and disquiet

In the aftermath of World War II, two antithetical models of economic organization confronted each other across an ideological divide that appeared to be unbridgeable. On one side stood the Soviet-inspired command economy, where an absolutist state owned the means of production and regulated the marketplace by setting prices, wages, and production goals. According to its defenders, communist central planning was designed to ensure economic equality, a decent standard of living for all citizens, and a more rational use of human and material resources. For Soviet propagandists, the selfishness inherent in unregulated capitalism had been responsible for the twentieth century's two horrific world wars, and for the economic collapse of the 1930s. A new economic paradigm was essential if humanity hoped to avoid future conflict, and it involved first and foremost strict state oversight and regulation of the economic appetite.

On the other side of the ideological divide were the defenders of Western-style market capitalism. Buffeted by the tragedies of the previous quarter-century and the broken promises of pre-World War I champions of laissez faire, where unprecedented wealth creation had not led to a more just or peaceful society, defenders of the market now insisted that their fundamental concern involved the preservation of political democracy and individual freedom. Under their reading of recent history, state control over economic affairs was the precursor to state abridgment of personal liberties – the short road to dictatorship. Although capitalism had suffered serious reverses during the Great Depression, the champions of the free market insisted that competitive economies alone undergirded democratic polities. For these thinkers it was no coincidence that open markets and limited regulations had powered the West to global preeminence simultaneous with the advent of universal manhood suffrage before 1900, and if democracy were to flourish in the aftermath of the most destructive war in human history, acceptable levels of economic welfare had to be provided under conditions that maximized initiative and rewarded innovation.

CLASSICAL LIBERALISM IN CRISIS

During the final decades of the nineteenth century and continuing to the outbreak of World War I, the developed nations of the West succeeded in creating the first truly global economy. While it might be argued that the move toward global integration had begun much earlier, with Europe's voyages of exploration in the early sixteenth century, the intense and systematic transfer of goods, services, labor, and capital around the world that has come to symbolize globalization did not make its debut until the steamship age. Transoceanic telegraph cables, refrigerated ships, and extensive railroad networks allowed businesses to communicate quickly across international borders and move goods – even perishables – cheaply and expeditiously to distant markets. Economies of scale were pioneered in the US and Germany as mass-production techniques were refined in large factory settings. Between 1870 and 1913 world trade increased by an average of 3.5 percent per annum, while world productive output grew by an average of 2.7 percent per annum. By the latter date exports accounted for a larger share of global production than they did at the end of the twentieth century. Britain accounted for 31 percent of world trade in 1913, Germany was a close second with 27.5 percent, while the US held third place with 13 percent.

With the formation of colonial empires in Africa, South Asia, and East Asia, Europe's great powers facilitated unprecedented levels of export-led growth, extracting primary materials from and selling finished products to colonial peoples around the world. "We must find new lands," Britain's Cecil Rhodes had intoned in the 1890s, "from which we can easily obtain raw materials ... and that will provide a dumping ground for the surplus goods produced in our factories." In addition to the movement of goods, capital also flowed freely across borders. Purchases of international stocks and bonds became commonplace, especially among investors in the US and Western Europe. During the 1870s an international monetary system based on the gold standard emerged. Several developed countries adopted a gold backing for their currencies, whereby a unit of a country's currency could be exchanged for an established amount of gold.

As the level of economic interdependence increased around the world, laissez-faire liberals insisted that the good of the whole was best served by the individual's unhindered pursuit of economic self-interest. The natural law of supply and demand would, over the long term, ensure balanced development and prosperity for all. The period of economic expansion that preceded World War I appeared to validate these guiding tenets of classical liberalism: government spending and personal taxes were low, budgets were balanced, prices and exchange rates were fairly stable, labor was mobile, and state welfare services were kept to a minimum. And for those who still questioned their prospects for a better life in Europe, the option of inexpensive passage to new lands and fresh opportunities in America and Australasia was now available.

The expansion of Western-dominated trade and investment came to an abrupt halt in August, 1914. Over the course of the next 40 years, the ravages of two world wars, separated by a worldwide economic depression, contributed to a sharp contraction in international commercial and financial activity. During the harshest years of the Great Depression, 1929–32, world trade dropped at an annual average rate of almost 10 percent, while production plummeted by over 6 percent. Countries erected high tariff barriers and set import quotas in an effort to protect domestic manufactures from overseas competition. They also devalued their currencies in a desperate attempt to boost export sales. Unhappily, the overall result of these measures was to aggravate inflation, cripple world trade, and ravage export earnings. Only the outbreak of World War II in 1939 arrested the slide into deeper economic crisis. Industrial production rose swiftly as government orders for military hardware intensified, while agricultural output rebounded once supplies for the troops became a national priority.

Building upon precedents set during World War I, governments in the capitalist West took steps to regulate key functions of their domestic economies, from wage controls, production quotas, and price fixing, to the mobilization of strategic resources and the rationing of consumer goods on the home front. The idea that national governments might effectively plan a country's economic development had been anathema to classical liberalism, but the wartime emergency seemed to suggest otherwise. At the very least, a willingness to experiment with a corporatist model of economic management was planted in the public mind by the considerable successes of government planning agencies during World War II. And at the heart of this emerging consensus in the West was a public desire to build a postwar world where the establishment of economic justice was a fundamental duty of the democratic state.

Europe's physical and psychological landscape in the summer of 1945 was integral to this call for greater economic justice. The market system had performed poorly during the 1920s and had virtually collapsed during the 1930s. For many Western observers, the Soviet-planned economy of the 1930s seemed to deliver both full employment and longed-for economic justice. At the time, few were aware of the full extent of the human costs involved in Stalin's Five Year Plans – the widespread malnutrition, the brutal elimination of the kulaks, and the deliberate starvation of millions of Ukrainians who resisted forced collectivization. Instead, the carefully controlled media reports coming out of the Soviet socialist utopia highlighted smiling peasants, dedicated factory laborers, and skilled managers all working in unison to beat every production target set by Stalin. From the perspective of the victorious powers in the West, both world wars had been justified on the grounds that a better, freer, more just society could be resurrected from the ashes of malevolent monarchism, dictatorship, racism, and genocide.

But Europe in the summer of 1945 was an unlikely candidate for renewal; as we saw in Chapter 1, the widespread destruction of homes, factories, roads and rail networks; millions of displaced refugees; millions more malnourished and near starvation; and an alarming level of despair about the viability of market economics, all posed extraordinary challenges to postwar leaders.

THE KEYNESIAN CONSENSUS

In Western Europe, and especially in Britain, some form of compromise between unfettered capitalism and Soviet-style collectivism was the desire of a population weary of war but committed to ensuring that the sacrifices made during the struggle against Nazism would not be in vain. The resounding victory of the Labour Party in the general election of May 1945 signaled the beginning of a new path for Britain's peacetime economy. Ironically, Churchill's surprising defeat in 1945 came in the wake of a five-year period in which his coalition government had virtually taken over the economy and realized efficiencies that had never been seen before in Britain. But Churchill was an inveterate opponent of state control in peacetime, and the British electorate turned to a Labour Party that was committed to the creation of a welfare state where major industries would be placed under the permanent auspices of the public sector. Labour leaders believed that government-owned industries could better mobilize human resources, encourage and invest in new technologies, practice efficiencies of scale, and make strategic decisions based on the wider public interest. Once in power, Prime Minister Clement Attlee's government nationalized the coal, iron, and steel industries. Railroads, utilities, and telecommunications were also placed under government jurisdiction, while a tax-supported national health system provided comprehensive medical and dental care for all citizens. At its height in the 1960s, the nationalized enterprises employed almost 20 percent of the county's workforce.

The major postwar spokesperson for this view of "managed" capitalism was the Cambridge-educated economist John Maynard Keynes. In a groundbreaking worked entitled *The General Theory of Employment, Interest and Money*, published in the midst of the Great

Depression in 1935, Keynes had argued that unfettered free-market principles actually enhanced the prospects for high levels of unemployment. There was, he argued, no natural balance between supply and demand that would guarantee full employment. As owners sought to increase profits by holding wages down, the ability of workers to purchase the goods which they produced was impaired. The result would be a lowering of domestic demand and a cycle of further salary cuts, layoffs, and bankruptcies. The social consequences of such a scenario would be disastrous, threatening the long-term viability of democratic states. Keynes called for governments to "prime the pump" of the economy whenever employment levels declined by investing in education, job training, public works, and health services. He also recommended direct financial support for the unemployed, even if this meant deficit spending in the short term. By hiring workers or supporting the unemployed with public funds, the consumer sector would rebound, the business climate would improve, and the national tax base would expand. In the end these increased tax revenues would address the short-term problem of the public deficit.

During the 1930s the American President Franklin Delano Roosevelt had adopted some modest "pump-priming" measures, but with mixed results. After the war, however, most governments in the West, including that of the US, adopted the Keynesian solution to recurring economic problems. Fearful that the Great Depression would return now that the wartime demand for military goods and services was over, Western governments adopted "managed market" strategies aimed at furthering job growth in the transition to a peacetime economy. The strategy seemed to work in Britain, where unemployment was reduced to 1.3 percent by the late 1940s, down from a high of 12 percent during the Great Depression. Similar successes were achieved in France, West Germany, and especially in the US.

Bretton Woods

It was obvious by 1944 that America's wartime allies would require significant financial assistance in the form of grants and loans in order to rebuild their shattered economies. Looking forward to the end of the conflict and eager to avoid future economic depressions, the US hosted a high-level meeting of financial experts representing 44 allied states in the summer of 1944. Gathering at the Bretton Woods resort in New Hampshire's picturesque White Mountains, the delegates set out to repair the damage that had been done in the 1930s after many countries abandoned the gold standard and indulged in disruptive currency devaluations. Two pivotal institutions were established at Bretton Woods: the International Bank for Reconstruction and Development, subsequently known as the World Bank, and the International Monetary Fund, or IMF. The purpose of the World Bank was to make reconstruction loans to member states either directly, or by guaranteeing separate loans made by private institutions. The IMF was charged with promoting world trade by allowing member states suffering from a temporary balance-of-payments problem to draw upon a common pool of emergency funds. In addition, a system of fixed exchange rates was created, making it easier for traders to exchange currency across borders. In place of gold the American dollar became the chief reserve currency of the noncommunist world. Signatories agreed that any changes in the exchange value of a national currency required the prior approval of the governing board of the IMF.

The Soviet Union had sent observers to the Bretton Woods conference, but Stalin never applied for membership in either organization. It was clear early on that neither the IMF nor the World Bank were interested in assisting states that adopted Marxist-style state economies. The US provided approximately one-third of the initial money available to both institutions, and the international headquarters for these agencies were located in Washington, DC. Americans assumed the key leadership roles, and the US banking community, source of so much of the private-loan capital, wielded inordinate influence over policy decisions. Private loans to member states often originated in New York, where lenders routinely prioritized American trade. Potential clients therefore had to structure their loan requests in a manner likely to advantage American commercial interests. In 1947, again at the urging of the US, the major Western powers concluded a General Agreement on Tariffs and Trade (GATT). Designed to prevent a reemergence of prewar protectionism in the noncommunist bloc, the inaugural agreement signed under GATT, together with subsequent meetings and negotiations, helped to stimulate robust cross-border trade for every member state. GATT provided the foundation for the establishment of the World Trade Organization (WTO) in 1995.

Together with Marshall Plan, World Bank, and IMF funding, the new trade protocols enabled Western Europe's war-torn economies to rebound, and living conditions improved dramatically during the 1950s. American reconstruction aid also energized Japan's recovery after 1945, and as the Cold War expanded, served the same function in Taiwan and South Korea. US aid enabled both of the latter states to industrialize in a manner that helped their economies to become competitive with the developed West. Taiwan received almost $1.5 billion between 1951 and 1965, while South Korea was the recipient of $6 billion between 1945 and 1978. As the world's largest manufacturer, however, the US benefited most from the overall reduction in tariffs and other trade barriers negotiated under GATT. Although its domestic market was huge, production for export, especially to European countries rebuilding from the ravages of war, played a significant role in ensuring a healthy employment picture in the US during the 1950s, and this in turn spurred the development of a mass consumer society.

Overall, the 20-year period between 1950 and 1970 represented an age of unprecedented expansion in production and world trade within the noncommunist bloc. Developments in the industrialized West during the 1950s and 1960s were especially encouraging. Part of the growth was due to increased military spending, especially by the US. In his farewell address to the nation in 1961, President Eisenhower warned his fellow citizens of the dangers inherent in the creation of a "military-industrial complex," but by that date the role of war, and preparation for war, had become central to the economic vibrancy of the world's wealthiest country. Another key factor in assuring growth was the availability of inexpensive energy sources, especially oil. In the postwar period, Europe and Japan reduced their use of coal and became heavily reliant upon imported oil. Between 1962 and 1972, for example, Europe and Japan increased oil imports from just over 6 million barrels per day to 18 million. By the latter date well over half of Europe's energy consumption was based on oil, and almost all of it was imported. New technology played its role as well. In 1965 an international agreement established a standard size for transport containers, making it possible for ships from every nation to move goods efficiently from port to port. Mechanized loading equipment lowered handling costs at the ports, while trucks were reengineered to handle standard-sized loads. Agribusinesses in developed states now produced for an overseas market, delivering foodstuffs in record time. Thanks to a series of innovations and inexpensive sources of energy (including the controversial advent of nuclear power), world output grew at an average annual rate of 3.9 percent and trade expanded at an average annual rate of 5.8 percent.

European integration

As discussed in Chapter 1, the US was eager to promote European political and economic union as a counterweight to possible Soviet encroachment. One-sixth of Marshall Plan aid had been targeted for the enhancement of trade within Europe, but little progress toward the free movement of goods, capital, and labor in Western Europe had occurred by the time the Plan was concluded in 1952. Nevertheless, the experience of collaboration in the use of American largess helped to reduce some of the traditional cross-border distrust that had been fueled by nineteenth-century nationalism. Prospects for European political integration were dim just after the war, especially in light of strong anti-German sentiment, but the possibility of gradual economic union, beginning with policies that directly advantaged every country, seemed within reach. In 1951 France, West Germany, Italy, the Netherlands, Belgium, and Luxembourg established a joint European Coal and Steel Community (ECSC), and this early success in the elimination of all restrictions on the exchange of key natural resources convinced both governments and a previously skeptical business community of the value of supranational economic projects.

In March 1957 the member states of the ECSC signed the Treaty of Rome, which called for a new organization dedicated to the complete elimination of tariffs and to the free movement of capital and labor across national frontiers. The new European Economic Community (EEC) was an immediate success in supranational governance. In 1963 the US concluded a landmark trade agreement with the EEC to lower tariffs, and during the 1970s additional states applied for membership in the organization, including Great Britain, Ireland, Spain, Denmark, Turkey, and Greece. And although the EEC limited itself to matters involving economic integration, it facilitated dialog on political assimilation though the establishment of a Council of Ministers representing the initial six member states, a Commission of Civil Servants appointed by their respective governments, and a European parliament whose members would oversee the activities of the Commission. By the early 1980s the EEC had a total population of 300 million and represented the largest free-trade zone in the world. Europeans who were wary of provincial nationalism and ashamed of its destructive past began to envision a future where a united Europe would become a major force in world affairs.

The ascent of Japan

The American occupation of Japan after World War II aimed to promote the same type of economic recovery under democratic principles that applied to Europe. Although the emperor was permitted to remain in office as a symbol of unity, he was no longer treated as a divine figure, and he cooperated fully with General Douglas MacArthur, supreme commander of the occupation forces. A new constitution, adopted in 1947, affirmed the principle of parliamentary government, renounced war as a instrument of policy, guaranteed individual civil rights, and adopted the practice of judicial review. An extensive land-reform program addressed the problem of rural poverty, transforming millions of laborers into owner-cultivators. Urban workers also benefited under the occupation: Labor unions were recognized, and the right to collective bargaining was endorsed. The goal was to break the stranglehold that a tiny minority of landowners and industrialists had enjoyed over Japan's economy since the early twentieth century.

But while General MacArthur was given full executive power, he worked closely with Japanese politicians and businessmen who were not associated with the wartime Japanese government. The large holding companies that controlled the country's major industries, the *zaibatsu*, were not broken up, despite the fact that they had supported Japan's expansionist policies before and during the war. Fear of economic chaos should the *zaibatsu* be dissolved, together with the fact that a number of large American firms, including Westinghouse and General Electric, had investments in the giant Japanese firms, blunted calls for retribution. Thus the framework for resuming Japan's march to economic modernization was largely in place by 1949, just as the communists triumphed in China, and as estrangement between the US and the Soviet Union intensified. In 1950 Japan became a strategic base of operations for the American struggle against communism in Korea, and the following year the Americans signed a security treaty with their former enemy. The occupation of Japan formally came to an end in 1952. For policy makers in the American State Department, Japan's economic rebound was essential to stem the rising tide of Soviet and Chinese communist influence in East Asia.

That rebound was not long in coming. Generous American development aid was deftly employed in the immediate postwar period, while American purchases of Japanese goods and services during the Korean conflict furthered the recovery. The Japanese government paid reparations to countries in Southeast Asia that had been occupied during the war, and these transactions facilitated the establishment of more permanent trade links, with Japan purchasing raw materials from Burma, the Philippines, and Indonesia. Even China, although unwilling to establish diplomatic relations due to Japan's recognition of Taiwan, engaged in a robust trade with Tokyo. During the 1950s and 1960s, Japan experienced a rapid demographic shift from the countryside to the cities. Whereas almost 40 percent of the labor force was employed in agriculture in 1955, only 12 percent was in 1975. The advent of mechanized commercial farms, coupled with a high demand for industrial labor, accounted for the dramatic conversion. Large electronics, automotive, and insurance corporations dominated the economic landscape, but small and medium-sized firms also played key roles. Although unionization had been encouraged during the occupation period, Western-style and industry-wide unions were less successful than their company-based counterparts. The latter stressed loyalty to one's employer in return for a promise of lifetime employment.

The national government carefully promoted specific industries by offering tax concessions and by imposing quotas and tariffs on imports. A strong domestic market was combined with an aggressive export sector by the early 1960s, where Japanese manufacturers emphasized quality and innovation. The automotive giant Toyota, for example, became one of the world's envied success stories in the late twentieth century. Operating largely out of Japan in the mid-1970s, 20 years later the company owned 9 parts plants in 7 countries other than Japan, 29 assembly plants in 25 countries, and 4 research and development facilities in 2 countries. By the year 2000, international sales of Toyota automobiles represented 60 percent of total sales, and one of their models had achieved the status of best-selling automobile in the US.

Thirty years after the end of the war, Japan boasted an economy second only to the US in terms of size, efficiency, and profitability. For much of that period the Liberal Democratic Party held the reigns of power and pursued a strongly pro-business agenda. Government subsidies and tax incentives for businesses, coupled with high import tariffs and cumbersome regulations that made it difficult for foreign firms to establish a foothold in Japan, contributed mightily to the country's prosperity. But these same policies also triggered a protracted dispute with its postwar benefactor, and in the 1970s and 1980s the US began to place quotas on the number of Japanese products allowed into its domestic market. Japan's economic growth slowed considerably during the 1990s, prompted by a downturn in urban property values that escalated during the 1980s. By 1996 the country was suffering from recession, and by the early twenty-first century, it had been displaced by China as the miracle economy of East Asia. Still, in combination with Europe and the US, Japan remained one of the world's most powerful economies, and one that was not burdened by the costs associated with the military establishments of the other great powers.

Consumer culture

Postwar Western prosperity raised vital questions respecting the ends of life. Before the Industrial Revolution in the West, the struggle to secure sufficient food and adequate shelter engaged the full-time energies of most human beings. The great majority of people were familiar with life on the margins; they expected to labor long hours each day in close touch with nature, and they resigned themselves to want and hunger and to the expectation that their children's world would be much like their own. This is still the case in much of the world today. But with the advent of industry, this centuries-old pattern was altered for a privileged few; machine technology separated people from nature and brought them into greater proximity to one another. A small consumer economy emerged in Britain during the eighteenth century, and by the end of the 1800s even members of the working class aspired to a modest role in the culture of consumption. Before World War I, a middle-class consumer sector was firmly in place across Western Europe, but it was during the 1920s in the US that the real boom in domestic consumables began to affect cultural expectations and definitions of the "good life." Automobiles, household items, clothing accessories, and electrical appliances began their momentous rise to the status of "basic necessities." The private automobile made possible the development of suburbs, enabling members of the white-collar middle class to continue working in the cities while establishing their residence in neighboring towns.

After World War II the culture of consumption spread to the working class in Western Europe. The enlargement of electrical power grids to accommodate private homes during the 1950s revolutionized domestic life; a bevy of mass-produced, labor-saving electrical products from washing machines to vacuum cleaners all saturated the market. Large high-street "department" stores, pioneered in the US but spreading quickly to Europe, made one-stop shopping possible, while vibrant competition led to the advent of discounting and seasonal product sales. Some stores in the US even offered consumer credit to valued customers, presaging the emergence in the 1950s of the third-party credit card. Companies such as American Express, Visa, and Mastercard began to realize enormous profits by charging high rates of interest for goods and services purchased on credit.

Americans led the way in this fast-paced consumer revolution. The US produced over half of the world's manufactured goods at the end of the war, and in 1950 its manufacturers accounted for almost 17 percent of global exports. Whereas global trade before World War I involved the transfer of primary products and raw materials, after 1945 finished manufactured goods filled the holds of massive container ships. International trade contributed to an enviable employment picture for Americans, and with an abundance of well-paid jobs, many families enjoyed a standard of living that was simply unimaginable for most of the world's peoples. A sophisticated advertising industry targeted men and women with disposable income, employing print media, radio, and finally television to sell myriad food and household products, a strategy that helped to strengthen existing gender roles that assigned women to "domestic" or "homemaker" duties. The science of selling things was even raised to the level of university study, as advanced degrees in marketing and business were conferred on ever expanding numbers of students. Faculty in these disciplines commanded salaries that rose well above the average for their peers in the humanities and social sciences, and the traditional liberal arts curriculum at many colleges and universities was reconfigured to allow for a greater focus on professional and applied subjects.

The sale of household products was assisted by the rapid increase in home ownership from 40 percent of American families in 1945 to 60 percent in 1960. And just at the moment when middle-class Americans seemed content to spend more of their leisure time in front of the television set, the travel industry succeeded in making annual holidays a status symbol and benchmark of material success. The building of an interstate highway system in the 1950s hastened the growth of private travel in automobiles, while the advent of regular jet service in 1958 inaugurated a new phase of the leisure industry. By the end of the 1950s middle-class Americans had secured the "essentials" of modern living, and producers began to focus their advertising on the need for householders to constantly upgrade and replace their goods with newer versions. Planned obsolescence found its way into boardroom strategy meetings, affecting everything from automobiles and buildings, to televisions and toasters. Even the fashion industry cultivated the need for constant change. Product durability gave way before an onslaught of advertising that intensified the "obligation" to adhere to seasonal shifts in taste. Targeting youth culture in particular, fashion designers and retail outlets enlisted the talents of entertainment and sports figures in order to bolster sales.

Each of these American trends had their European counterpart, albeit delayed due to postwar reconstruction. Rationing, for example, remained in place in Britain until 1954. But the pace of recovery quickened during the second half of the decade, and by the early 1960s French, Italian, West German, and British families enjoyed many of the creature comforts that were available to their upstart American counterparts. Traditional local markets and shops faced increasing competition from larger retailers who practiced economies of scale, but despite the loss of intimacy associated with traditional neighborhood trade, living standards in Europe had reached enviable heights in a remarkably short period of time. Even the Soviet-dominated countries of Eastern Europe experienced modest growth, especially in the category of household conveniences like refrigerators and washing machines. The same could not be said for Europe's former colonies. Indeed, as late as 1970, the modern consumer economy remained largely limited to the US, Western Europe, Australasia, and Japan. Electrification had yet to make significant inroads in most areas of the world, while private motorized transport along paved roads was unimaginable. But the indelible example had been set, and by the 1980s images of the Western lifestyle were beamed around the world through electronic media. Consumer culture was redefining *Homo sapiens* as *Homo economicus*, and most of humanity was left out of the competition.

NORTH AND SOUTH, RICH AND POOR

The Keynesian consensus reached the status of near-orthodoxy in the capitalist West in the early 1970s. Even President Richard Nixon, a moderate Republican, declared himself a Keynesian in 1971, adopting deficit spending and wage and price controls in an effort to curb rising inflation and boost employment. Limited government intervention in and regulation of national economies had paid conspicuous dividends in the West, especially in the consumer sector. But not all nations in the noncommunist world reaped the benefits of the regulated market economy. There have always been material imbalances between societies, but in the post-World War

II era, and especially during the last quarter of the twentieth century, disparities in the distribution of the world's resources reached extraordinary levels. In 1960, the total income of the richest 20 percent of the population was 30 times the poorest 20 percent, and by the end of the century it was 82 times that of the poorest 20 percent. In December 2004 the British-based international aid agency OXFAM claimed that rich nations had broken a pledge, first made in 1970, to make available 0.7 percent of their gross national incomes for aid to poor countries. The organization alleged that in 2003 wealthy nations contributed only 0.25 percent of their incomes to aid, and in the case of the US, only 0.14 percent. OXFAM reminded rich nations that their poor neighbors were also paying out over $100 million in debt repayments daily. The glaring imbalance was increasingly referred to as the "North–South Divide" in light of the fact that the wealthy nations of the world were located primarily in the Northern hemisphere, while their impoverished counterparts were to be found south of the equator.

Postcolonial economies

At the end of World War II, a mixture of altruism, support for democracy, and fear of Soviet intentions led the Americans to invest in the rebuilding of Western Europe and Japan. Elsewhere in the postwar world, levels of American assistance were prioritized on the basis of whether or not the aid would strengthen anticommunist governments, even if those governments repudiated or paid mere lip service to democratic principles. Once Western Europe and Japan had rebounded, however, Western government agencies and private lending institutions offered modest levels of direct aid and loans to developing states. The hope was that the resulting infrastructure projects, educational facilities, and agricultural improvements would stimulate domestic economic development and permit the receiving states to meet their obligations in a timely manner. Unhappily, the development model that had been so successful in rebuilding postwar Europe, involving a rapid infusion of technical assistance and investment, and aimed at specific projects like roads, buildings, and power plants, was not transferable to most of the postcolonial world. Poor countries simply lacked the political and intellectual assets – including the rule of law, a skilled workforce, an established business sector, and a competent government – that were needed before significant development could take place.

Despite the efforts of the Soviet Union to influence political developments in the postcolonial world, the vast majority of Europe's former colonies remained squarely within the camp of the Western capitalist system. Most newly independent states and their Western-educated leaders refrained from interfering with the property and investments of their former overlords, opting instead to allow for continuing access to resources and cheap labor in the expectation that export earnings would hasten the development of a diversified domestic economy. Political independence was a significant achievement, but new states needed overseas markets for their primary commodities, and long-established trade relationships with the West provided the logical starting point. From the perspective of the former imperial powers, an ongoing trade relationship with ex-colonies was important in terms of securing primary resources, but it did not rise to the level of a strategic imperative. Even at the height of empire most First World trade had been carried on with other developed countries, not with backward colonies. Indeed many colonies had become economic drains on the imperial center, with administrative and military costs far outpacing the revenues generated through one-sided trade relationships. Still, it was undeniable that the colonizer benefited most from the relationship, and after independence the imbalance continued, as most Western aid was tied directly to the purchase of goods and services originating in the donor country.

Development economics

Many of the poorer countries attending the 1944 Bretton Woods Conference had pushed for the adoption of a worldwide economic development scheme, but the leading powers dismissed these efforts. Western academics then took up the cause, asserting that only massive state intervention and foreign assistance could help newly independent states to achieve modest levels of economic well-being for their citizens. These proponents of what came to be known as "development economics" claimed that poor countries faced insuperable barriers to growth in a world where industrialized economies dominated existing markets. In particular, developing countries lacked a trained workforce, experienced political leaders, and strong constitutional and legal traditions. Most were agricultural export economies, where low levels of productivity were coupled with low levels of savings and investment. Breaking out of these conditions required unprecedented amounts of aid from the international community. More controversially, development economists believed that poor states should adopt trade protectionism in order to foster domestic industrial growth, a policy known as import substitution, while rich countries should extend preferences to goods imported from their poorer neighbors as a measure of added assistance. Development economics was anchored in the belief that global economic well-being was in the interest of every state, and that a temporary period of massive investment in the developing world would, over the long term, advantage all peoples.

India's example

Over three centuries of British involvement in India's affairs, first under the auspices of the East India Company and then under direct crown control, had done little to address the crushing poverty of the masses. Unlike the vast majority of his countrymen, Prime Minister Jawaharlal Nehru had grown up in privileged circumstances: His father was a successful barrister and one of the founders of the Congress Party, and the young Nehru was sent to England for his public school, university, and legal training. Returning to his homeland two years before the start of World War I, Nehru established a close friendship with Gandhi, who by this time had already become a champion of the dispossessed. Under the Mahatma's influence, Nehru began to question an imperial order that virtually ignored the desperate condition of the laboring peasantry. During the 1920s he became convinced that the struggle against poverty must be the central obligation of any future Indian government, and with independence he began the fight with a call for rapid industrialization under state auspices. This priority had been set while he had been imprisoned in a British jail during World War II. There he composed *The Discovery of India,* a book that was first published in 1946 and which argued that Britain had "deindustrialized" India during the eighteenth century by imposing high tariffs on the export of Indian finished textiles.

Nehru associated unregulated capitalism with the remnants of colonialism; thus he and his closest allies in the Congress Party insisted that state planning was both more reflective of Indian communal values and more likely to catapult the nation into the twentieth century. Impressed by the platform of Britain's Labour Party and by the apparent successes of the Soviet command economy and its five-year plans, the Congress Party under Nehru's leadership adopted a mixed economy where the state owned and operated new industries and services, like automobile manufacturing, power-generation plants, and air transport. The government heavily regulated other industries, avoiding outright nationalization, and permitted a private sector in small business and manufacture. Overseeing the direction of the big push toward modernization was a heavily bureaucratic government planning commission. An element of faith was involved in Nehru's vision for a planned economy, a faith that highly trained technocrats could lift India's 350 million citizens out of their frightful poverty and into the age of plenty.

Nehru's preference for state control and centralized planning meant that export-led growth and foreign investment were discouraged. India's share of world trade actually fell during the 1950s and 1960s as the government strove for industrial self-sufficiency. Unfortunately, the focus on industrialization led to a neglect of the agricultural sector. Land reform was overlooked, and by the time of his death in 1964, Nehru's country was heavily dependent on food imports from the US. In addition, commission-mandated quotas, permits, and myriad licenses, instead of jump-starting India's quest for modernization, actually frustrated many would-be entrepreneurs. Critics began to refer to the system as the "permit raj," a bureaucratic labyrinth where even a company's decision to increase output required official state approval. And while Indian universities graduated a higher number of scientists and engineers than most developed countries, government investment in primary education remained well below levels of spending on national defense. Low literacy rates and high fertility rates translated into more poverty for millions across this multilingual country. The government finally turned its attention to agriculture in the mid-1960s, introducing new fast-ripening varieties of wheat and rice, chemical fertilizers and pesticides, and more mechanized equipment. But even while the threat of famine was removed during this "green revolution," the ineluctable growth in population frustrated efforts to reduce poverty. Millions fled into urban centers seeking work, creating massive housing, sanitation, and public health problems.

Africa's dilemma

Despite these considerable shortcomings, India's political democracy and managed economy served as powerful models for other colonial peoples through the 1960s. In Europe's African colonies, the calls for independence that began after World War II were strengthened by the example of India's independence struggle and its Herculean efforts to modernize through state planning. Unhappily the anticipated parallels between Africa and India overlooked the fact that the British had built a considerable transportation and communications infrastructure in South Asia. Railway lines connected the major cities, roads radiated out from urban centers, and telegraph and telephone service was available. In addition, highly trained members of the Indian Civil Service were in place to assume control over this infrastructure, making it possible for the new government to undertake large state projects with ample intellectual resources. Such was not the case in Africa. Indeed at the close of World War II it was Africa more than Western Europe that was in dire need of direct financial assistance from the US. Although Africans had contributed mightily to the struggle against Nazism, the widespread poverty and lack of access to medicine and education outstripped anything facing beleaguered Europeans. Rich in mineral, agricultural, and human resources, Africa's colonial overlords had failed miserably in terms of preparing the colonies for independence, and the dire economic backwardness of the continent stood as a harsh indictment of the entire colonial project.

Of course there would be no equivalent of the Marshall Plan for Africa, just as there would be no postwar assistance for Latin America. Most of the 30 African states that had gained their independence by the early 1960s adopted versions of the Keynesian managed economy, but firmly within the context of integration within the existing capitalist system. They could hardly have chosen otherwise, especially given their pressing need for loans, development grants, technical assistance, and markets for their primary products. Newly independent African states were early customers at the World Bank, and they had a seat at the table for GATT tariff-reduction talks. Despite these linkages, African leaders, like their Indian counterparts, were wary of freewheeling capitalism. Convinced that government was best fitted to supervise development on behalf of the population, leaders like Kwame Nkrumah of Ghana, Jomo Kenyatta of Kenya, and Julius Nyerere of Tanzania erected socialist alternatives to the exploitative free-market capitalism of the defunct colonial regimes. Agreeing with Western development economists, they argued that central governments alone could marshal the requisite human and fiscal resources to transform an economic landscape that for decades had been exploited by Europeans whose only interest was profit.

In most new African countries, public marketing boards were charged with buying domestic agricultural and mineral products at set prices and selling these products overseas. The goal was to increase export earnings during periods of high demand, and in turn to use part of these earnings to cushion the blow for peasant producers when international demand slackened. All key export commodities were channeled through monopolistic marketing boards, with most of the profits from foreign trade to be used by the government to jump-start industrialization. It was an ambitious agenda, but in one newly formed African state after another, the rhetoric of "African socialism" was sadly belied by official mismanagement and corruption. Regulatory bureaucracies grew, but little actual development took place. As economic conditions worsened, military governments replaced civilian ones, but even the generals failed to arrest the slide. For producers whose crops were purchased by the government at below market prices, an alternative black market undermined the moral high ground that had been assumed by the proponents of the state-controlled economy.

Some African leaders, like Egypt's Gamal Abdel Nasser and Ghana's Nkrumah, sought to finance economic development by taking advantage of Cold War superpower rivalries. In 1955 Nasser entered into an agreement with the Soviet Union and its East European satellites to exchange Egyptian cotton and rice for modern military equipment. Not to be outdone, the British and Americans pledged $70 million in economic aid to build the massive Aswan Dam on the Nile, a project that doubled the country's electrical power and expanded its core of arable land through irrigation. In Ghana, Nkrumah pushed for the construction of a massive dam on the Volta River that would provide ample electricity for future factories. The World Bank, Britain, and the US, together with private Western aluminum firms (interested in Ghana's large bauxite reserves) were all involved in financing the project, eager to keep Ghana out of the Soviet sphere of influence.

Conditions worsened for most African countries when the price of oil escalated in the 1970s. Oil-producing countries like Nigeria, Libya, and Algeria gained a short-term advantage from the increases, but the world recession undermined demand for other export commodities, and numerous countries found themselves unable to continue established development initiatives. Turning to the IMF and to private lenders for assistance, African debt to the industrialized world mounted during the 1970s and early 1980s. When combined with rapid population growth, drought, and attendant malnutrition, the plight of African governments intensified. By the mid-1980s Western lending institutions, together with the IMF, were insisting that governments abandon their commitment to the welfare state and drastically reduce services to the neediest of their citizens. Imports were decreased, swollen bureaucracies were dismantled, and government-controlled enterprises shed. The overall result of these austerity measures was a cycle of decline and dependency on the West that erased all pretense of genuine sovereignty.

In the midst of this unfolding catastrophe, the Organization of African Unity (OAU) attempted to rally the member states of the UN to support the adoption of what the OAU called a New Economic Order. Emerging out of the 1973 annual meeting of the OAU and informed by development economics, member states appealed to the world's wealthiest nations to reduce their tariffs against products from the developing world and establish fixed commodity prices, forgive existing Third World debt, and provide a massive increase in total development aid. Nonaligned countries swiftly endorsed the proposal, and in 1974 even the General Assembly of the UN voted in favor of what would have amounted to an unprecedented transfer of global wealth. It was an audacious campaign, but it took shape at an inauspicious moment. Recession and inflation in developed countries during the 1970s soured the political atmosphere regarding foreign assistance and more generous trade relations. Western intellectuals who had become disillusioned with development economics began to embrace "market-conforming" economic policies as the surest road to prosperity. It was becoming clear to Africa's leaders that the postcolonial decision to remain within the orbit of the capitalist West had not paid lasting dividends. Africa's inability to "catch up" with the developed world was increasingly viewed as the product of a playing field that was anything but even.

Also during the 1970s, a number of regional economic cooperation units were established in sub-Saharan Africa. They were designed after the model of the EEC and sought to free the member states from their dependency on the developed West. Oil-rich Nigeria made a strong bid to lead a West African association in the 1970s, for example, but its efforts were hampered by declining oil prices in the early 1980s. In addition, the 1970s witnessed the expansion of the Cold War to Africa and an escalation of regional conflict that undermined the pan-Africanist vision of the OAU. In 1974 the Soviet Union gained air and naval bases in Somalia and South Yemen in return for military assistance and training. But when the pro-Western Emperor Haile Selassie of Ethiopia was overthrown by communists that same year, Moscow's offer of military assistance to the new regime offended neighboring Somalia. By 1977 the Somali leader Mohammed Said Barre had invaded Ethiopia, expelled all Soviet personnel, and turned to the US for aid. The horn of Africa, desperately poor and lacking effective leadership, became a client-state region in the wider Cold War.

Superpower rivalry also had a harmful impact on development efforts in the south of the continent. After the Portuguese withdrew from Angola and Mozambique in 1974, the Soviets inserted 20,000 Cuban troops into Angola to buttress Marxist fighters who were engaged in a bloody conflict with American-backed guerrilla groups seeking to rule the country. The communists eventually triumphed, but little in the way of economic development aid was forthcoming from Moscow. Indeed the expansion of Soviet influence in Africa during the 1970s, involving a dozen countries, hundreds of Soviet technical and military advisors, and thousands of Cuban troops, served only to exacerbate the continent's economic difficulties. By the early 1980s, it was becoming clear to the pro-Soviet regimes in Libya, Angola, Ethiopia, Mozambique, and Guinea-Bissau that their economic woes, for decades attributed singly to Western neo-colonialism, were not about to be addressed by their allies in the Kremlin.

Latin America

During the course of the nineteenth century, the economies of Latin America were heavily dependent upon the overseas export of primary products. Brazilian, Colombian, and Cuban coffee; Argentinian beef; Chilean copper; and Guatemalan bananas were sold to Europeans and North Americans, while large companies based in the US won control over production in a variety of sectors. Half of Latin American trade was destined for the US at the start of World War II, but in the postwar period most leaders on the continent, irrespective of their political orientation, favored a policy of import substitution as the best road to further industrialization and economic autonomy. Tariffs were raised in an effort to foster domestic industries, and during the 1950s and 1960s manufacturing output expanded at a rate of 6 percent per year. From 3.6 percent of total world exports in 1960 to over 17 percent one decade later, this rapid growth in manufactured exports strengthened hopes that Latin America was at last developing a mature and diverse economic profile, one capable of competing with the developed economies of the industrialized West.

At the end of the 1970s, manufacturing in Argentina, Brazil, Uruguay, and Mexico assumed one-quarter of each country's GNP, and the future looked promising. In Mexico, the state-owned petroleum company began to realize record-breaking export earnings. As a result, President José López Portillo launched an ambitious development program, spending millions on infrastructure projects, transportation, and manufacturing. Since the country's proven oil reserves were extensive, projected earnings based on international sales boded well for the government's strategic plan. Securing loans now became easier, and by 1982 the government had assumed a total debt of more than $85 billion. The other significant trend during the 1960s and 1970s involved Latin America's decreased dependence on the US as a trade partner. At the start of the 1980s, 25 percent of manufacturing exports were destined for US ports, but an equal percentage found their way into a wide range of markets worldwide. Imports from the northern colossus also declined, and more Asian and European products were made available to the Latin American market. Foreign investment from the US slowed but overall foreign investments in the region intensified.

Unfortunately, the period of economic growth and greater autonomy from the US did not last. During the oil boom of the 1970s, oil-producing states had deposited a large portion of their handsome profits in Western banks. Private credit institutions, impressed by Latin America's recent economic performance and its stable, if authoritarian, governments, made generous loans to states in the region. Latin American governments were keen to pursue these loan opportunities since it freed them from any "conditionality" policies of the IMF and World Bank. Overall Latin American debt jumped from $2.3 billion in 1970 to $340 billion in 1983, the latter figure accounting for more than half of the foreign debt owed to private banks worldwide. Heading robust economies, Latin American political leaders were confident that they could meet their obligations as long as domestic economic growth continued. But the onset of a worldwide recession in the late 1970s and early 1980s led to a slackening of demand for products from Latin America. And when a decline in oil prices hit in the 1980s, two of the world's biggest petroleum producers – Mexico and Venezuela – found it difficult to meet their loan payments.

A debtors' globe

When, in the summer of 1982, Mexico announced that it could no longer afford to make payments on its $90-billion foreign debt, Western banks braced themselves for a wave of additional shocks administered by states in a similarly precarious position. They did not have to wait long. Within a year 40 additional countries, many of them in Latin America, followed Mexico's lead and declared that they were unable to make either principal or interest payments on debts held by First World private banks and governments. By 1983, the nations of Latin America, Africa, and Eastern Europe owed the West $810 billion, up from $64 billion just 13 years earlier. It became clear that if the debt was not repaid, major banks in the developed world might fail, plunging the world into global economic crisis. And if borrowers defaulted, their chances for securing future cash to import food, develop industry, and provide training for workers would evaporate.

Responding to the crisis, private creditors, together with the IMF and the World Bank, called for debtor nations to adopt rigorous new austerity measures, "structural adjustments," before any future loans would be considered. The debt crisis signaled the end of development economics and undermined confidence in the ability of sovereign states to manage the economy. Structural adjustments normally included mandatory cutbacks in basic social services to the most needy, reductions in the size and scope of government authority over the economy, and a return to export-led growth. Poor countries seeking new loans were obliged to eliminate trade barriers and to end subsidies for nascent industries. At the same time, developed states continued to subsidize their own agricultural producers, thus making it harder for developing states to earn export income by selling their agricultural products overseas. At the end of the century some poor countries were spending more on foreign debt service than on domestic social services. Partly in response to these perceived inequalities, in September 2003 a number of developing states walked out of a meeting of the WTO over the issue of ongoing state subsidies for Western farmers.

NEOLIBERAL ECONOMICS

Oil shocks and stagnation

In the quarter-century after World War II, the industrialized West had enjoyed full access to cheap supplies of imported oil from the Middle East, where two-thirds of the world's proven reserves were located. Britain's influence in Iraq prior to the seizure of power by the nationalist Ba'ath party in 1963, and America's leverage in Iran, together with the compliance of the absolute monarchy in Saudi Arabia, ensured that oil supplies to the West remained affordable and abundant. This changed suddenly with the outbreak of the 1973 Arab–Israeli war, and America's airlift of supplies to Israel. Led by Saudi Arabia, the member states of the Organization of Petroleum Exporting Countries (OPEC, founded in 1960) announced restrictions on the sale of oil to Europe and Japan, and a five-month embargo on the sale of oil to the US. This was followed by the quadrupling of the price of OPEC-produced crude over the next two years, a development that sent shock waves through the world economy. And the price escalation continued for the remainder of the decade: In 1973 the average price of a barrel of oil was $3.73; seven years later, after further disruptions caused by the Iranian Revolution, it was $33.50.

The oil embargo against the US created a short-term inconvenience for American consumers who waited in long lines at petrol stations, but more fundamentally the decision of OPEC to raise prices led to the most serious economic downturn in the West since the Great Depression. The US relied on oil imports to satisfy 40 percent of domestic energy needs by the early 1970s, while the figure in Europe and Japan was over 80 percent. Higher oil prices led to inflation and deep recession. In the US, for example, the inflation level in 1974 reached its highest point since World War I, while unemployment hovered just over 9 percent, its highest since the end of World War II. Neither the Republican administration of Gerald Ford (1974–6), not the Democratic administration under Jimmy Carter (1976–80), were able to spend their way out of what was increasingly described as a period of "stagflation." For his part, President Carter took to referring to an American cultural malaise, a posture interpreted – and successfully exploited – as defeatism by his Republican opponent in the 1980 presidential race.

The oil shocks had a disproportionate impact on developing countries that relied upon imported oil to stimulate their economies. They were now obliged to borrow on international markets in order to maintain the flow of oil. Assuming new debt, oil-importing nations in Africa and Latin America found their economic well-being tied directly to lending institutions in the world's richest states. The World Bank also entered the picture, making emergency loans to countries like Brazil, Hungary, and Poland, but not before these sovereign states agreed to the imposition of strict guidelines on domestic economic policy. By the early 1980s the strain on debtor nations threatened to undermine the entire international banking structure. Lending institutions engaged in a frenetic round of restructuring and loan-rescheduling schemes in an attempt to stave off massive defaults. Despite these efforts, some debtor states found it difficult to pay even the interest on loans contracted after the initial escalation of oil prices.

In the Arab oil-producing states, on the other hand, the windfall of the mid-1970s signaled the beginning of a new age of economic development and social change. Oilfields, many of which had been under the management of Western interests, and where profits were shared 50–50 with host regimes, were nationalized in Iraq, Libya, Saudi Arabia, Kuwait, Venezuela, and Iran. Each of these states, together with small Gulf sheikhdoms like Bahrain, Qatar, Oman, and the United Arab Emirates, undertook large-scale building and modernization efforts. In a few short years the capitals of the Gulf States became modern cities replete with commercial towers and costly public buildings. Urban development, and new employment opportunities in the cities, spurred a rapid growth in migration from rural areas (see Chapter 5). In sparsely populated kingdoms like Saudi Arabia and Kuwait, foreign migrants from non-oil-producing Muslim countries provided much of the manual labor force for the varied undertakings, while skilled professionals from the West assisted the various royal families with infrastructure projects. Employment in the public sector mushroomed, allowing monarchs to buy off traditional rivals, placate the population, and stay in power. The Saudi royal family, for example, used oil revenues to extend educational opportunities and improve health care. A Saudi middle class emerged whose strong appetite for foreign products helped to forge a robust consumer culture.

The example of the OPEC cartel, using the export of strategic raw materials as a political weapon, convinced other resource-rich developing states that they too might leverage their products in order to redress the historic economic imbalance between North and South. It was hoped that the massive transfer of wealth from Western industrial consumer states to the oil-producing countries might be repeated with raw materials like bauxite, cobalt, copper, and tin. The two largest copper-producing states, Zambia and Chile, soon nationalized all foreign-owned copper mines. In the case of Chile, the decision to nationalize strengthened US covert support for a military coup that overthrew the leftist government of Salvador Allende in 1973. Many of these developing states, frustrated by their ongoing dependency on the North, came together as the "Group of 77" in the UN, and with Soviet backing, they demanded higher prices for their raw materials and for a broader reparations scheme designed to make amends for decades of alleged imperialist, neocolonial exploitation.

Thatcher and Reagan

In the Western democracies, the high interest rates, high energy costs, inflation, slow economic growth, rising unemployment, and labor unrest of the mid-1970s contributed to a growing sense of disenchantment with government-led solutions to economic problems. Despite the proliferation of regulatory agencies, the Western economies continued to perform poorly. A mineworkers' strike in Britain during 1973 led to disruptive power cuts while inflation reached 15 percent. Edward Heath's Conservative government fell in the wake of the strike, but its Labour counterpart was equally unsuccessful in stopping the slide. In the US, Richard Nixon's resignation in 1974, coupled with the fall of South Vietnam to the communist North in 1975, intensified public distrust of big-government solutions to major domestic and international problems. By the end of the decade voters throughout the capitalist West were increasingly attracted to alternatives that questioned the viability of the postwar interventionist consensus. With the election of Margaret Thatcher as British Prime Minister in 1979 and Ronald Reagan as President of the US in 1980, a movement toward deregulation and market economics gathered strength.

In Britain, the new government embarked upon a decade-long effort to privatize national industries and curb the power of the unions. For Margaret Thatcher the critical moment in her drive to overturn the postwar consensus occurred in 1984, when the government took on the National Union of Mineworkers (NUM), led by the militant Arthur Scargill. Coal had been one of the first industries nationalized by the Attlee government back in 1947, but by the early 1980s its place in the British economy had declined dramatically, with inefficient pits costing the ratepayers almost $1.3 billion per year in subsidies. Thatcher recognized that the miners had been instrumental in the downfall of Heath's Conservative government in 1973, but she was determined to use the inefficient and costly practices in the coal industry as an illustration of everything that was wrong with the welfare state. When the miners struck in March 1984, the government was prepared for a long struggle. It took more than a year for Thatcher to prevail, but in the end the miners returned to work and the pit closures began. Telephone, oil, gas, steel, and coal were all sold off during the Thatcher years, and by 1992 two-thirds of all state-owned industries had returned to the private sector. Reagan followed a similar course in the US, cutting taxes and overseeing the deregulation of the airline, trucking, railroad, and telecommunications industries. For the conservatives of the 1980s, government had become the nemesis of economic well-being, an impediment to growth rather than its handmaiden.

Soviet blues

The American and British examples were soon adopted across Europe. The introduction of the single European market in 1992 facilitated the privatization juggernaut, as national giants like Volkswagen and Renault, Lufthansa, and Deutsche Telekom were sold to private investors. The greatest shift, however, came in the communist bloc. Back in 1961, Nikita Khrushchev had boasted that Soviet industrial output would overtake America's by the early 1980s. The communist ideal of labor on behalf of the wider society, rather than work to satisfy the demands of self-interested shareholders, would inspire new levels of productivity. But Khrushchev's boast turned out to be mere bombast. Guided by inflexible Soviet Cold War priorities, the Eastern Bloc refused to participate in the capitalist economic structure, and by the 1970s it was clear that the Soviet-style command economies had become stagnant, slow to innovate, and incapable of addressing basic consumer demands. Economic conditions during the 1970s seemed to improve as oil and natural gas revenues burgeoned, but when prices declined in the 1980s it was apparent that the communist bureaucrats had failed to employ export profits in a creative manner. Thanks to the myriad inefficiencies of collectivized agriculture, the Soviets were obliged to import wheat from the West during the 1970s, a humiliating admission of the failure of state planning. Technology also lagged; the early 1980s computer revolution in the West, for example, had no counterpart in the Soviet bloc. Industrial innovation, basic scientific research, and business risk-taking were discouraged by aging Soviet leaders who instinctively associated unorthodox ideas with political subversion.

The consumer market remained largely stillborn during the decades of Soviet ascendancy, with shoddy goods, lack of variety, poor service, and long delays all commonplace. An increasingly apathetic population seemed resigned to the inefficiencies of state-owned enterprises. Even with 1970s stagflation in the West, the Soviet Union fell further behind its Cold War rival, and when the Reagan administration embarked upon a major military buildup after 1981, Gorbachev's government found itself hard-pressed to compete. With the implosion of the Soviet Union and the collapse of communist ideology worldwide, the virtues of capitalism and the promise of the unfettered marketplace informed government policies around the globe. Socialist governments sold off companies that had been nationalized decades earlier. In Russia, President Boris Yeltsin privatized thousands of state-owned companies, and upward of 40 million Russians became shareholders. The transition was anything but seamless. Millions of Russians lost their jobs as the state cast off its holdings, while the fortunate few who secured lucrative franchises embraced a lifestyle of conspicuous consumption that was deeply resented by ordinary Russians. Even in China, where the communist state structure survived, the government of Deng Xiaoping had lost faith in the command economy. Thousands of inefficient state factories were subject to the rigors of the marketplace as generous subsidies ended. Companies were allowed to sell shares, institute efficiencies (often including redundancies), and find their own way in a competitive global market.

Markets triumphant?

The victory of the market-based reforms undertaken by the Thatcher and Reagan governments was affirmed, ironically, by the resounding victory of the Democrats under Bill Clinton in 1992, and by the triumph of "New" Labour Party under Tony Blair in Britain's 1997 general election. Clinton managed to defeat an incumbent president who had violated a pledge not to raise taxes, and who appeared out of touch with the needs of working families. Once in office the new president succeeded in winning congressional approval for a deficit reduction bill, but his effort to create a national health-care system gave conservative Republicans new life. After a long battle with the Republican-controlled Congress over tax cuts and a balanced budget in 1995, a battle that led to a temporary shutdown of the federal government, Clinton announced in his January 1996 State of the Union address that "the era of big government is over." By the end of his second term in office, Clinton's administration had achieved a balanced federal budget and the private-sector economy was booming. In Britain, Tony Blair ran on a platform that accepted the privatization revolution undertaken by the Conservatives over the previous 17 years. New Labour abandoned the philosophy that had long privileged state-led development. No renationalization or central planning took place, no government subsidies for unproductive enterprises reemerged, and no plans for promoting economic equality were drawn up. Clinton and Blair presided over a massive shift in the popular understanding of government's role in the economy, a shift made all the more dramatic in that it involved principles at odds with the values of their respective political parties since the 1940s.

A similar pattern emerged in South Asia, where India abandoned its inward-looking search for modernization in the early 1990s. Although the country had managed to achieve some significant milestones under the export-averse state-managed economy, more than half of the population remained mired in desperate poverty. The Congress Party's focus on industrialization was paying dividends for some, especially in the electronics and technology sectors. Close to 200 million Indians had achieved middle-class status and enjoyed the fruits of a growing consumer sector in the major cities, while others had leveraged their educational training to secure jobs in the US and Britain. Rajiv Gandhi, a former pilot for state-owned

Air India, was elected Prime Minister in the wake of his mother's assassination in 1984 and sought to reduce the burdens of the "permit raj." But it was not until the early 1990s – after the assassination of Rajiv and the end of the Nehru–Gandhi dynasty, and in the wake of the Soviet implosion – that the government took a series of bold steps to liberalize the Indian economy. The Soviets had been India's leading trade partner and ideological mentor on the economic front for close to four decades. The sudden failure of the Soviet command economy undermined faith in the long-term viability of its Indian stepchild, especially in light of the fact that India's managed economy looked anemic in comparison to East Asian states like South Korea, Indonesia, and Singapore. Embracing international trade and aggressively promoting manufactures overseas, these states, with a fraction of India's human resources, had made enormous strides in raising standards of living for their citizenry.

During the 1990s India's tariff and trade barriers were reduced, government subsidies for domestic manufactures were eliminated, and the noisome licensing system was scaled back. Potential foreign investors were courted by government ministries, even in such traditionally state-dominated sectors as transportation and telecommunications. By the end of the decade satellite television was beaming images of the latest Western consumer products to an Indian middle class that was now some 300 million-strong, American fast-food giants like McDonald's were doing a brisk business in vegetarian burgers, and the southern city of Bangalore had become a major global center for software research and manufacturing. The coalition governments that had ruled from Delhi since the erosion of the Congress Party monopoly on power, while prone to internal disagreement on a host of issues, maintained a united front on the need for market-based reforms. And when Congress finally returned to power in 2004, its reform-minded leadership eagerly embraced the precepts and practices of the market economy.

GLOBALIZATION AND DISQUIET

In October 2003, the American conglomerate United Technologies announced that one of its largest businesses, Carrier Air Conditioning, would close its manufacturing facility in central New York state, lay off some 1200 workers, and transfer their jobs to Singapore. Carrier had been located in the city of Syracuse, New York, since the 1930s. At its peak, the company was the city's largest employer, providing solid incomes for close to 7000 men and women, some of whom represented three generations within the same family. In a last-ditch effort to keep the Syracuse facility open, local political leaders and the governor of New York offered the company generous tax incentives, but in the end the chief executive officer of United Technologies stated that the company could not pass up the opportunity to build its refrigeration units three times cheaper in Asia.

The Carrier story was a familiar one at the end of the century, and it encapsulates one of the key dilemmas of globalization. In addition to the profit-and-loss dimension of the individual business decision, the phenomenon of international corporate migration involved questions of local and national identity, and the often conflicting claims of shareholder and local community. In the relentless pursuit of higher returns for the former, the complex question of whether or not larger networks of national, regional, and local responsibility should inform business decisions was raised by vocal opponents of increasing globalization. These opponents alleged that corporate migration was driven exclusively by greed, as businesses sought to reduce costs and avoid new health, safety, and environmental regulations. Nations that competed for foreign investment found themselves in a desperate "race to the bottom," offering ever larger incentive packages to First World companies that command enormous reserves of capital, technology, and productive capacity.

Multinational corporations

International businesses have existed for centuries. The Dutch and English East India Companies established a global presence in the early seventeenth century, while joint-stock companies sponsored overseas colonization efforts in England's Virginia and Massachusetts Bay colonies. In some respects, these early transnational enterprises were more powerful than their more recent counterparts like IBM,

Daimler–Chrysler, and SONY. The English East India Company, after all, became the de facto political authority in eighteenth-century India, deploying its own military forces and reducing the venerable Mughal dynasty to the status of supplicant. These early crown-sanctioned companies also enjoyed monopoly trading privileges in designated regions of the globe. Prior to World War II, almost all transnational businesses were engaged in extractive enterprises, exporting agricultural and mineral products to the West from colonies and underdeveloped trade partners.

Since 1945 the profile has changed dramatically. Multinational corporations became synonymous with manufacturing, financial services, entry-level jobs for millions of people in host nations, and rising levels of concern about the commitment of business to the very concept of the nation-state. Breakthroughs and improvements in technology accelerated the dynamic trends in globalization. Most recently, the introduction and rapid adoption of computer technology made business communications easier, and allowed for improvements and efficiencies in financial operations and inventory control. On the factory floor, increased use of robotics reduced the need for human hands in the assembly process. The advent of the Internet, fiber optics, satellites, microelectronics, air-freight services, and inexpensive ocean transport all made it possible for producers to locate manufacturing in low-wage regions of the world. And as the manufacturing sector introduced more labor-saving or labor-replacing technologies, or alternatively relocated from First to Third World countries, service-related jobs in the First World increased, bringing with them lower wages, few if any benefits, and declining levels of job satisfaction.

Most of the internationals were First World entities. As the EEC proved its durability during the 1960s, and as tariff regimes were lowered under GATT, increasing numbers of corporations sought to extend their influence across international borders. By 2000 there were almost 40,000 transnational corporations operating in a variety of states around the globe. Some of them, like Exxon-Mobile, General Electric, and Hitachi, rivaled large independent nations in terms of their capital and material resources. Giant companies controlled large portions of the world's investment capital, technology, research and development facilities, management expertise, and access to markets. While no longer wielding direct military power or controlling territory, massive economic might translated into political influence wherever multinationals established a presence. In such a setting, where profit dictated location and relocation, the idea of corporate citizenship, of material obligations to the wider host community, lost ground in the ceaseless pursuit of efficiency and profit.

The former Soviet-dominated Eastern European countries became a favorite destination for Western outsourcing in the 1990s. Wage levels were not as low as those in South and East Asia, but they were approximately one-third of averages in Western Europe, and proximity to the West meant lower transportation costs. This was especially important to automakers that were dependent upon the shipment of heavy parts to the final assembly point. Even Asian firms were attracted to the location and labor costs in the former Soviet-bloc countries. The Taiwanese computer-assembly firm Foxconn Electronics, for instance, opened a factory in the Czech Republic in 2000 in order to erase the average 30-day shipping period to Western European clients. While direct foreign investment worldwide lagged during 2002, in Eastern Europe it rose by 16 percent, from $25 to $29 billion. Honeywell International, an American firm based in New Jersey, was so impressed by the level of scientific and engineering skills amongst Czech college graduates – together with their willingness to work at wage levels much lower than those in the US – that it based a company research centre at the Czech Republic's Academy of Sciences. In 2001, beleaguered US Steel lobbied successfully with Congress and President Bush to raise tariffs against foreign imports, while simultaneously expanding its operations overseas with the purchase of a mammoth Slovakian steel mill. Even the manufacture of weapons defied national boundaries. In 1996, for example, the American aerospace company Goodrich purchased a plant in Poland that was used to build parts for sophisticated F-16 jet fighters. During the 1990s the US became the indisputable leader in the international arms sales market, filling orders for 40–50 percent of global demand. By this final decade of the century, the sale of weapons had become a centerpiece of the international economy, with many states spending more on arms purchases than on domestic education or health care combined.

The internationalization of business placed into question the appropriate "nationality" of commodities. By the close of the century fully half of the products built in the US contained components produced in other countries. The Ford Focus automobile built in Mexico for sale in the US market was just as familiar as the Honda Accord automobile (ostensibly Japanese) that was manufactured in the US for the same consumer. By the year 2000 it was estimated that half of all imports and exports in the world economy involved transactions between parent firms and their foreign subsidiaries. Again in the case of the world's greatest economic power, 20 percent of the goods sold by American companies were actually produced overseas. And manufacturing was not the only sector that "outsourced" operations to low-wage, non-unionized countries. Western-owned commercial services also tapped into cheap labor pools. Insurance and utility companies transferred processing, research, and claims operations overseas during the 1980s, and by the mid-1990s computer software support was typically located half a world away from the customer. By the early 1990s it was estimated that multinational corporations controlled one-quarter of the world's economic activity outside of their home states, including half of world trade in manufacturing and 80 percent of the world's land cultivated for export crops.

A better world?

The supporters of globalization and economic liberalization were many during the 1990s, from governments in North America, Europe, and Japan, to the award selection committee for the Nobel Prize in economics, to television media and the op-ed columns of major newspapers. Champions of globalization maintained that the benefits derived from the more efficient use of resources, labor, and capital outweighed any potential liabilities, including the dislocation involved when jobs shifted from rich to poor nations. They insisted that opening up international trade and manufacture would lead to a faster pace of development in poor countries and an overall improvement in the quality of life for the citizens of these states. And the movement of capital, assembly, and production facilities from the industrialized North into low-wage countries of the South would result in less expensive goods on the world market together with greater employment opportunities for predominantly rural, agrarian populations in developing regions.

The defenders of multinationals also pointed to the fact that large internationals tended to pay higher wages when measured against domestic firms, imposed higher labor standards, and afforded the host nation capital and technology otherwise unavailable. In Turkey during the 1990s, for example, multinational firms paid their employees 124 percent of the average domestic wage. Similarly, the Republic of Ireland reversed decades of economic decline once it began to attract foreign technology and service firms. By the early 1990s Ireland's "Tiger" economy had become the envy of Europe. And when the southern Indian state of Kerala began to play host to international computer software companies in the late 1980s and 1990s, a vibrant middle class quickly emerged. The positive effects of globalization were also felt by urban dwellers in China, Taiwan, South Korea, Singapore, and Malaysia, as job options expanded and new opportunities for social mobility were created.

Despite the sanguine predictions, however, most of Africa, Latin America, and South Asia realized few immediate benefits from the spread of First World business and manufacturing. In 2001 the World Bank listed 41 countries as heavily indebted and poor. Of these, 33 were located in sub-Saharan Africa. After the end of the Cold War, aid flows from rich nations to poor neighbors dropped sharply, falling 25 percent between 1991 and 1998 alone. It appeared to many leaders in the world's poorest countries that the rhetoric of economic globalization was replacing traditional aid commitments from affluent states. During the 1990s the number of people living in poverty worldwide increased by almost 100 million, during a period when total world income increased by an average of 2.5 percent each year. As the gap between the wealthiest and poorest countries continued to widen in the post-Cold War environment, critics of economic globalization became more vocal. By the end of the century meetings of the WTO, the IMF, and the World Bank became the sites of popular protests, demonstrations, and street violence. Many of the protesters pointed to the expansion of business across international borders as compounding, not lessening, economic disparities between states.

A disconcerting conclusion

In the year 1500, the overall gap in average per capita income between developed and developing states was approximately 3 to 1. By the end of the twentieth century the gap had become a cavernous 30 to 1, with the lives of the poorest on the planet more desperate than the most impecunious peasant of the late Middle Ages. At the beginning of the twenty-first century the World Bank estimated that half of the world's population, approximately 2.8 billion, were limited to incomes of less than $2 per day, and 1.2 billion of these survived on less than $1 per day. Almost half the population of sub-Saharan Africa struggled on less than $1 per day, certainly not enough to ensure clean water, sufficient food, or minimum medical care. Even the modernization of agriculture in parts of Africa benefited only large- and medium-scale farmers who could afford chemical fertilizers, hybrid seeds, and petroleum-driven machinery. Landless peasant laborers, on the other hand, found themselves forced off the land by the "green revolution." Millions crowded into cities that lacked the basic infrastructure, and the employment opportunities, to absorb internal migrants. Even in the wealthiest nations, 10 percent of the population typically lived below the poverty level. Focusing on the persistence of poverty amid plenty, in 2000 the World Bank published a report on world development that called into question the value of market liberalization to antipoverty efforts. Russia stood out as a glaring test case, since that country's shift to free markets in the 1990s had been accompanied by a tremendous surge in poverty levels. Sadly, the evidence from the century's final decade seemed to suggest that the expansion of wealth mantra, absent government intervention, had done little to lift all boats. Thanks to globalization, more humans became involved in the generation of goods and services around the world, but fewer than 20 percent of the world's people consumed 85 percent of those goods and services.

The arrival of First World multinationals may have provided a partial solution to the problem of urban unemployment in developing countries, but at high cost with respect to host government concessions in the form of tax exemptions and unrestricted repatriation of profits. Critics alleged that many host countries became little more that company towns or a gigantic shop floor, where environmental concerns were ignored, where labor unions were forbidden, and where output had little or no relation to needs of the domestic population. Even in developed countries, the negative impacts of globalization were borne exclusively by the poor, men and women whose work skills were easily replicated in low-wage countries. One troubling result of states negotiating with multinationals from a position of weakness was a significant shifting of tax burdens from holders of mobile resources (multinationals) to middle- and lower-class individuals and householders. Between 1986 and 1995, the standard corporate tax rate in countries belonging to the OECD fell from 43 to 33 percent. From the 1960s through the 1990s, taxes on capital grew less than 1 percent, while taxes on labor grew by more than 8 percent. As multinationals became more central to one of the key functions of government – ensuring economic growth – they became akin to sovereign powers. States found themselves in the unenviable position of having to compete with each other for the privilege of having a powerful multinational set up shop within their territorial borders.

In addition to the growing disparities between rich and poor states, the social and psychological costs of a material culture that equated profit and individual advancement with a life of fulfilment and meaning were largely overlooked in the scramble for success. Some supporters of economic globalization carelessly identified development, and especially Western market capitalism, with the totality of human progress. They downplayed the environmental costs and the depletion of nonrenewable resources associated with an economic creed that associated consumption with contentment. And those costs were significant. Even if the most optimistic forecasts of development theorists were to be achieved, during the 1980s and 1990s it became clear that the Western standard of living was ecologically unsustainable given current resource use. At meetings of the WTO in Seattle (1999) and Prague (2000), thousands of protesters took to the streets in vocal, and occasionally violent, opposition to the broader human and environmental damage associated with economic globalization.

The celebration of market forces that epitomized the 1990s in the Western capitalist democracies was accompanied by other insecurities. For millions of middle-class professionals, the absence of job security and rising stress levels in the workplace became the unpleasant companions of economic good times. The fate of the "Asian Tiger" economies of South Korea, Singapore, Taiwan, and Malaysia served as a sober reminder of the fragility and fickleness of the market. Deregulation of world financial markets had prompted banks and investment firms to extend large loans to these rapidly emerging Asian countries in the early 1990s. For a brief moment, they became great success stories as their free-market economies boomed, especially in the area of real-estate speculation. Signs of overinvestment in real estate emerged in the late 1990s, however, and in 1997 and 1998 panicked investors began to call in loans. Over $100 billion left the region within a 12-month period, leaving a number of countries in serious financial straits. Declining confidence in the market as the best platform for growth and prosperity was coupled with the contraction of government welfare provision for the neediest in society, and the callousness of employers whose workforce decisions were informed solely by shareholder priorities.

For many even in the affluent West, the rewards of competition and acquisition, and the relentless pursuit of wealth as an end in itself, seemed unsatisfactory. Economic growth has always been fundamental to the task of freeing humankind from hunger and poverty. And changes in objective material conditions have most often been associated with changes in subjective well-being, or levels of personal happiness. The connection between higher levels of income and happiness is most compelling when the shift in material conditions is at the most basic level, when, for instance, an individual is able for the first time to secure access to adequate food, shelter, education, and health care. For the poor agricultural laborer in India, the prospect of landownership, the availability of clean water, electricity, and private transportation in the form of a bicycle would typically translate into the enhancement of subjective well-being. But the inference becomes more tenuous when applied to persons who already live in unprecedented comfort, and this was the condition of the majority of women and men in the industrialized North during the last quarter of the twentieth century.

As the per capita income of the world's wealthiest states grew, levels of satisfaction with the quality of life in consumer economies did not keep pace. In fact detailed surveys conducted in the US between 1972 and 1991 suggested a trend in a negative direction, with no statistically significant improvement in average happiness despite a doubling of GDP per capita. In Western Europe during the same period, where GDP per capita rose between 25 and 50 percent, the survey results were similar. And in Japan, where per capita income skyrocketed fivefold between 1958 and 1987, affording millions of consumers access to automobiles, electric appliances, and countless other durables that were simply unavailable after World War II, the survey data indicated no improvement in subjective well-being. At the beginning of the new century, the call for "growth" continued unabated in the developed countries, with politicians of every political persuasion glibly championing the culture of getting and spending. But the prospect that material needs might one day be satiated, and that the achievement of a particular level of material comfort would still the desire for even more, appeared unlikely.

Indeed the wonders and efficiencies of new technology, especially manufacturing, information, and medical technology, appeared to do little to advance personal happiness, to liberate its beneficiaries from the more elemental fears of a rudderless existence. Levels of job dissatisfaction, even within the fortunate middle class, continued to rise even as technology transformed the workplace. Divorce rates increased, civic engagement languished, and clinically diagnosed depression became a widespread feature of middle-class professional culture. The economist Joseph Schumpeter once described the essential dynamic of capitalism as "creative destruction." By the end of the twentieth century the phrase was applicable to more than material conditions. The modern consumer culture, aside from its deleterious impact on the natural environment, had raised important value-questions that had not been addressed in a serious manner by any of its champions. In 2000 the highly respected historian of religion Huston Smith argued that the paradox of unhappiness amid plenty pointed to a deeper spiritual crises in the developed world, one that began with the eighteenth-century Enlightenment and intensified after World War II. The question of whether or not the free market could ever advance the cause of economic justice worldwide, or, more importantly, whether it could produce a life that was both fulfilling and meaningful in the widest sense, remained unanswered at the start of the new century.

5

WHEN BORDERS DO MATTER: INTERNATIONAL MIGRATION AND IDENTITY

KEY TOPICS

States and refugees   *Globalization and identity*
Provisional guests   *Global equity and migration*

One of the great ironies of globalization at the start of the twenty-first century involved voluntary and involuntary human migration across national frontiers. On the one hand, the postwar period was characterized by a sharp increase in both the number of international migrants and in the range of sending countries. With the world's population burgeoning from 1.6 billion in 1945 to just over 6 billion in 2000, more humans – perhaps as many as 180 million – were living outside the land of their birth than at any previous period in modern history. On the other hand, at the very moment when ideas, money, manufacturing, and even pollutants moved ever more seamlessly across international borders, restrictions on the movement of humans across those same borders became more rigorous. Exclusionary immigration regimes were imposed in all First World nations after the end of World War II, and in the wake of the September 2001 terrorist attacks against the US, calls to make immigration policy and enforcement a political priority intensified. In the developed countries, border controls were tightened, visa policies were scrutinized, and the rules of state membership and naturalization were reevaluated.

Even before 9/11, the 20 percent of the world's population that consumed 85 percent of global goods and services seemed conflicted about extending the benefits of First World citizenship to new-comers from overseas. With population projections indicating that there would be upwards of 8 billion people on the planet by 2025, and with the most dramatic growth set to take place in poor coun-tries, the potential advantages of a generous immigration policy in the aging and demographically stagnant North seemed compelling. Gainfully employed immigrants could offset the reduced numbers of native-born workers, contribute to state-mandated retirement schemes that supported the growing ranks of the elderly, and pro-vide new ideas and creative energy in market-driven economies. But these long-term benefits of international migration were typ-ically overlooked in the media rush to point up the myriad dangers of immigration. Much of the discussion focused on the potential social disruption caused by newcomers, their alleged reluctance to assimilate, proclivity for criminal behavior, and disproportionate need for welfare benefit. In the year 2004, globalization remained largely a matter of product, not people, and especially not people who lacked education, specialized skills, and considerable financial resources of their own.

This was not the pattern that was anticipated in the aftermath of World War II. In 1948 the UN adopted a nonbinding "Universal Declaration of Human Rights" that was intended for "all members of the human family," irrespective of their nationality or their polit-ical circumstances. Among the political, social, and economic rights outlined in the Declaration, three specifically involved human migration. Article 13, Section 2 claimed that every person "has the right to leave any country, including his own, and to return to his country." Article 14 declared a right "to seek and to enjoy in other countries asylum from persecution," while Article 15, Section 2 mandated that no one "shall be arbitrarily deprived of his national-ity nor denied the right to change his nationality." Work on the Declaration began in 1946 and was prompted in large part by the horrors witnessed during World War II, especially against innocent noncombatants. But its framers, led by former First Lady Eleanor Roosevelt, also looked forward to a world where freedom of move-ment across borders would strengthen international understanding, enhance respect for cultural differences, bolster workforces in needed areas, and provide relief to those who found themselves without hope in the land of their birth.

By defining international relocation as a universal human right, the authors of the UN Declaration challenged a key component of the Western Enlightenment heritage. Since the late eighteenth century, one's identity and core allegiance had become increasingly tied to the territorial nation-state. The goal of modern secular nation-building involved first and foremost the unification of diverse cultures and languages under a shared identity and within defensible borders. Loyalty to the centralizing state, and to the values represented by the state, became the ideological nexus around which the principle of citizenship was organized. Sovereign countries were defined in part by their borders, their claims on specific territory irrespective of the cultural, linguistic, and religious features of the citizenry. The experience of modern warfare helped to solidify the allegiance of citizens to the state, as nationalism was used by political leaders in order to rally popular support and encourage sacrifice. Now in 1948, under the auspices of the UN, the peoples of the world were being asked to make their borders more permeable, to welcome the distant stranger and to think in terms of global citizenship. It was a bold challenge, and within the context of the gathering storm that was the Cold War, few nations were prepared to accept it.

The increased pace of international migration in the postwar decades, irrespective of the emergence of more restrictive national policies, prompted a vigorous debate among policy makers, intellectuals, and the media in the world's industrial democracies. Those who harbored misgivings over the level and diversity of international migration since the 1950s employed a range of arguments. Some scholars and pundits alleged that poor and ill-educated newcomers would place an inordinate stress on the fiscal resources of receiving countries: urban infrastructures would be unable to cope with new populations; labor markets would be saturated and wages for native workers would be forced down; law enforcement would be undermined; and welfare services would expand, leading to escalating tax rates. A residual fear of the "other," long associated with the introduction of minority cultures into established societies, lay at the core of these critiques and was aimed especially at South–North migration. In the 1990s, respected American political scientists like Myron Weiner and Samuel Huntington warned of an impending security threat associated with the failure of developed states to police their borders. They were joined in their appeal by the distinguished historian Arthur Schlesinger, who insisted that the rapid pace of American immigration represented a serious challenge to America's long-term political unity. Newcomers – most of them poor – appeared unwilling or unable to embrace the dominant language and culture, and in democracies a shared set of cultural values was deemed essential to political success. "The contemporary ideal is shifting from assimilation to ethnicity," mused Schlesinger, "from integration to separation." Sadly, much of the criticism echoed sentiments expressed one century earlier in the US, as large numbers of poor, non-Protestant, and non-English-speaking Europeans arrived to upset the Anglo-Protestant consensus. But memories fade, and in the wake of the "war on terrorism" declared by President Bush and endorsed by many world leaders, constraints on the voluntary and involuntary movement of people across international borders intensified. By the early twenty-first century, the "problem" of legal and illegal migration flows from poor to rich states had become integral to a much larger debate over global terrorism, the outsourcing of First World jobs to developing countries, and the need for potential newcomers to embrace the dominant culture.

STATES AND REFUGEES

There have always been refugees, people driven from the land of their birth by natural disaster or the animus of fellow humans. The Jews of ancient Egypt; the Prophet Muhammad and his early followers in Medina; Buddhists in Muslim-controlled northern India; Native Americans at the time of the European incursions – the pattern of forced displacement is as common in human history as it is distressing. What distinguished involuntary migration after 1945, however, was its sheer geographical sweep, its numerical scale, and the existence of agreed (but largely unenforceable) international standards on how migrants should be treated. Just as the concept of the sovereign nation-state reached its apogee in the mid-twentieth century, the number of people who were forced to flee their homeland due to persecution, war, disease, and famine reached unprecedented levels. By the end of the century, television images of desperate people in flight from Kosovo, Rwanda, Liberia, Haiti, and Iraq had become part of popular consciousness in the West, and a sense of resignation over the unfolding of new refugee emergencies took the place of an original postwar hope that the root causes of displacement might be addressed through the coordinated efforts of the international community.

Most states in the modern era demanded a high level of ideological commitment from their citizens, and in undemocratic countries, those who did not conform and who lived to tell the tale were subject to harassment, abuse, and banishment. During World War II, upward of 25 million Europeans became refugees, most fleeing Nazi violence and Soviet oppression. Repatriation proved difficult; five years after the end of the war there were still almost eight million refugees in West Germany alone. In East Asia, Japanese aggression compelled the flight of millions, destroying communities and shattering local economies from Korea to Burma. In South Asia, an estimated 17 million Indians and Pakistanis fled from their homes after the tragic partition of the subcontinent in the fall of 1947, and in China approximately two million Nationalists abandoned the mainland for the island of Taiwan ahead of Mao Zedong's advancing Red Army in 1949. Requests for political asylum rose sharply in the West after 1945 and continued as the Soviet Union tightened its grip across Eastern Europe. But while an international convention at the Hague recognized the right of persons to leave their homeland, no parallel right of ingress was confirmed. States retained the power to reject any and all applicants, including refugees, and admissions criteria increasingly revolved around the political orientation of the sending country.

In the years immediately after the war, the international community struggled to address refugee crises on a case-by-case basis. Only in 1951, when the UN established the Office of the United Nations High Commissioner for Refugees (UNHCR), did a formal international protocol emerge for the treatment of displaced persons. Refugees were defined as persons living overseas who had a well-grounded fear of persecution at home due to their race, religion, nationality, political views, or membership in a social group. While there was no enforcement mechanism, the 1951 UN Convention Relating to the Status of Refugees obliged host governments to refrain from returning people to their home country when there existed a legitimate fear of persecution. UNHCR was given the mandate to find solutions to refugee crises and to protect those who found themselves displaced, and its activities grew exponentially over the second half of the century. From an original budget of $300,000 and a staff of 33 in 1951, UNHCR was responsible for more than $1 billion by 2000 and maintained offices in more than 120 countries. During the height of the Cold War in the 1960s and 1970s, the number of international refugees expanded as a result of regional proxy wars between the superpowers, and UNHCR intervention always came at the risk of alienating one side or another. And while these larger geopolitical motivations for regional wars abated in the post-Cold War era, new identity and ethnicity-based conflicts took their place, adding yet another complication to the difficult relief work of the UN.

During the first years of its existence, UNHCR focused most of its resources on the settlement of displaced persons in Europe. After the Soviets crushed an uprising in Hungary in 1956, for example, the agency successfully resettled 200,000 refugees in Western Europe. But superpower conflicts repeatedly exacerbated the worldwide refugee crisis over the next three decades, particularly in developing nations, and this fact led to a reorientation of the UN mission. As the world's political leaders began to take sides in the Cold War, internal ideological divisions fueled domestic upheaval and the displacement of peoples in Eastern Europe, Africa, Asia, Central America, and the Middle East. Civil wars and political unrest in countries as geographically diverse as Vietnam, Korea, Angola, Somalia, Cuba, and Nicaragua fueled the outflow of civilians and created humanitarian emergencies in neighboring states that were poorly prepared to deal with the influx.

American policy and refugees

The experiences of two countries in Southeast Asia – Vietnam and Cambodia – illustrate something of the scale of the disruption. After the communist takeover in North Vietnam in 1945, almost one million residents, the majority of whom were Roman Catholics, fled in advance of state-ordered collectivization and religious persecution. Two decades later, as the government of South Vietnam fell to the communist North, over 140,000 South Vietnamese government and military personnel, together with their families, escaped the country and were eventually resettled in the US. Many who were unable to flee in the chaos surrounding the collapse of the American-backed government were despatched to reeducation labour camps by the triumphant communists. Cambodia also fell to communist insurgents in 1975, and under the barbarous rule of Pol Pot, cities were emptied and rural labor camps were established where over one million Cambodians died of starvation and overwork. Those who managed to escape crossed over the border into Thailand, where they were assisted by UNHCR. Most of the refugees refused to countenance a return to the "killing fields" of their native country. Neighboring Vietnam invaded Cambodia in 1979 and overthrew the hated Khmer Rouge regime, but by that date, thanks in no small measure to an American embargo and an additional regional military clash with China, Vietnam joined Cambodia as one of the poorest countries on earth. Driven to desperation, 250,000 Vietnamese of Chinese ethnic origin fled to Southern China, where they too were assisted by UNHCR and by the government of China.

Hundreds of thousands of additional Vietnamese fled their homeland in small boats between 1979 and 1982. After enduring harrowing experiences at sea, those who survived landed in Hong Kong, the Philippines, Malaysia, or Thailand. These Vietnamese "Boat People" were unwelcome refugees, and in some notorious cases their small craft were towed back out to international waters by the authorities. Those who were allowed ashore were housed in crowded detention camps pending a resolution of their status. Most of the exiles, some 630,000, were eventually resettled in the US, Australia, France, and Canada. By the mid-1990s there were over one million persons of Vietnamese, Cambodian, and Laotian origin resident in the US alone. Many of the new immigrants, while grateful for the opportunity to rebuild their lives, were deeply conflicted over the role of the Americans in their native land. And while relations between the US and Vietnam improved markedly during the first Bush and Clinton administrations, with a resettlement agreement in 1989 facilitating the return of over 100,000 Vietnamese over the next eight years, a strong case of "refugee fatigue" had gripped the Western world, with some observers declaring that many of those who fled Vietnam had been economic migrants, not legitimate refugees.

Another locus of the Cold War refugee phenomenon was Central America. In Cuba, the Castro revolution led to the flight of more then 800,000 people to the US, beginning in the early 1960s. And during the bloody civil conflicts of late 1970s and 1980s, as many as 385,000 Salvadorans, Nicaraguans, Hondurans, and Guatemalans entered Mexico illegally, with most living on the outskirts of the country's major urban areas. By the mid-1980s approximately 200,000 Guatemalans had made their way across the Mexican border into the US. Most of the migrants from Central America were fleeing the death squads and political repression of right-wing military governments that were supported by the US. The triumph of the leftist Sandinista government of Nicaragua in 1979, for example, led to a redoubling of US support for conservative, and antidemocratic, regimes in the region. Refugee flows reflected Cold War priorities, as asylum applications from opponents of the US-backed Salvadoran regime were routinely rejected by immigration authorities, while a more generous posture was adopted with respect to opponents of the Sandinista government in Nicaragua. In 1982 fewer than 600 of the 3000 refugee slots allocated for Latin Americans were filled, and most of these were awarded to Cubans seeking political exile.

The first Gulf War

Military conflict in the Middle East has always been coupled with the disruption of civilian life, but the 1991 war to free Kuwait from Iraqi occupation led to an unprecedented level of displacement owing to the large numbers of guest workers located in the region. The Americans had supported the brutal Iraqi dictator during the eight-year Iran–Iraq war of the 1980s, but when Hussein's troops overwhelmed oil-rich Kuwait in 1991, an international coalition of oil-dependent states, led by the US, forced the Iraqis out. Estimates run as high as five million people forced to move during the crisis of 1990–1. Migrant workers in Kuwait and Iraq were the first to flee, with most entering the nearby Kingdom of Jordan. The Saudis then expelled all Yemenis resident in their kingdom, fearing that these guest workers sympathized with Saddam's regime and might desta-bilize the Saudi government. After this first Gulf War, an uprising by Kurds in northern Iraq was put down in ruthless fashion by the forces loyal to Hussein. Over one million Kurds fled to Iran, while another half-million set out to cross into Turkey. Refused asylum by the Turkish authorities who worried about their own restive Kurdish population, the UN approved the establishment of safe zones in both northern and southern Iraq that were protected by American, British, and French forces. The Kurdish safe zones remained a fixture of the Iraqi political landscape until the overthrow of the Saddam dictatorship in the spring of 2003, at which time many expatriate Kurds returned to reclaim their lands in the north. The Kurdish refugee crisis was a post-Cold War phenomenon, but it illustrated the difficulties involved whenever a regime attempts to "cleanse" itself of potentially dissident populations within its national borders.

Jews and Muslims

For world Jewry, the life of the refugee was woven into the very fabric of a uniquely tragic history, and in the aftermath of World War II, the creation of a national homeland in Palestine precipitated one of the more intractable disputes in modern international affairs. The Nazi employment of modern science and technology in pursuit of the elimination of an entire people resulted in the murder of more than six million innocents before the war ended, but while it was certainly the most gruesome display of anti-Semitism in history, the marginalization and mistreatment of Jews had deep roots in European life, stretching back to ancient Rome. Between 1880 and 1948 over four million Jews left their homes in Eastern Europe, Russia, and a variety of Muslim-dominated countries for destinations in Western Europe and the US. More often than not the moves were occasioned by some element of persecution. By the latter date a small minority of the refugees had settled in British-occupied Palestine. Most of the migrants were inspired by a Zionist movement that had secured a key endorsement from the British government in 1917 for the establishment of a territorial Jewish homeland in Arab-dominated Palestine.

The British encouraged Jewish relocation to the mandate territory of Palestine during the 1920s, mostly as a counterweight to

Muslim influence in the region. The pace of migration quickened during the 1930s as Nazi policies hardened in Germany. By 1940 there were half a million Jews in the region, prompting Arab fears that Jews would eventually become the majority population. With support from Western financiers, some Jewish settlers formed communal farms called *kibbutzim* and achieved remarkable levels of agricultural efficiency and output. Others built factories and transformed the city of Tel Aviv into a vibrant commercial centre. And all insisted that their presence in the region represented a progressive and democratic beacon of hope for every resident, including the majority Arab population. After 1945, the remnants of European Jewry found little reason to believe in a better future on the war-torn continent. Most Zionists were convinced that the creation of a sovereign Jewish state in Palestine would put an end to centuries of involuntary diaspora, facilitating an ingathering of the oppressed now scattered throughout the Christian and Muslim world. In the US, the Truman administration agreed, and when a sovereign Israeli state was declared immediately upon the British withdrawal in May 1948, the US was the first country to recognize the new democracy.

Israel's Arab neighbors viewed Jewish settlement in Palestine as a blatant example of old-style Western imperialism. With a deplorable and centuries-long record of anti-Semitism in the Christian West, it was argued, Europeans now sought to excise the problem by foisting Jewish refugees upon the Muslim inhabitants of the Middle East. Immediately attacked after its Declaration of Independence by a coalition of Arab countries, seasoned Israeli forces, many of whom had trained and fought alongside the British during World War II, won a decisive victory and even expanded the borders of the country beyond those established by the UN. The fighting continued for nine months before the UN finally brokered an armistice. In the wake of this first Arab–Israeli war, upward of one million Palestinians were expelled from their ancestral homes in Israel, creating an enormous refugee problem for regional powers and for the UN. In 1950 the UN established a special "Relief and Works Agency for Palestinian Refugees in the Near East" in order to address the crisis, but half a century later it was still at work, recognizing 3.5 million Palestinians who were scattered across the region, denied the right of return to Israel, and without effective leadership in the quest for a sovereign state of their own. Lacking that leadership, and without a strong advocate on the world stage, increasing numbers of Palestinians became radicalized, and their frustration was shared by the wider Muslim community of states.

Although the majority of the world's ten million Jews continued to live outside of Israel at the end of the twentieth century, the tiny state became one of the most prominent destination points for Jewish migrants, and many of these were legitimate refugees fleeing persecution in their home countries. Only a sprinkling of America's six million Jews elected to emigrate to Israel, but Jews from Russia, North Africa, and Eastern Europe found safety and a sense of national purpose in the new country. The greatest wave of refugees came from the former Soviet Union. While only 200,000 Soviet Jews were allowed to relocate during the four decades of the Cold War, in 1990 alone that same number – often entire families – departed for Israel. A nation of immigrants, the majority of whom had never been accepted on equal terms in the lands of their birth, Israel emerged as a refugee success story. Unhappily, that signal success had not been without enormously tragic consequences for Arabs. The Palestinian question became and remains the refugee dilemma with the highest profile in the early twenty-first century, one that acts as a fundamental divide between the wider Muslim world and the democratic West. As we have seen, efforts by the US to intervene in the conflict during the 1990s were unsuccessful, and although most Israelis acknowledged the right of the Palestinians to their own sovereign state, irredentist elements on both sides were unwilling to renounce the use of force in order to achieve their ends.

A South Asian emergency

The largest cross-border movement of refugees in the second half of the twentieth century occurred in South Asia during the 1971 Bangladeshi war of independence from Pakistan. An estimated ten million people from war-torn Bangladesh crossed into the Indian province of Bengal between April and December of 1971. Indian authorities, recognizing that in some districts of West Bengal the refugee population outnumbered the local residents, announced that it would not accept any permanent settlers. UNHCR and the Indian government took the lead in coordinating relief efforts in the hundreds of squalid refugee camps that were established along the border with Bangladesh, but the work was compounded by the spread of cholera through the camps during the summer monsoon season. The UN Secretary-General issued an urgent call for humanitarian assistance, and the international community responded generously by midsummer with a total pledge of $70 million.

The humanitarian crisis was compounded by deteriorating political relations between India and Pakistan. Mrs. Gandhi's government claimed that the Pakistanis were attempting to crush the independence movement in Bangladesh through the forcible removal of a significant part of the country's Hindu population. Bilateral relations deteriorated over the course of the crisis, and when war erupted in early December, the Indian army fought its way into Bangladesh and swiftly overwhelmed the Pakistani army. With independence secured, India announced that all refugees would be obliged to return to Bangladesh, and by February 1972 over nine million had been repatriated. The following year a UN-brokered agreement was reached that allowed for the repatriation of Pakistanis living in Bangladesh and Bengalis who had been living in Pakistan at the time of the independence struggle. A massive airlift, the largest in history, was organized and over 230,000 people were flown home by 1974, all with the assistance of UNHCR. The returning refugees were now citizens of one of the world's poorest countries, and once the population transfer was complete, the eyes of the international community turned elsewhere.

Africa's refugee predicament

Over 95 percent of the world's refugees in the half-century since the end of World War II have been from developing states, and the vast majority of these were located in sub-Saharan Africa. Often fleeing one impoverished postcolonial state for an equally destitute neighbor, the refugees placed impossible economic burdens upon their unprepared hosts. By the early 1960s, the focus of UNHCR shifted away from the settlement of East Europeans in Western countries, to the problem of repatriation on a wider African stage. In 1969 the

Organization of African Unity established its own refugee convention, extending the definition of refugee beyond the narrow confines of those who feared persecution at home to include those who fled war and communal violence. The impact of the Cold War in aggravating refugee flight in Africa was enormous. The long struggle for independence against Portuguese rule in Mozambique, for example, forced the relocation of 1.7 million people outside the country by the time that the war ended in 1992. Over one million of these refugees sought shelter in tiny Malawi, a country that was ill prepared to support the destitute newcomers. Sadly, the end of the Cold War had little effect in reversing the trends. Ancient ethnic and religious antagonisms that lay dormant during the decades of superpower conflict reemerged in a virulent fashion during the 1990s, precipitating new disasters in states that already faced enormous challenges from illiteracy, endemic poverty, desertification, and the spread of AIDS. By the end of the century Africa's refugee population had exceeded 20 million, four times the total just two decades earlier. Having lost most of its strategic value with the end of the Cold War, the world's most powerful nations appeared unalarmed by the scale and the human costs of involuntary migration in this enormous continent.

In the Horn of Africa, the end of the Cold War meant that states like Ethiopia could no longer count on Soviet assistance in its protracted struggle against Somalia, while in Sudan, Africa's largest country, the US closed its military facilities and canceled further military and economic assistance. The country's military government came under strong Islamist influence in the early 1990s, supported Iraq during the first Gulf War, provided training facilities for the Saudi fugitive Osama bin Laden, and imposed Sharia law on the Christian majority living in the south of the country. The latter act of intolerance triggered a full-scale civil war, with the US providing military support for the neighboring countries of Eritrea, Ethiopia, and Uganda that offered sanctuary to the Christian rebels. The result was colossal displacement, human suffering, and death. In a nation of 22 million, estimates of displaced persons reached as high as seven million caused by environmental degradation, drought, and military upheaval. Close to one million Sudanese, many driven from their homes, died from hunger and disease during the conflict.

In neighboring Somalia, the picture was equally gloomy. The overthrow of President Said Barre in 1991 triggered a return to clan-based military conflict throughout the country. Within a year more than two million people had been displaced, and almost half of these crossed illegally into ill-prepared Ethiopia and Kenya. In December of 1992 an American-led UN force of 20,000 entered Somalia with a humanitarian mandate to provide food for a population on the verge of starvation, but the mission quickly took on a political component as UN forces attempted to remove the warlord Mohammed Farrah Aidid. After a series of military clashes in the capital city of Mogadishu which left 18 US soldiers dead, UN forces were withdrawn and the dissolution of the state continued. Lacking a central government that could protect international aid workers, the suffering of the Somali population disappeared from the headlines during the 1990s.

The Rwandan genocide of 1994 and its immediate aftermath epitomized the confluence of ethnic rivalry and post-Cold War politics. As we read in Chapter 2, in the spring of 1994 a systematic campaign of genocide against the Tutsi claimed the lives of approximately one million people. Fully aware of the scale of the violence, the international community failed to intervene, and a multinational peacekeeping force of 2500 was reduced to 250 as the genocide unfolded between April and July. And when the Tutsi-dominated Rwandan Patriotic Front eventually triumphed in the bloody fighting, more than two million Hutus who feared retribution retreated across the border into Zaire. Here they established makeshift refugee camps that, according to Rwandan authorities, also housed many of those responsible for the genocide.

Conditions in the refugee camps were appalling, with cholera claiming the lives of tens of thousands. Intent on reaching the perpetrators of the genocide, the Tutsi government in Rwanda plotted the overthrow of Zaire's president, the despotic Mobutu Sese Seko. During the Cold War, Mubutu had enjoyed the unqualified support of the US, France, and Belgium, but in the 1990s his political value to the West had evaporated. Casting their lot with the insurgent leader Laurent Kabila, the Rwandan government felt betrayed after Mubutu was ousted in 1997 and Kabila failed to close the refugee camps, despite the fact that exiled Hutu rebels were now launching attacks from these bases. Seeking to replace their erstwhile ally Kabila with a more pliable neighbor, Rwanda joined forces with Uganda in a military offensive against Congo. The conflict immediately escalated into a major regional war involving eight states and plunging Congo into deeper political and economic chaos. And in the midst of the carnage the issue of the Hutu refugees was almost forgotten, their fate of small concern to the wider international community.

Europe's recent refugees

The modern nation-state was conceived as an entity that would transcend ethnic and religious differences, and to a large degree this Enlightenment ideal had triumphed in the developed West, allowing the formation of states where allegiance to a set of political principles facilitated the union of peoples who embraced different faith perspectives and cultural traditions. However, some attempts at multiethnic and religious nation-building after World War I proved in the end to be untenable, and in one case, the failure of state formation to erase centuries-old antagonism led in the 1990s to Europe's largest refugee problem since the end of World War II. The Kingdom of the Serbs, Croats, and Slovenes emerged out of the deliberations of the Versailles Peace Conference in 1919. Renamed Yugoslavia in 1929 in order to better reflect the fact that this Balkan state also included Montenegrins, Albanians, Macedonians, and Bosnians, the country's numerous ethnic minorities continued to quarrel amongst themselves, with the Orthodox Christian Serbs claiming a leadership role over the Roman Catholic Croats and Slovenes and the Muslim inhabitants of Bosnia-Herzegovina. As we saw in Chapter 3, the country was held together after World War II under the forceful leadership of Josip Broz Tito, who, while a communist, managed to remain outside of the Soviet Bloc. Tito encouraged internal labor migration, and this resulted in a significant level of residential mixing among the country's various ethnic groups. The formula succeeded as long as Tito was alive, but after his death in 1980 the old rivalries resurfaced. The 1991 collapse of the Soviet Union heartened all those in Yugoslavia who wished to dissolve the federation into its respective ethnic parts.

Between 1991, when the ethnic fighting began, and 1995, when the Dayton Accords were signed, more than 2.5 million people in the former Yugoslavia had been reduced to refugee status. The Dayton Accords guaranteed the right of all refugees to return to their homes, but less than one-fifth felt confident enough to do so. Two years later the brutal policy of ethnic cleansing resumed in Serbia's southern province of Kosovo, where more than one million ethnic Albanians fled from their homes there into neighboring Albania. Three-quarters of these refugees managed to return to their burned-out homes after the war, but a NATO peacekeeping force had to be inserted to protect both sides in the ethnic struggle. Only with the defeat of Miloşevič in the Serbian elections of 2000, and his subsequent arrest and trial at the International Criminal Tribunal in the Hague, did the specter of further displacement and death recede.

PROVISIONAL GUESTS

The most significant international migration flows since the 1950s took place across the frontiers of adjacent states in the developing world. But there was also considerable movement from the less developed and more heavily populated regions of the globe to the industrialized, demographically stagnant, and prosperous First World. Fleeing poverty, war, environmental degradation, and political, ethnic, and religious persecution, millions have sought improvement for themselves and their loved ones in the relatively peaceful and unmistakably affluent North. And as the bounty of the democratic North was beamed electronically into rural towns and villages around the world through television and (more recently) the Internet, the preferred destination points of potential migrants were easily identified.

The results were unprecedented, most immediately for Western Europe. For over 400 years Europeans had been the world's principal migrants, expropriating and settling land in the underdeveloped Americas and Australasia and shaping the political, economic, social, cultural, and religious life of these continents. Native populations had been decimated by infectious diseases early on in the process, and expansive and dynamic transplant civilizations were created. Now after 1945, with lower rates of fertility and a high demand for unskilled labor to rebuild war-torn economies, Western Europe became a net immigration zone, inviting former colonial subjects and peoples from less developed regions of Southeastern Europe to join in the task of restoring the continent's economic greatness. The invitations continued to be issued, with varying levels of misgiving and suspicion, until the early 1970s, when a general economic downturn transformed once valuable human assets into unwelcome neighbors.

Guest workers and remittances

The history of production for a mass market is also the social history of human migration. Whenever the concentration of capital in the form of productive enterprise occurs, the concentration of manpower follows. The transatlantic slave trade enabled cash-crop producers in the Americas to maintain a viable labor force after the decimation of the native population through disease. With the abolition of slavery in the West by the mid-nineteenth century (Brazil being the exception), a system of indentured servitude emerged to fill key jobs in agriculture and manufacture. Often the indentures were drawn from one colonial holding and assigned to work in another; Indians, for example, labored in British-controlled South Africa, Uganda, and the Caribbean. Other indentures left oppressive conditions in a country under semicolonial status and found work in a cash-crop appendage of empire; this was the case for thousands of Chinese who accepted indentures in the Dutch East Indies. With the start of industrialization in nineteenth-century Europe, internal migration from rural areas to crowded urban centers became a normal feature of domestic life. Thanks to a rising birthrate during these decades, there was little need to recruit additional industrial workers from overseas. Even the departure of between 50 and 60 million Europeans for new lives in North America during the decades of intense industrial expansion did not hamper recruitment for industrial workers.

The manpower shortage that affected the entire European continent after World War II prompted a new phase in labor migration, one designed to allow for maximum flexibility and organized around the concept of temporary guest workers. As we saw in Chapter 1, Western Europe's initial reconstruction financing was met by American Marshall Plan dollars, but additional labor was needed to restore the continent's industrial base. Levels of unemployment were low in Europe during the 1950s and 1960s, and demand for workers provided unique opportunities for Turks, Greeks, Italians, Moroccans, Tunisians, and Algerians to assist with rebuilding in West Germany, France, Belgium, the Netherlands, Britain, and Luxembourg. Necessary but in general unwelcome in Europe's rich northern states, these temporary workers were expected to return to their respective countries once their services were no longer required, and as a result civil rights and employment options in the host countries were severely limited. Few Europeans anticipated that large numbers of migrant workers would end up as permanent residents, and fewer still could have anticipated the impact of family reunification plans that were introduced during the 1960s. Two groups were pivotal in changing the relationship between the guest worker and the host country: Beginning in the 1960s, business groups and civil right activists together supported the adoption of more liberal residency rules. Employers in particular were eager to retain low-wage workers in a highly competitive environment. The result was a changed continent: By the mid-1970s, when the guest-worker programs were ended across Western Europe, genuinely multicultural societies were being formed.

Labour recruitment in West Germany

Prior to the erection of the Berlin Wall in 1961, most of West Germany's labor needs were met by migrants fleeing from the communist-controlled East. Immediately after World War II, some eight million people of German ethnic origin were forced out of Eastern Europe and settled as refugees in the American-, French-, and British-occupied zones of defeated Germany. A subsequent flow of East Germans enabled the "economic miracle" of the Federal Republic to begin, but after construction of the Wall in 1961, West German authorities turned to southern Europe and Turkey for assistance. A Federal Labor Office was established and recruitment stations were opened in a number of Mediterranean countries.

Prospective guest workers were tested for occupational skills, and underwent medical examinations and criminal background checks. Only then were they referred to employers who had registered with the Federal Office. The initial guest workers typically arrived in groups and lived in hostels near their designated worksite. They were not allowed to apply for citizenship, and the type of employment that was available to them was carefully restricted. By 1973 many of the Federal Republic's 2.6 million foreign workers were Turkish, and generous reunification policies led to further immigration of family members even after the original recruitment programs were dismantled. By 1982 one-third of the foreign population of the German Federal Republic (4.7 million) was Turkish, and almost two-thirds of these were dependants of men who had initially been admitted to the country as guest workers.

For political leaders in most sending countries, the European guest-worker system of the 1950s and 1960s was viewed solely as a means of addressing widespread domestic unemployment. It was also anticipated that many guest workers would receive specialized job training while living overseas and return with marketable skills that would contribute to domestic economic development. For their part, many guest workers hoped to save enough money over the course of their sojourn to enable them to purchase land or to establish a small business at home. One unanticipated benefit of the programs for sending countries involved the scale of remittances, or money sent home to families by the guest worker. In the case of the Turkish Republic, for example, remittances from overseas workers represented the largest component of export earnings during the late 1960s.

The need for migrant labor in Germany was sharply reduced after the fall of the Berlin Wall in 1989. The destruction of the Wall and the reunification of the country was expected to lead to rapid economic integration and prosperity. The initial high expectations were not met, however, and within a year many East German businesses collapsed. The full employment guarantees of the old communist regime in the East were replaced by the harsh forces of the marketplace in the West. As a result many Germans and other Eastern Europeans relocated. There were approximately five million foreigners resident in West Germany in 1989, and although not citizens, they competed with Germans for access to housing, social services, and jobs. In good economic times, tensions between citizens and resident foreigners was muted. Beginning in 1989 and continuing over the next four years, however, an additional two million migrants arrived in the West. Some were asylum seekers, but most were economic migrants. Frustration at the lack of employment opportunities in the new Germany led to a rash of anti-immigrant violence in the early 1990s, often led by groups of neo-Nazi youth.

Britain and France

Prior to World War II, Britain's government approached immigration issues on an ad hoc basis. Irish laborers enjoyed the right to come and go without restrictions, and the handful of additional immigrants who arrived from other nations and colonies faced few impediments. But severe labor shortages experienced during and after the war led to the establishment of a more centralized protocol under the Labour government. A "volunteer worker" program was established for Europeans seeking employment in the UK, and the scheme attracted approximately 90,000 workers between 1945 and 1951. From the early 1950s, additional migrants from Ireland and newcomers from the disintegrating empire made their presence felt in Britain's domestic labor market. Across the Channel in Belgium, around 60,000 workers from Southern Italy arrived in 1946, finding employment in coal mines and in steel and iron production. They were later joined by newcomers from Spain, Morocco, and Turkey. And in the Netherlands, 300,000 former colonists from the East Indies returned after Indonesia secured its independence.

Before 1962, colonists and citizens of the Commonwealth States were free to emigrate to the UK and were accorded the opportunity to apply for British citizenship. Over 3.2 million had relocated to the former center of empire by the early 1960s, with most settling in the country's industrial cities where they assumed jobs in manufacturing or established small service-oriented businesses. Large ethnic enclaves of nonwhites emerged in urban areas, and racial tensions intensified. In response, a restrictive Commonwealth Immigrants Act was passed by Parliament in 1962, and six years later additional controls were placed on nonwhite British passport-holders from

Asia. While family reunification provisions remained in force for another decade, the trend against immigration from Commonwealth nations intensified, until by 1981, under the British Nationalities Act, new migration was limited to those possessing needed professional skills. British employers, not aspirant employees, had to apply for the work permits, and their duration was set by state authorities. Illegal immigration became a serious problem in the late 1990s, although it did not prompt the level of antiforeign sentiment that developed across the Channel in France.

The French government first sought to centralize the process of labor recruitment, travel, and registration by establishing a National Office of Immigration in 1945. Prospective employers were obliged to channel all requests for guest workers through the National Office and to pay a fee for the service. Two million Europeans entered France as guest workers between 1945 and 1974, and they were subsequently joined by almost 700,000 dependants. In addition to guest workers who had entered the country legally, a large number of undocumented workers arrived from across the Pyrenees in Spain and Portugal. Some of these workers were both economic and political migrants, fleeing the dictatorships that ruled both countries until the mid-1970s. Undocumented workers were the most flexible, and the most vulnerable, in the Western European labor pool. Like Britain, migrants from France's former colonies were able to enter without hindrance until the 1960s, and by the onset of the recession of 1973 there were almost 850,000 Moroccans, Algerians, and Tunisians living in the country. By the end of the decade France was home to a total of 4.5 million legal migrants and their dependants.

The colonial legacy was especially significant in shaping migration patterns between France and Algeria. As a French colony until 1962, Algerians relocated freely to mainland France while Algerian Muslims were made French citizens. Even after independence, labor migration continued, and by 1970 the Algerian community in France numbered close to one million. During the early 1970s, tensions between the majority population and North African migrants grew, and the French government ended all further recruitment of foreign labor. Still, remittances from Algerians living in France constituted an important source of income for some regions in the former colony, and levels of illegal migration to France remained high. The presence of North Africans from Algeria, Morocco, and Tunisia during periods of elevated unemployment contributed to the emergence of nativist political sentiment in France. High levels of unemployment among migrant groups, together with growing resentment among the lowest-paid members of the French working class, led to the growth of a strong nativist political movement during the 1980s. The anti-foreigner program of Jean Marie Le Pen won considerable backing by the 1990s. His anti-immigrant National Front Party won 15 percent of the vote in the 1995 presidential elections. Seven years later, during a fourth challenge for the nation's highest office, Le Pen qualified for the second round of presidential elections, and while he lost decisively to incumbent Jacques Chirac, he won almost 17 percent of the vote in the initial round.

Even after Western Europe's recruitment of guest workers ended in the mid-1970s, liberal policies respecting family reunification translated into higher immigrant populations over the next decade. In Belgium, for example, the foreign population grew from 453,000 in 1961 to 851,000 in 1977, a figure that represented just under 9 percent of the country's total population. The children of migrant parents were not accorded citizenship, but the naturalization process was not onerous. The impact of guest workers on the workforce of tiny Switzerland was even greater. There were only 90,000 foreigners working in the country in 1950, and many of these crossed the border on a daily basis from adjacent countries or were employed as seasonal help. By 1973 the Swiss government had liberalized its policies in the face of stiff competition for workers, and the 900,000 foreigners living in the country represented one-third of the labor force and one-half of all factory workers. When the recession of 1973 hit, many guest workers in Switzerland had already been accorded the right to remain in the country and to be reunited with their families.

Guest workers in the oil kingdoms

As European guest-worker schemes came to an end in the wake of the "oil shocks" of the 1970s and the resulting downturn in most Western economies, migration patterns became more diverse. The pace of industrialization in Asia quickened, while in the oil-producing kingdoms of the Arabian peninsula, massive development projects were undertaken. Both areas of the globe became new destination points for contract laborers, but if welfare provision and settlement rights were restricted in the case of Europe's guest workers, then conditions for temporary labor in the new receiving zones were nothing short of exploitative and abusive. It is easy to criticize the Western democracies for their postwar labor recruitment policies, but whatever the limitations of the original vision regarding the status of guest workers and their families, the policies did evolve over two decades, resulting in the transformation of the same democracies into truly multicultural societies, countries where religious freedoms and cultural distinctions were permitted.

Nothing so generous occurred in the oil-producing states of the Middle East, even when migrants shared the faith tradition of their hosts. While the Western receiving countries generally softened their residency policies under pressure from employers and civil rights activists in the 1960s, no such movement emerged in the sparsely populated Gulf states. In fact the issue of civil rights, so loudly contested on behalf of guest workers in Europe during the 1960s, was barely audible in the autocratic oil kingdoms. Most of this region was still under indirect Western control at the end of World War II, and prior to the 1970s little economic development was undertaken. Levels of education remained low, and women were largely excluded from the workplace. But the economic landscape of the region changed dramatically after the 1973 Arab–Israeli war and the OPEC-inspired spike in world oil prices. The wealthiest of the oil kingdoms – Saudi Arabia, Kuwait, Bahrain, Qutar, Oman, and the United Arab Emirates – possessed neither the manpower nor the skill levels needed to transform windfall profits into meaningful improvements in infrastructure. As a result, they were obliged to turn to skilled and unskilled guest workers from overseas in order to complete a bewildering range of internal development projects. In the case of Saudi Arabia, workers initially came from neighboring Arab states, but by the 1980s migrants from South and East Asia began to play a significant role as Saudi authorities grew distrustful of foreign Arabs. Anxious that their own small population might be overwhelmed by non-Saudis, wary of Palestinian migrants who were eager to bring the oil kingdoms into the struggle for a Palestinian homeland, and worried that the rhetoric of Pan-Arabism might end in the redirection of oil revenues outside of Saudi Arabia, the monarchy turned to a safer, less politicized workforce, one that would also work for lower wages.

As a result, semiskilled and unskilled men and women from Pakistan, India, Bangladesh, Sri Lanka, the Philippines, Thailand, and South Korea were admitted in large numbers, with women playing a significant role in the nursing and domestic-servant sectors. On the eve of the first Gulf War in 1991, there were over three million Asian workers in the Gulf, and two-thirds of these were based in Saudi Arabia. By the mid-1980s, approximately 30 percent of the Saudi population was foreign-born, and nonnationals constituted 60 percent of the labour force. The government remained the largest employer in the Kingdom during the final quarter-century, providing salaries for over 40 percent of the workforce, or some four million people. Not surprisingly, more than half of all jobs were located in the construction, oil, and service sectors. The upward trend in foreign recruitment ended during the economic downturn of the mid-1980s, and almost half a million Muslims were forcefully repatriated immediately after the first Gulf War. Once the sovereignty of Kuwait was restored, however, the policy of heavy labor recruitment was reinstated.

The commodification of guest workers reached unprecedented levels of efficiency in the Arab oil kingdoms during the 1970s and 1980s. No one was allowed entry without a specific and preapproved work contract, and most permits expired after one or two years. Housing and health-care arrangements for the worker were outlined in the initial agreement, and personal conduct was strictly regulated. Dependants were prohibited from entry, and the kingdoms refused to accept any requests for asylum or citizenship. Absent any migrant advocacy groups in the host countries, worker misconduct resulted in swift deportation. High wages, normally ten times what might be earned at home, were the sole incentive for those willing to live under such tightly regulated conditions thousands of miles from home. For those family members who remained behind in poor countries, the remittances often made the difference between destitution and a tolerable existence. Despite the higher incomes, however, significant wage differences between native and guest workers were commonplace, and there was no legal recourse for the guest worker who felt aggrieved by salary discrimination. Unlike any other receiving area in the world, the Arab oil kingdoms were able to maximize the economic potential of guest workers while denying them any basic social, economic, or political rights.

East Asian migrants

Labor-driven migration in Asia has existed since the colonial period. Chinese and Japanese workers were recruited to the western US, Canada, and Australia during the second half of the nineteenth century, but restrictions were imposed during the 1880s and the total number of transplants was modest. Indentured Chinese workers also played a significant role in European colonies in Southeast Asia. But the pace of Asian migration did not reach truly significant levels until the 1970s, when as the result of war in Southeast Asia the refugee problem expanded. Then, as a handful of countries in the region industrialized at a rapid pace, the need for unskilled labor increased dramatically. Still, in terms of total population in the Asian Pacific region, international migrants in the 1990s were few, perhaps six million working both in the region and around the world. Women represented a significant portion of this number, approximately 1.5 million. Asian women typically found themselves working in the service fields, either as domestic servants or in the hotel industry, as well as in the unskilled textile and electronic-assembly sectors.

Not surprisingly, the "Tiger economies" of Singapore, Hong Kong, South Korea, Malaysia, and Thailand became the preferred destination points of most Asian guest workers during the heady 1990s. Most of the transplants worked in the booming construction, transport, and service industries, often assuming the lowest-paid jobs. In the early 1990s almost one-fifth (around 300,000) of Singapore's labor force was foreign born. The Malaysian government claimed in 1997 that there were as many as two million "illegals" living in the country, most from neighboring states. The Philippines became the predominant sending country in the Asian Pacific region during the 1990s. Four million Filipinos worked overseas, with about half of these living permanently in the US and the other half working as temporaries around the globe. By the middle of the decade official remittances financed more than half of the country's external trade deficit. Since the Asian financial crisis of 1997, host governments in the region have attempted to put an end to labor recruitment and in some cases have worked to repatriate foreign workers.

GLOBALIZATION AND IDENTITY

As we observed in Chapter 4, the accelerated pace of globalization after the dissolution of the Soviet Union allowed more businesses in the developed world to relocate units of production to low-wage countries. Fostering economic conditions that would slow the rate of migration from these countries to the industrialized North was one anticipated result of the new global economy. Workers in China, Vietnam, Brazil, and Mexico, it was argued, could anticipate a quality of life that mirrored the affluent North if only world productive output could be more equally distributed across international borders. Free-trade agreements and other multilateral partnerships would, in the long run, eliminate the "pull" factors that had contributed so much to the movement of unskilled workers across international borders. Similarly, balanced economic development would enable highly skilled professionals to find meaningful employment in their home country after years of advanced training, often at state expense. The flight of educated talent to the developed North, the so-called "brain drain" that for decades undercut the ability of new states to modernize, would come to an end as domestic opportunities expanded.

The Chinese case

As a percentage of total population, the number of Chinese migrants to other countries was small during the nineteenth and twentieth centuries, but their impact on receiving countries was, and continues to be, enormous. Fourteen million Chinese lived as expatriates at mid-century, and approximately 40 million were living abroad in the year 2000. Most of the migrants became urban dwellers in a variety of states in Southeast Asia. Chinese nationals emerged as successful middleman minorities in Indonesia, where they constituted 5 percent of the population, and in Thailand, where they represented 10 percent of the total. By the early 1990s, ethnic Chinese living outside of China led family-owned firms that together produced as much wealth as China itself. Immigration to the US was aided in 1943 by the repeal of the racist Chinese Exclusion Act of 1882, which had interdicted new migrants and denied those already in the country the opportunity to apply for citizenship. Anti-Chinese sentiment abated during World War II, as the US allied itself with the Nationalist forces of Chiang Kai-shek, and Chinese residents regained the right of naturalization. The communist government of Mao Zedong forbade its citizens the right to emigrate, but after the death of Mao in 1976 some restrictions on travel were lifted. This relaxation especially benefited students, and in 1992, in response to the Tiananmen massacre of 1989, almost 50,000 of them took advantage of an offer of permanent resident status in the US.

As we have seen, Deng Xiaoping made no apology for the crackdown at Tiananmen, but he also recognized that full-scale modernization in China required both capital and technology, and that securing these assets would oblige the country to abandon its autarkic command economy and open itself to the capitalist West. The Chinese leadership was impressed by what export-led growth had done for South Korea and Taiwan, and during the 1980s and 1990s Beijing aggressively courted foreign investors, new trade and manufacturing partnerships, and technology transfer. Foreign firms were invited to China, awarded special tax concessions in specific coastal cities, and encouraged to produce goods for export utilizing a low-wage workforce. Japan became China's biggest trade partner during the 1980s, but in the 1990s American textile and clothing manufacturers established themselves in the country, and by the start of the new century China had become American's principal source of these products. "Made in China" labels were omnipresent in the malls and outlet stores of the industrialized democracies of the North, affording consumers lower prices while facilitating a major rural–urban migration in China as peasants from the countryside sought to improve their lives in the factory setting. In the 1990s the US became the world's largest foreign direct investor in China. The Clinton administration (1992–2000) not only relaxed Cold War restrictions on technology transfer to China, but also admitted thousands of Chinese students to leading universities around the country. By the year 2000 there were over 80,000 Chinese students in the US. Most would return home at the end of their training, hopeful about the future and not infrequently finding employment in foreign-owned firms located in their native land.

Millions of Western tourists and business people traveled to China during the 1980s and 1990s, further solidifying the country's integration into the global economy. Indeed, by 2000 tourists and business travelers worldwide accounted for a larger number of border crossings than labor migrants and refugees combined. Highly skilled foreign workers represented a wide variety of transnational corporations whose production facilities were located, and relocated, in low-wage markets around the world. China's entry into the WTO in 2001 meant that 1.3 billion people were poised to become part of a wider network of economic opportunity, and China's communist leaders were anticipating that future development would obviate the need for emigration. They also hoped that domestic improvements would put an end to a wave of illegal smuggling of immigrants to the US that in the early 1990s was estimated to have involved around 100,000 persons per year. The nefarious trade produced estimated annual profits in the range of $3 billion.

By the start of the twenty-first century, part of the project had been achieved, but with mixed results. The need to bring low-wage labor into the developed states for certain types of service work was on the brink of elimination. By the end of the century, telephone call centers designed to assist clients in the New York, London, or Berlin were just as easily located in Manila as in Minneapolis. Customer service representatives located in South Asia were trained in "American" English before going live to answer questions and take orders from consumers located half a world away. In the South Indian state of Kerala, trained software consultants provided valuable technical support to clients in Europe and North America. By 2001, the US had lost a quarter of a million call-center jobs to firms located overseas. Often these firms were American-owned and keen to take advantage of skilled college graduates who flocked to service jobs at wages that were a fraction of levels in the US. But the paradigm had its limits, especially in light of burgeoning populations in the nations of the South and the seemingly insatiable demand of employers in some sectors of the developed economies for "flexible labor."

Mobile Latin Americans

From the start of Spanish and Portuguese colonization in the early sixteenth century until the beginning of World War II, Central and South America had been immigration zones, accommodating hundreds of thousands of Europeans and their descendants. In the so-called "Southern Cone" consisting of Argentina, Chile, Paraguay, and Uraguay, the majority population was of European stock. Argentina was the destination point of almost half a million Italians after World War II, but in general the era of European settlement ended in the 1930s. To the northwest, in the Andean region, the majority population was *mestizo* or mixed European–Indian descent. And in Central America the Indian and *mestizo* populations constituted the majority.

Intraregional migration flows within South America have been overshadowed by the continent's relationship with the US, but seasonal migrant labor across international boundaries was commonplace throughout the course of the nineteenth and early twentieth centuries. After 1945 these movements were increasingly dictated by employment opportunities in urban centers and in new industries. In Venezuela, for example, the development of the oil industry in the 1970s attracted almost half a million documented workers from other Latin American states, in addition to large numbers of illegal workers from Colombia. Argentina also absorbed approximately 600,000 migrants from neighboring Uruguay, Paraguay, and Bolivia during the 1970s and 1980s, despite the fact that the country was becoming more authoritarian. Even with this significant European settlement and later cross-border migration within the continent, however, postwar Latin America and the Caribbean basin became a net exporter of human resources, and the majority of these women and men relocated to the US. Dramatic population increases, slumping economies in the 1980s, and the resultant high levels of unemployment contributed to the movement, but the rise of military government in the Southern cone and protracted civil wars in El Salvador, Guatemala, and Nicaragua also played a significant role.

Identity in the US

The US was the quintessential immigrant nation. With the exception of laws which excluded felons, persons with mental illness or severe physical handicaps, unaccompanied children, and anarchists, the borders of the country were open to newcomers. And employment was normally available to all who sought it. Fifteen percent of the population was foreign born in 1910, and by that date most of the new arrivals were non-English speakers from Southern and Eastern Europe. A literacy requirement was imposed in 1917 that adversely impacted these sending regions, and in that same year an outright ban on all Asian immigration was adopted. By the 1920s, political calls for additional limits on transnational movement intensified. Two ethnically based Quota Acts were passed in 1921 and 1924 which further disadvantaged countries outside of Northwest Europe. The 1924 quota was based on 3 percent of the nationals already living in the US at the time of the 1890 census, a date guaranteed to favor immigrants from northern Europe. The 1924 legislation, which limited the total number of new immigrants from Europe to 150,000, also stressed the importance of racial homogeneity and cast doubt on the success of the "melting pot" argument. Over the next two decades immigration levels to the US were very low, with fewer than 50,000 persons entering the country per year during the Depression and World War II.

Although national origins quotas were retained after 1945, US admissions policies began to reflect emerging Cold War ideological divisions. The 1952 Immigration and Nationality Act provided for the exclusion of Communist Party members and "fellow travelers" while simultaneously allocating small immigration quotas to Asian countries that might be drawn into the Cold War conflict. The category of "alien" now assumed an ideological as opposed to an ethnic emphasis. By the early 1960s it was becoming obvious to many lawmakers that the quota system of the 1920s was at odds with the foreign-policy priorities of both major political parties. Presidents Truman, Eisenhower, and Kennedy called for changes more in line with the realities of the day, and in 1965 the Congress finally responded. The Immigration and Nationality Act of that year reflected both the priorities of the emerging civil rights movement and America's changing relationship with the noncommunist world. Family reunification and the recruitment of skilled professionals now took priority in admissions decisions. In the 30 years after 1965, more than 20 million migrants arrived, making the US the largest receiving country in the world at a time when entry requirements were becoming more rigorous in most developed countries.

Thus even with the adoption of entry restrictions after World War I, the US remained a nation of immigrants whose multicultural profile served as a source of strength and creativity. But the sending profile changed decisively after World War II, thanks in large measure to the family reunification terms of the 1965 legislation. Whereas over two-thirds of all legal immigrants to the US were from Europe in the 1950s, by the 1990s this number had dropped to 17 percent. In 2000 the population of 288 million included 26 million who were foreign born, half of whom were from Latin America and another 30 percent from Asia. Overall, residents of Hispanic origin represented 11 percent of the population and were poised to overtake African-Americans as the nation's largest minority group.

A common border

The upswing in Latin American migration to the US actually began during World War II and focused on what for decades had been a flexible and vulnerable source of Mexican labor. Shortages in the US agricultural sector led to an agreement between the US and Mexico in 1942 to allow Mexican laborers to work on US farms. Although initially designed to meet a wartime emergency, this "bracero program" continued for another two decades and involved approximately five million Mexicans. It also spurred much illegal migration from a country whose population burgeoned from 20 million in 1940 to nearly 70 million in the early 1980s. Hundreds of thousands of undocumented workers were rounded up and expelled during "Operation Wetback" in 1954, but the cross-border flows continued. When the bracero program was finally suspended, illegal border crossings intensified. American farmers in the Southwest and California continued to ignore the law, while immigration officials typically looked the other way, especially during harvest season. At the start of the 1980s, American border patrol officers were apprehending close to one million undocumented Mexicans per year, and by 1986 the number of arrests reached 1.8 million.

Those Mexican workers who managed to elude the Immigration and Naturalization Service continued to find ample employment opportunities in the agricultural, service, and industrial sectors of the US economy, and business interests lobbied hard to prevent any diminution of this of cheap and malleable labor source. Their efforts enjoyed mixed success. The 1986 Immigration Reform and Control Act imposed legal sanctions on employers who knowingly hired or recruited illegal aliens, but the legislation also authorized resident status and eventual eligibility for citizenship to undocumented workers who had been in the country since before January 1, 1982. More than three million Mexican immigrants applied under the legalization program, with most applicants concentrated in just five states. Supporters of the legislation hailed its passage as a decisive step in the drive to regain control of the US–Mexican border, but after an initial decline in the number of arrests along the border, rates began to climb again in the early 1990s. Few employers were prosecuted and fined under the law, and it was not until the US economy suffered reverses in the early 1990s that calls for more rigorous enforcement were heard. In California, one of the principal receiving states, the economic downturn triggered a wave of hostility directed against undocumented Mexicans. In 1994, California voters passed Proposition 187, called the "Save our State" initiative, denying undocumented residents access to public schools and non-emergency medical services. The constitutionality of the referendum was challenged in the courts, but the message was clear: undocumented workers were welcome only as long as their services supported a robust economy.

From the perspective of migrants and family members who remained behind, curbs on migration had a significant economic impact, not unlike the situation of Turkish guest workers in Germany. Remittances from the 15 million Latin Americans living in the US totaled $20 billion in 2000, with almost half of this amount accounted for by Mexicans. For the Mexican economy, this represented an amount equal to tourism revenues and about two-thirds of that earned from the sale of oil. Similarly, remittances from the million Colombians living in the US equaled 50 percent of export earnings from coffee. By the start of the twenty-first century, migration flows to the US from Latin America, and especially from Mexico, resumed their surge. In 2005 there were some 10 million undocumented Mexican workers in the US, and many of these were living not in traditional destination states like California and New York, but increasingly in rural states like Kansas and North Carolina. Making significant economic contributions to the construction, agri-cultural, and services industries, and parenting children who are accorded instant US citizenship, these migrants live outside the circle of civic life, remaining, in a sense, peoples without a state.

GLOBAL EQUITY AND MIGRATION

The scale and variety of migration at the turn of the new century was without precedent in human history. Since the birth of modern nationalism during the period of the American and French Revolu-tions, when subjects were transformed into citizens, allegiance and a sense of belonging have been associated with the nation-state. It was assumed that armies no longer fought to promote the inter-ests of monarchs, but instead on behalf of a set of abstract ideals associated with the purportedly universal "rights of man" together with larger national interests. "Belonging" to the nation-state required that each citizen, irrespective of cultural, geographic, or religious identity, commit to the defense of these shared values.

Every modern nation-state claims authority over territory, bor-ders, and people. Indeed, belief in the indivisible sovereignty of states has been at the core of political consciousness in the West since the Enlightenment, and the principle was eagerly embraced by newly independent states in Africa, South Asia, and East Asia during the postcolonial era. But the growth of supranational entities like the EU, together with the rapid pace of economic globalization and efforts toward international economic cooperation, have prompted debate over the moral legitimacy of the exclusionary state system. With one-quarter of the world's population living in poverty, and with the gap between rich and poor states growing wider under conditions of economic globalization, the call for more open borders on grounds of moral principle gathered force during the 1990s. The democratic states of the North will continue to admit newcomers from overseas. But of the three broad quota categories – refugee, family reunification, and economic migrants – most receiving states will focus their attention on the recruitment of highly skilled professionals, those women and men who are most likely to have an immediate positive impact on the host nation's economic, scientific, and intellectual well-being.

It is highly unlikely that any developed state will ever again permit the mass immigration of unskilled and semiskilled labor that was characteristic of the early stages of industrialization. Indeed stopping, or at least regulating such unwanted migration has become one of the most important functions of modern states, deemed essential to national security, the maintenance of social peace, and the preservation of jobs for citizens who lack special training. But this political imperative is more often than not at odds with the needs of employers who are keen to hire foreign workers for low-wage menial jobs that are often eschewed by native workers. This became an acute tension in the agricultural and hospitality sectors of the US economy in the late twentieth century, contributing to an unprecedented rise in the Hispanic population.

Opponents of international migration argued that opening borders was no solution to grinding global poverty, and that instead it was the responsibility of sovereign states to redouble their efforts to assist developing countries achieve a sound economic future for each citizen. International immigration will never significantly address the problems associated with the North–South divide. No matter how targeted admissions policies become, the poverty, hunger, environmental degradation, and political instability facing the majority of the world's population at the start of the new century will not be ameliorated by flight across international borders. Global economic injustice was unlikely to be remedied by moving desperately poor people to rich countries. Increasingly, it appeared to observers that only a fundamental redistribution of global resources could address the problem of poverty in a serious and sustained manner.

Prospects

One of the major questions facing sovereign nations at the start of the twenty-first century involves the extent to which nongovernmental entities – be they legal corporations, criminal cartels, religious communities, or transnational terrorist organizations – pose a threat to the integrity of traditional territorial states. Can the military resources of modern states, unparalleled in scale during the postwar decades, continue to protect a citizenry from nonstate opponents, from the priorities of multinational economic interests, or from the powerful impress of a set of dominant cultural values? Will identity politics, ethnic division, and religious intolerance invalidate the idea and practice of state formation predicated on shared political principles? And can states, should states, interdict the movement of peoples across international frontiers, especially common borders? Do the almost 200 member states of the UN have a broader commitment to uphold agreed human rights conventions even when such commitments entail the admission of the unwanted? Of the approximately 150 million people living outside of the country of their birth in 2000, about 15 million could be defined as refugees who feared persecution if they were to return home. In terms of the total, the refugee numbers look modest, but with respect to the human costs incurred by the displacement, the level is distressing and the prospects for improvement inauspicious. "Identity" – driven conflicts, where racial, ethnic, and religious communities strove to equate a particular tradition with the right to full citizenship, showed few signs of receding in the new century. And as countries around the world tightened requirements for those seeking entry on economic grounds, asylum-based requests predicated on human rights codes that transcended citizenship rights intensified.

A number of indicators suggest that transnational migration will continue to increase even as border controls are tightened and resentment of "the other" grows. World population is projected to increase from 6 to 10 billion during the first half of the twenty-first century; world poverty is not being addressed effectively; low-intensity military conflicts continue to trouble many developing states; religious intolerance remains a worrisome constant; the exploitation and abuse of women persists in too many cultures; and environmental degradation has yet to fully engage the attention of the leading industrial powers, each of whom continues to equate "progress" with development and the manipulation of nature for human purposes. Voluntary and involuntary migrants, and especially the poor and unskilled, face a world where there are no open spaces, uninhabited and unclaimed lands, destination points where the only admission requirement is a commitment to hard work and a wish to begin anew. On a planet where sovereign nation-states have made claims on every habitable place, and where the defense and security requirements of the homeland lend themselves to the rhetoric of exclusion, the fate of transnational migrant is very much in doubt.

Part III
Body and spirit

6

SCIENCE, TECHNOLOGY, AND THE ENVIRONMENT

KEY TOPICS

Population and healing
Energy and power
Goods, services, and culture

Debate over the
environment
Uncertain future

The postwar years were marked by a wide range of advances in science (defined as efforts to understand the natural world) and technology (the application of science to achieve specific objectives), the sum of which transformed the natural environment and humanity's place in it. In some fields, particularly health sciences, communications, aviation, and computers, developments that occurred during World War II or earlier were brought into widespread practical use. During the war years, national economies were heavily regulated by government, and basic scientific research assumed a level of strategic importance equal to military operations in the field. Governments recruited and employed unprecedented numbers of highly trained specialists in engineering, physics, biology, chemistry, metallurgy, and electronics, providing these researchers with state-of-the-art facilities as part of the overall war effort. Risk taking and innovation in pure and applied science were both encouraged and generously funded by states engaged in a struggle for national survival.

The practical results were impressive by any standard. The ability to establish the position of aircraft from the ground through reflected radio waves, or radar, for example, had first been explored in the early 1930s. Britain's vulnerability to aerial bombardment hastened the government's willingness to accelerate the research, and a limited-range defensive radar system was initially employed in September 1939, just as the continent descended into darkness. Radar was expanded after the war, and it remained the principal means of guiding the growing number of commercial aircraft and ships for the remainder of the century. German scientists and engineers worked to perfect missile and jet-engine technology, and while their efforts came too late to affect the outcome of the war, both technologies were available to advanced nations by the early 1950s. The collaboration of American, British, and German refugee scientists on the secretive Manhattan Project set the organizational stage for postwar government research into the peaceful uses of nuclear power. The very research laboratory outside Chicago where Enrico Fermi achieved a controlled chain reaction with an experimental reactor became the center of a postwar effort to build a reactor that could produce electrical power. In terms of medicine, plant research by scientists at Oxford University led to the discovery of the plant mold penicillin just before the US was attacked by Japan in late 1941. The potential of penicillin for treating battlefield wounds and the onset of septicaemia and/or pneumonia led the US to embark upon a crash program for development during the conflict, and when the drug was made available to the general public after 1945 it became a symbol of a new private–public collaboration.

These advances and many others, research on which was accelerated by the wartime emergency, had unparalleled effects upon the lives of people in the more developed countries of the world after 1945, with the average citizen living a longer and more comfortable life than did the most wealthy individuals of the past. Breakthroughs in medical science extended the average lifespan and tackled age-old diseases; communication technologies provided continuous and varied information and entertainment; and agricultural improvements (especially chemical fertilizers and economies of scale) augmented food supplies across international borders. The relationship between science and its political and cultural *milieu* became more intimate, with funding agencies expecting tangible strategic and economic return on investment. Science was increasingly identified with technology and engineering, and the reputation of the scientist as *savant*, willing and eager to reflect on the broader philosophical implications of basic research, declined.

In its place emerged the model of the scientist as employee within a larger corporate or governmental system, working to strengthen the nation's defenses and the corporation's stock value. In the less developed nations, Western scientific advances had an uneven and less dramatic effect – although the immense increase in the destructive power of weaponry, particularly portable high-tech weaponry, made itself felt in every corner of the planet irrespective of national income. Some scientists in the West protested the postwar militarization of science, establishing organizations such as the Federation of Atomic Scientists and the Union of Concerned Scientists. But during the Cold War their voices were largely eclipsed by advocates who pointed both to the need for credible deterrence, and to the many important civilian by-products of military research.

The postwar acceleration of scientific research and technology, not surprisingly, had its foundation in the otherwise debilitating Cold War. The great struggle between the Soviet Union and the US for economic and military superiority in the wake of World War II involved a crucial technological dimension. In the postwar era, it was clear to everyone that new technologies could, as the atomic bomb had in 1945, change the landscape of international relations overnight. The constant fear haunting the leaders of both the US and the Soviet Union was that the other superpower would discover some new technology, either of great economic or military force, which would enable them to sweep their opponent aside and assume paramount influence over world affairs. Consequently, through the means available to them, both superpowers, and to a lesser extent the other more developed nations, sought to avoid being left behind in the race for technological advancement.

In the Soviet Union, scientific research was conducted almost exclusively at state-run institutions. While such work was often brilliant, and occasionally resulted in real technological advances which the West was hard-pressed to answer, the Soviet scientific community was often hamstrung by a bloated bureaucracy and constant political interference. An unedifying example of such interference was the "Lysenko affair" of the late 1940s, in which a plant breeder of humble origins named Trofim Lysenko posited that learned tendencies could be passed to offspring through the genes. Such a contention would normally have been tested through experimental methods, and shown to be false; but the idea appealed to Stalin, and hence became the official position of the Soviet Union until it was quietly abandoned years later. Many Soviet geneticists who took issue with Lysenko were sent to the gulags, victims of the totalizing state. The Soviet scientific system was also limited by state secrecy laws; when a terrible nuclear accident occurred at a reactor near Chelyabinsk in 1957, preliminary research on the effect of nuclear discharges was undertaken. But Soviet authorities never acknowledged the disaster during the Cold War, and the research findings remained a closely guarded secret. It was only later revealed that in the aftermath of the accident over 270,000 civilians in more than 200 villages had been exposed to deadly radiation.

In the US and Europe, the encouragement of scientific research took the form of public fiscal support for universities and institutes, coupled with the awarding of long-term government contracts to private firms. Thus the development of a substantial scientific infrastructure, an interlocking system of publicly supported universities, colleges, and research institutes, provided both educated workers and research data to a vast array of businesses hoping to profit from their activities. The market-based economic system of the Western powers meant that numerous corporations and research groups were constantly seeking ways to exploit any new scientific finding or technological advance, and the competition between them for government contracts became intense. The widespread acceptance of what scientists call the "hypothetico-deductive method," in which hypotheses are developed, tested, and refined, all within an atmosphere of peer-reviewed communication of results, contributed to the rapid spread of new techniques worldwide. And with the advent of the Internet in the 1990s, information exchange leapfrogged national and ideological boundaries with remarkable ease.

Advances in science and technology, particularly in the West, had substantial economic benefits too, especially for highly trained professionals in targeted industries. They also, however, exacerbated the disparity of wealth between the richest and the poorest citizens of the world. While new agricultural technologies, for example, meant that hunger was no longer a problem in the West, thousands of people still starved to death at the turn of the twenty-first century. Material prosperity had not "trickled down" to the poorest nations, with millions of people across the planet still subsisting on much the same diet, and living in much the same manner, as they might have 500 years earlier. The only difference between life in 1500 and 2000 for the poorest of the poor was that the images of affluence for the fortunate few were now widely available, thanks to global electronic communications.

Thus the unprecedented prosperity and technological marvels of the postwar era raised some previously unasked, and unanticipated, questions. Through technology, and the scientific management of economic systems, at least some in the West thought that it might be possible to arrange society so that everyone would have adequate food, health care, shelter, and clothing. For critics of Western affluence who argued that ending hunger and want captured the essence of what it meant to act morally, more developed countries had an obligation to give of their plenty to the people of the poorer countries until everyone enjoyed the basic necessities. But a strong counter-argument was made by champions of market economics after the collapse of the Soviet Union revealed the true extent of the failures of centralized planning. By the close of the century, a wide-ranging debate around the issue of human flourishing could not be engaged without references to science and technology. Sometimes the solutions provided by science and technology had unforeseen consequences, both environmental and societal. Sometimes technologies were so successful that they placed enormous strain on natural resources and on social systems. And sometimes technological fixes to the problems facing humanity were simply inadequate to the challenge, especially when those challenges involved the preservation of humankind's fragile habitat.

POPULATION AND HEALING

Perhaps the most eventful material achievement of the twentieth century has been the extension of the human lifespan, to the point where for the first time in history the most common age at death ceased to be infancy and shifted decisively to old age. Indeed by the year 2000 the global average age at death was 67, and in developed states of the North it was 75. As we have seen, there were over six billion people on the planet at the start of the twenty-first century, more than double the population at the end of World War II. Most of this unprecedented expansion took place outside of the nations of the North, where only 15 percent of the total lived in 2000. In China, the world's most populous country, a State Family Planning Commission worked to implement a one-child-per-family policy, but enforcement varied by province. Rural families took particular exception to the policy owing to their need for labor. The most dramatic growth occurred in Africa, South Asia, and Latin America, precisely those areas of the world where state structures were often weakest and where economies were least able to accommodate the additional population. And this growth outside the North occurred despite the fact that many of the newest medical therapies remained largely unavailable to the world's poorest inhabitants.

Prolonging human life

No single factor accounts for the remarkable postwar shift in longevity, but better nutrition, sanitation, access to clean water, health care, wealth, education, and lifestyle choices all played conspicuous roles, albeit in different combinations depending upon location and cultural tradition. The most basic changes sometimes had the greatest impact. Increasing access to sources of clean water, for example, was arguably the most important health advance in the postwar world. Clean drinking water is especially important for young children, whose small bodies are less capable of withstanding the impact of severe diarrhea. Beginning in the early twentieth century, most cities in the richer nations had built water-filtration plants and adopted chlorination processes that killed harmful water-borne microorganisms. Sewage-treatment plants also contributed to the overall improvement in water supplies. These technologies were spread unevenly in the developing world after World War II, but once in place the quality of drinking water improved dramatically. At the start of the twenty-first century millions of people in poor countries still died from diseases connected with impure water, but greater provision of this precious resource had become a priority of governments worldwide.

Increased agricultural output and improved diet also saved lives. Researchers reached a consensus that malnutrition had a decisive impact on people's immune systems, making the chronically malnourished particularly susceptible to diseases like cholera, pneumonia, and tuberculosis. Efforts to increase staple crop production, and to transport food to people facing severe drought, all met with greater success after 1945. Key to the increases were fuel-intensive mechanization, the expansion of irrigation beyond the immediate confines of river systems, crop breeding, and the introduction of chemical fertilizers and pesticides. Instead of increasing acreage under the plow, farmers now concentrated on bolstering total harvest per acre. The so-called "Green Revolution" of the 1960s, where rich countries introduced high-yielding, disease-resistant strains of staple crops like wheat, rice, and corn to poor countries, had a dramatic impact in densely populated states like India. And it took far fewer farmers to produce crops for a burgeoning global population. At the close of the century less than 10 percent of the population in Europe, North America, Japan, Australia, and New Zealand worked in the agricultural sector, and most of these farmers produced a single crop for a larger national and international market. By the 1980s just one American farmer fed approximately 80 people, and due to the consolidation of farmland by agribusinesses, only 2–3 percent of Americans could fairly describe themselves as family farmers.

China's demographic profile is illustrative of the impact of new approaches to agriculture outside of the developed West. After Mao's government put an end to decades of civil unrest, confiscated and redistributed arable land, and established large collective farms, significant improvements in agricultural output were realized. By the 1990s, new high-yield strains of rice and maize accounted from almost 95 percent of total output. The enlarged food supply and improved sanitation increased life expectancy and reduced infant mortality. The population surged from 700 million in the mid-1960s to just over one billion in the national census of 1982. It would have been even higher if the horrific famines associated with the Great Leap Forward in 1960–2 had not led to the premature deaths of between 15 and 30 million Chinese. The census also revealed that China's population was extremely youthful, with over

200 million Chinese women in the childbearing years. Some economists argued that the material abundance that would result from the communist-planned economy would comfortably accommodate the larger numbers; but less optimistic forecasters warned that without a family-planning policy, China's hope for vibrant and sustained economic development would be thwarted.

Assault on disease

Another remarkable milestone in the quest to extend life was reached by the year 2000, as infectious communicable diseases ceased to be the leading cause of death in the developed world. The advent of antibiotics, or "killer bacterias," beginning with penicillin in 1941, enabled doctors to shift their attention away from lethal infections and toward chronic noncommunicable organ diseases – illnesses associated with the cardiovascular system or various cancers normally linked with advanced age. The World Health Organization (WHO) played an invaluable role in this work, overseeing vaccination campaigns around the globe that drastically reduced the incidence of childhood killers like measles, tetanus, tuberculosis, whooping cough, and diphtheria. In 1977, the WHO proudly declared victory in the battle to eradicate smallpox, the fearsome scourge of millions for centuries, and hopes were raised that additional ancient enemies would be vanquished by modern science. Even in cases where germs had already compromised the body, scientists developed aggressive drug therapies that were lethal to specific infections but harmless to body tissue. Supplementary vitamins addressed problems associated with dietary deficiencies, and helped to ward off a number of diseases like scurvy (with vitamin C). Toward the close of the century, research into the genetic mechanisms of disease held great promise, especially in terms of offering preventative strategies for patients with genetic predisposition to certain diseases.

But there were also troubling setbacks. In the late nineteenth century researchers had identified the causal parasites responsible for another great killer, malaria, and in 1955 the WHO committed itself to the ambitious goal of malaria eradication. Armed with residual insecticides like DDT, a 1948 Nobel Prize-winning poison, the WHO set to work to eliminate all malaria-bearing mosquitos by intensive spraying of DDT in affected areas. Unfortunately, the campaign did not account for the fact that malaria parasitizes other creatures, nor did it consider the impact of human migration by individuals already infected. By the end of the century the disease had been effectively eradicated in the developed North, but remained a threat to millions in Africa, Latin America, and South Asia. In the mid-1980s the WHO estimated that ten million preventable infant and child deaths still occurred annually.

Undeterred, in 1979 a still optimistic WHO launched an ambitious crusade titled "Health for All by the year 2000." The focus of the effort was on the creation of primary health-care facilities where the poor could be treated before the onset of serious illness and the need for high-cost specialized treatment. Unfortunately, the culture of primary care practice, with its emphasis on preventative, frontline medical treatment, ran counter to the research-oriented, high-tech orientation of the major medical centers of Western Europe and the US. Specialized training in the North became the goal of many medical students around the world, to the neglect of the less glamorous but altogether essential work of local primary care. Thus in spite of the remarkable postwar antibiotics revolution, infectious diseases remained the most common cause of death in the developing world as late as the mid-1990s. Of the roughly 52 million persons who died in 1995, for example, more than 17 percent were victims of bacterial, viral, or parasitic infections. When the new millennium began, half a billion cases of malaria were reported, and two to three million people, mostly youngsters, continued to die from this preventable and treatable disease. The same could be said for tuberculosis, which still claimed the lives of an estimated three million persons per year. Indeed, even infant measles and neonatal tetanus were responsible for more deaths per year than the high-profile HIV/AIDS virus, but little was made of these disturbing statistics in the media. Clearly nothing near an equitable distribution of medical therapies had been achieved by the WHO and its supporters.

These shocking disparities were not unrelated to global economic development and the aid policies of developed states in the North. During the 1980s and 1990s, both the World Bank and the IMF played a crucial, if indirect, role in compromising the level of wellness and health-care provision in the developing world. As we saw in Chapter 4, the heavy borrowing undertaken by poor states during the 1960s and 1970s placed them in a untenable position during the recession of the 1980s. These postwar development dollars were most often used to enhance production of primary crops that were exported to the North, to the neglect of foodstuffs needed by the growing domestic populations. When the recession struck the North, demand for products such as coffee and cocoa declined, and developing states found it difficult to meet their loan repayments to private institutions. The IMF and World Bank provided assistance, but only on condition that debtor countries commit to "Structural Adjustment Programs" that involved cutbacks in public services like education and health care. By 1989, some $178 billion was moving from developing states to the developed North for debt servicing, while only $61 billion was going in the opposite direction in the form of loans and assistance. And the world's wealthiest country, the US, was spending less than one-tenth of one percent of GNP on assistance to poor countries. The results were both predictable and distressing. By the year 2002, one-fifth of humanity, or 1.2 billion people, still lived in desperate poverty, while 2.5 billion lacked access to proper sanitation and thus remained highly vulnerable to infectious disease. Even in the world's wealthiest countries, the gap between rich and poor in terms of access to medical care remained large. In the US, for example, although almost 15 percent of GNP was devoted to health care in 2001, close to 40 percent of the population remained uninsured, a status that effectively denied them access to the most advanced – and expensive – treatments and technologies available.

Technology, medicine, and the quality of life

Not surprisingly, the greatest of the high-tech diagnostic and therapeutic advances occurred in the world's wealthiest countries. Many of the breakthroughs were crucial to the extension of life, but the ability to prolong life was often unrelated to the quality of life. More people in the North lived longer lives after World War II, but morbidity rates also increased as the aged required additional care during their seventies and eighties. Children who were responsible for elderly parents turned increasingly to institutionalized solutions, fostering the growth of nursing homes and retirement communities where levels of care and compassion varied widely. But even as the demographic projections in the West grew more alarming, with the proportion of retired people expanding just as the number of wage earners who funded pensions and health schemes declined, medical research continued to move forward aggressively on a variety of fronts, offering innovative solutions to human suffering. And some of the most dramatic, headline-grabbing achievements took place in the operating theater.

Surgery in the pre-anaesthetic, pre-antiseptic age was the "treatment" of last resort. While as old as humanity, surgical technique before the hospital revolution of the mid-nineteenth century was the monopoly of the barber surgeon, a manual skill, not a liberal art, undertaken by individuals whose steady income derived from cutting and shaving hair. Prior to the introduction of anaesthesia in the 1840s, the emphasis in surgery was on speed and precision, using sharp knives, amputating saws, and cauterizing irons. Most surgeries were limited to simple, if extremely painful, procedures such as lancing boils, bloodletting, and drawing teeth. Still, mortality rates were extremely high, with the patient most often succumbing to trauma or complications associated with post-operative infection. The growth of teaching hospitals during the nineteenth century, with their sterile operating theaters, combined with the regular employment of anaesthesia and antiseptics at the close of the century, redefined the role of the surgeon, elevating those who undertook invasive procedures to the very pinnacle of the medical profession. Operations on the major body cavities were now undertaken with increasing regularity, and with ever more encouraging results. The surgeon's art was further refined during the two world wars, when emergency medical units were established near the front lines to treat the life-threatening wounds suffered by combatants. After 1945, surgical interventions to remove pathological matter and to restore and/or replace damaged organs became commonplace. The operating theater, according to historian Roy Porter, became "the high altar of the hospital," while the surgeon emerged as the "high priest of medicine," especially in popular culture. By the 1970s surgeons were specializing in urological, neurological, thoracic, orthopaedic, and pediatric problems.

Beginning in the mid-1980s, laparoscopic surgical techniques were introduced in major research and teaching hospitals. Fiberoptic light and minute cameras allowed the surgeon to manipulate delicate instruments through tiny incisions while watching a video monitor. The new technique still required manual dexterity and precision on the surgeon's part, but by avoiding a large incision, post-operative discomfort was lessened and the recovery period abbreviated in most cases. Presurgical anaesthesia, while available at the end of the nineteenth century, became the province of a highly trained specialist in the postwar decades. Traditional inhalation techniques were complemented by intravenous and spinal methods; the former was of great value when the surgery involved the head or neck, while the latter allowed the patient to retain consciousness. In developed countries, local anaesthesia became commonplace even for minor operations and for routine dental treatments. A host of additional applications, all discovered before World War II but only made widely available in developed states since the 1950s, contributed mightily to the diagnosis and treatment of disease. X-ray technology was refined in the 1970s with the advent of the CAT (computerized axial tomographic) scanner, providing doctors who specialized in brain disorders with a three-dimensional image of the skull. Whole-body scans followed with the introduction of MRI (magnetic resonance imaging), a noninvasive process that avoided the radiation side effects associated with X-rays.

There were dozens of additional breakthroughs. Heart disease, for example, had for centuries been a major killer. By the early 1990s, surgeons were undertaking about 200,000 heart-bypass operations annually; they were also implanting the same number of pacemakers, small devices that could adjust arrhythmic heartbeat by electrical impulses. The introduction of the electrocardiograph enabled cardiologists to monitor the heart's four main cavities for irregularities, and use of the device became standard for anaesthesiologists during surgery. The cardiac catheter, fist used on a patient in 1940, allowed specialists to insert a narrow tube into a vein and on to the heart. By injecting a radio-opaque substance into the catheter and then taking an X-ray (angiocardiogram), physicians were able to pinpoint areas of blockage. And beginning in 1964, doctors began removing small blockages in the coronary arteries through a balloon technique called angioplasty, thus avoiding the greater risks associated with heart surgery. Organ transplants became another tool in the treatment of major illness. Lung, liver, and bone-marrow transplants all enjoyed modest rates of success, although a lack of suitable donors, high incidences of organ rejection, and the very high cost of the surgical procedure limited the impact of transplant surgery in reducing mortality for most sufferers.

The business of medicine

Before World War II, the medical profession in developed countries of the North was centered around the individual doctor–patient relationship. Hospitals were few, most physicians were self-employed and earned their livelihood from fees, and their emphasis was placed squarely on primary and palliative care. The same could be said for pharmacology; the proprietor of the small owner-operated apothecary shop or drugstore normally worked closely with local physicians in providing medicines to patients. After 1945, the culture of medicine changed dramatically, thanks in no small part to the example of government intervention in many sectors of the economy during the war. In the US, the success of large government-funded research undertakings like the Manhattan Project convinced many politicians that public funding for the battle against disease could yield equally impressive results in a very short span of time. The National Institutes of Health (NIH) was established in 1948 with a state-of-the-art facility in Bethesda, Maryland, and a federal budget of $26 million. The agency funded research efforts at university medical schools and private laboratories in the expectation that new diagnostic instruments and treatment regimes would improve the lives of all citizens. The expectations of the supporters of NIH were more than met during the following 50 years. Effective treatments for a range of diseases, including kidney failure and forms of childhood leukemia, together with high-technology advances like the intensive-care unit, prosthetics, and manufactured implants, all enhanced the ability of physicians to heal. By 1997 the National Institutes of Health enjoyed an annual operating budget of $12.4 billion and leading medical centers in the US were attracting research professionals from around the world.

Emerging from the long struggle against fascism with pledges to enhance the lives of all citizens, nationalized health-care systems were adopted by most developed states (the US was the one notable exception). Politicians and medical practitioners increasingly stressed the importance of prevention, health education, infant care, and the need for government intervention to encourage appropriate lifestyle choices. Britain's Labour government undertook what was perhaps the most comprehensive reform of medicine immediately after the war when it created the National Health Service (NHS). Led by Minister of Health Aneurin Bevan, the NHS established universal medical benefits and free hospital treatment for all, and despite the reservations of local authorities who lost control of municipal hospitals, and physicians who resented their new status as state employees, the overwhelming majority of the British public applauded the new system. By the 1970s the benefits provided by NHS had become part of the fabric of the welfare state, and while better health care for the poor did not lower overall health costs, few politicians were prepared to question the emerging inefficiencies in what was an increasingly bureaucratic system.

The US followed a different path. Although most politicians rejected British-style national health, during the 1960s private health insurance was offered to most workers in the US through employer-paid plans; by 1970 a majority of Americans enjoyed some form of employer-based coverage. And in 1965, the federal government created the publicly funded Medicare and Medicaid programs, enabling the aged and the poor to gain regular access to physician and hospital services. As more Americans began to take advantage of the new services and treatments, however, spending on health care as a percentage of GNP rose sharply. The costs associated with health care in the early 1950s were quite low, averaging 4.4 percent of GNP in 1950. As this figure climbed to 7.4 percent in 1970 and then to 13.6 percent in 1995, corresponding rises in insurance premiums associated with medical interventions led some employers to reduce the level of benefits available to their employees. Skyrocketing costs— especially for hospital services and prescription drugs – also called into question the long-term viability of the Medicare system for the elderly. While many applauded the fact that the increased access made possible by insurance and government programs represented an undoubted social good, the best way to pay for the latest diagnostic and therapeutic advances became a contentious political issue.

The unanticipated costs associated with medical breakthroughs, and the growing set of ethical dilemmas involving access to new treatments and procedures, is illustrated by the treatment of kidney disease. In the early 1960s an American physician pioneered a dialysis treatment that enabled patients with long-term kidney failure to live in reasonable comfort. But the treatment was very expensive, and no insurer would offer coverage. Only persons who could afford the approximately $30,000 per year were even considered for acceptance into the first treatment facilities. This rationing of high-tech health-care services soon caught the attention of members of the US Congress, and in 1972 a new provision was added to the Social Security Act that afforded every patient access to kidney dialysis. By the mid-1990s almost of a quarter of a million Americans were receiving the lifesaving treatment, at a total cost to taxpayers of some $8 billion per year. A similar story could be told for cancer treatments. During the last quarter of the century, $20 billion was spent on cancer research in the US alone, but it continued to be a major killer, especially among older adults.

Treatment of the most recent global epidemic, AIDS (Acquired Immune Deficiency Syndrome), provides another disturbing case in point, placing the cost factor into global perspective. Since it was first identified in 1981, this highly contagious disease has been responsible for the deaths of some 16 million people. Spread by the virus called HIV (human immunodeficiency virus), more than 70 million people worldwide were infected by the year 2000. While in no sense comparable to mortality rates associated with diseases like malaria, which continues to take the lives of 1.5 million infants each year in developing countries, AIDS has had a devastating impact on certain populations, and no more so than on young people in sub-Saharan Africa, where about 8 percent of the population was infected by the year 2000. More than half of the people infected with HIV worldwide are below the age of 25. By the end of the century, the annual cost of the medication designed to stabilize the HIV/AIDS condition of a person in developed countries was approximately $50,000 per year, a sum that made such treatment impossible for most of those afflicted by the disease.

The culture of big business spread swiftly to the health-care arena during the 1950s. Increasing specialization, the advent of state-managed health-care systems, the burgeoning of large metropolitan hospitals with their highly skilled physicians and ability to purchase the latest technology, the growing propensity of patients to seek specialized hospital care, the advent of drugstore chains where pharmacists became hourly employees, and escalating insurance costs all contributed to a seismic depersonalization of the doctor–patient relationship. Medicine as corporate enterprise reached its apex in 1990s America, where some 4.5 million people were involved in health care, but where only one in seventeen of this total was a physician. Clinical researchers, lab technicians, accountants, and patient-service representatives made up the vast majority of the professional staff. Hospital conglomerates, pharmaceutical companies, insurance providers – including government agencies – all have stripped the physician of his or her once-valued autonomy. In the case of the for-profit pharmaceutical industry, the argument that cutting-edge research required enormous initial investment meant that some of the new wonder drugs were beyond the reach of many patients. By the 1990s the large US-, German-, British-, and Swiss-based companies were realizing great profits for drugs that were geared toward an affluent Northern market. These included treatments for common allergies, impotency, and hair loss – all totally irrelevant to the life needs of most humans.

Health-care issues moved to the center of political debate in the more favored nations during the 1980s and 1990s. In the US, First Lady Hillary Clinton caused a legislative furor in 1992 when her husband appointed her to head up a health-care reform initiative. Critics swiftly branded the Clinton proposals as socialized medicine, the very type of "nanny state" that had been put on the defensive in Britain by Prime Minister Margaret Thatcher during the previous decade. Thatcher repeatedly criticized the shortfalls of the NHS, and while she pledged to preserve the principle of national health (despite the closure of clinics and the long waiting lists for elective surgery), she simultaneously encouraged citizens to "opt out" and pursue private health-care options. The Prime Minister herself set the example by eschewing the NHS for private medicine.

Other countries faced more difficult challenges as their economies faltered. In Egypt, for example, Nasser's postcolonial government promised that every citizen would be afforded access to free government-sponsored clinics. And meaningful progress was made during the 1950s and 1960s, as rural and urban clinics were built with public money. But severe budget cuts during the 1980s reduced public spending on health care to a mere 1.7 percent of GNP. An even more alarming pattern emerged in Russia in the decade after the fall of the Soviet Union. Survival rates had increased markedly in the Soviet state between 1945 and 1965, increasing by one year for every calendar year. But with the breakup of the empire in 1991, the economic downturn and cuts in the health-care system of the new Russian federation led to an actual fall in life expectancy, down from a high of 64 years in 1965 to 59.2 years in 1995. Even where government support remained strong for preventive medical care, national campaigns for good health ran up against powerful corporate interests around the globe. In particular, the powerful tobacco industry skillfully employed both the print and electronic media in a successful effort to link cigarette smoking with a youthful and exciting lifestyle. Only in the 1990s did tobacco advertising come under strict regulation in the developed countries of the North, but by that time the biggest growth markets for tobacco were in the developing world, especially China. A 2002 study coauthored by the WHO and the Atlanta-based Centers for Disease Control and Prevention found that 14 percent of students around the world between the ages of 13 and 15 smoked cigarettes. The highest rates were found in developing countries, and many of these young people revealed that they had been first introduced to smoking by free samples made available by tobacco companies.

From eugenics to genetics

The scientific study of biological inheritance was a major preoccupation of researchers in the late nineteenth century, and when a cousin of Charles Darwin coined the word "eugenics" (from the Greek root meaning "good in birth") in 1883, hopes were high in Europe and America that better breeding practices might improve the human stock. Eugenics was particularly popular among middle-class professionals who saw it as a solution to urban degradation, crime, poverty, and disease. Convinced that humans were determined in large measure by their inherited "germ plasm," eugenicists discounted the role of environment in shaping basic character and advocated on behalf of public policies that would reduce the fertility rates of those groups deemed to be biologically inferior. One of these policies involved forced sterilization, adopted in over 20 states in the US after World War I and upheld by the Supreme Court in 1927. Speaking for the Court's majority, Justice Oliver Wendell Holmes opined that three generations of imbeciles were enough. The most comprehensive and pernicious sterilization campaign, of course, took place in Nazi Germany, where a 1933 law made sterilization compulsory for those deemed to be suffering from hereditary diseases like feeblemindedness and physical deformities. A quarter of a million Germans were "treated" during the first three years of the program, and Nazi racial theory increasingly informed decisions about appropriate target populations. By the start of the war in 1939, the eugenics program had expanded into a brutal euthanasia campaign against those deemed to be unfit. The horror of the wartime extermination camps soon followed.

In the postwar environment, those few who continued to embrace eugenics worked under the disturbing shadow of the Holocaust. But just as their theories were discredited, a new type of genetic research began to engage the public's attention. At Cambridge University, research into the role of deoxyribonucleic acid (DNA) in the makeup of chromosomes advanced the discussion of how genes control the development of organisms. The American James D. Watson and his British counterpart Francis Crick published their double-helix model of the structure of DNA in the journal *Nature* in 1953. Within a decade it was widely recognized that all genes consist of a code that is part of their chemical structure. The code instructs each cell respecting what proteins to assemble. Since some proteins were associated with known diseases, a comprehensive knowledge of the genetic code would be invaluable to the medical profession. In the 1990s, the US government allocated $3 billion to a multiyear study called the Human Genome Project whose goal was to identify the approximately 30,000 genes in human DNA and determine the sequences of the three billion chemical base pairs in the body.

Involving the research facilities of 18 countries, the massive project was completed in 2003, 50 years after Watson and Crick's pathbreaking work on the fundamental structure of DNA.

The potential human health applications of the Human Genome Project were enormous. Since all diseases have a genetic component, identifying and treating errors in genes became the principal challenge, and opportunity, for a new growth industry called biotechnology. At the start of the twenty-first century, biotechnology firms began developing sophisticated diagnostic tests for pinpointing disease-causing genes. The pharmaceutical industry entered a new, and controversial, arena of drug therapy where healthy genes are introduced to replace or supplement defective genes in the patient's body. Extending the technique, first developed in the 1970s, of recombinant DNA, which allowed for the removal of single genes from one organism and their insertion into another, scientists offered new hope to patients suffering from a range of serious illnesses.

But while disease intervention was the most exciting result of the DNA revolution, the wider social and ethical implications of the new science were intensely debated. Influential social and religious conservatives objected to what they saw as an effort to interfere with nature by manipulating the genetic profile of human beings, while others feared that the new knowledge would merely resurrect eugenics for the twenty-first century. Any technology that was capable of identifying diseased genes might tempt those in positions of political power to once again interfere in reproductive behavior. By the end of the twentieth century, issues of personal privacy also emerged around genetic research. While few objected to the fact that law-enforcement agencies were using a person's genetic signature to help determine the guilt or innocence of accused criminals, major debate arose over a patient's medical right to privacy. By the late 1990s, life and medical insurance companies began to demand access to medical records in order to determine the genetic risk factors of potential clients. Some employers followed suit, determined to avoid hiring those with characteristics deemed inappropriate. The sharing of genetic information compromised not only the individual whose records were being evaluated, but potentially their offspring as well.

ENERGY AND POWER

One of the principal motives for Japanese imperialism in the 1930s was the military government's desire to secure new, more reliable sources of energy for the country's dynamic industrial economy. Fear that such access would be denied contributed to the fateful decision to attack the US in December 1941, just after Washington imposed an embargo on the sale of oil and other strategic goods to the resource-poor island. The following year in the European theater, Hitler ordered his forces to capture the Soviet Union's distant Caspian oil fields, a gambit dictated in part by the dictator's drive to ensure future industrial growth in Germany. Since the end of World War II, nonhuman energy has become an indispensable foundation of the modern lifestyle, and powerful states have used their diplomatic and military muscle repeatedly to ensure adequate supplies. More humans used more energy in the final half of the twentieth century than at any time in history, and for millions living in the favored nations, life without abundant, low-cost energy is now simply inconceivable. Reliance upon electricity reached the stage where even a temporary disruption or blackout resulted in a government hearing or official investigation. Heating, cooling, lighting, transport, communications, manufacturing, food production and distribution – all depended on power that was generated largely by nonrenewable fossil fuels such as coal, oil, and natural gas. The Internet alone accounted for nearly 10 percent of total energy consumption by the end of the century, and this single technology was poised to grow exponentially every year. The developed world's appetite for energy-dependent products and conveniences appeared limitless at the turn of the century, even though their dangerous side effects were well understood by the scientific community.

The world profile of energy production and use has changed dramatically since the mid-1800s. Traditional biomass fuels, including wood, charcoal, and agricultural residues, made up the bulk of productive capacity for most of humanity across the centuries. Industrializing states like England and Germany turned to abundant coal reserves in the nineteenth century, and it became the dominant, and the dirtiest, energy source from the 1890s until the end of World War II. Indeed, while biomass fuel consumption grew only modestly from 700 million tons in the year 1700 to 1.8 billion tons in 1990, coal mining grew from 10 million tons in 1810 to one billion tons in 1910, a hundredfold increase. Oil emerged as the favored product during the late 1940s, and it has remained the most sought-after fuel, despite the fact that user states rely on steady imports from a politically volatile region of the world. Crude oil extraction jumped from less than 10 million tonnes in the 1880s to a remarkable three billion tonnes in the 1980s. And natural gas production increased one thousandfold during the same century.

Not surprisingly, global inequities were conspicuous in energy use as rich nations employed a range of tools to pursue and secure ever larger portions of the world's nonrenewable resources. By the end of the 1990s, developed industrial states used six times more commercial energy per capita than developing countries; consumption of energy in North America alone was ten times greater than levels in Asia and Africa. The 5 percent of the world's population living in the US was responsible for one-quarter of the globe's fossil fuel emissions by the year 2000, but few consumers seemed alarmed by the imbalance. For one-third of humanity, the modern energy revolution remained an irrelevancy at the end of the century. Lacking access to electricity and petroleum products, almost two billion of the earth's inhabitants continued to rely on traditional sources of energy, especially wood and animal products. But forecasts anticipated a dramatic change over the next quarter-century, as developing states like India, China, and the nations of South America and Africa seek to power their modernization programs with the same fuels that transformed the North during the nineteenth century.

Of special interest to many of the developing states was the potential of new sources of power to expand food production and meet the basic nutritional needs of growing populations. The carrying capacity of the earth expanded rapidly after 1945 thanks to new sources of energy. The spread of internal combustion engines and electrification, together with the employment of fertilizers like synthetic nitrogen, resulted in great leaps in productivity even as rural populations declined. Engines were used to expand irrigation, to extract water from aquifers, and to power a wide variety of tractors and harvesters. During the twentieth century the amount of land under cultivation worldwide increased by one-third, but the total crop harvest expanded almost sixfold. In the US, the 40 percent of the total workforce in agriculture was reduced to a mere 2 percent in the early 1990s. And while two-thirds of the workers in China, India, and Indonesia were still engaged in agricultural pursuits at the end of the century, this figure was poised to decline rapidly with the spread of mechanization.

The envied model for success

Since the end of the war, plans for economic growth in the developed North have been predicated on the unrestricted exploitation and use of nonrenewable resources. In the case of the US, the world's greatest superpower had achieved its dominant status during an era of cheap and abundant energy. Throughout the boom period of the 1950s and 1960s, the price of coal and oil, when adjusted for inflation, actually declined in the US, and the prospect for even lower costs through the development of nuclear power was bright. The US only began importing oil from the Middle East in the 1950s; prior to this decade levels of domestic production were sufficient to meet the vast bulk of demand. Domestic oil producers even managed to convince Congress to impose import quotas during a mild recession in 1958, thereby enabling the American companies to preserve existing profit levels.

Since the overall cost of energy dropped during the period 1945–73, it was easy for political leaders in the developed states to champion the virtues of conspicuous consumption. Many utilities encouraged customers to use as much electricity and natural gas as possible in return for generous rebates. Large, inefficient vehicles dominated automobile showrooms, while commercial buildings and private homes were constructed with scant regard for overall efficiency. As demand for newer and better appliances, tools, and automobiles intensified, the production and distribution of energy became a very big business, with the decisions of powerful international energy corporations affecting the economies of sovereign nation-states large and small. By 1992, 5 of the world's top 25 nonfinancial multinationals were oil companies, 5 were vehicle manufacturers, and 3 were electronics manufacturers.

Oil shocks?

The fivefold increase in oil prices that began in 1971 – and reached its peak in the 1973 OPEC oil embargo – temporarily arrested the West's remarkable postwar economic growth. And a second round of oil price hikes following the toppling of the Shah of Iran in 1979 led to inflation and worrisome levels of unemployment during the early 1980s. But even in the face of record price increases, the industrialized states of the North took few steps to reduce their dependence on imported oil. The US established a massive strategic reserve by storing oil in underground salt caverns along the coastline of the Gulf of Mexico, but when President Jimmy Carter admonished his fellow citizens to embrace conservation as the moral equivalent of war, few were prepared to respond in a meaningful way. And as oil prices began to moderate during the 1980s, the old patterns resurfaced. Indeed by the final decade of the century consumers in the West had returned with enthusiasm to the 1960s penchant for ever larger, inefficient vehicles. The "Sport Utility Vehicle" (SUV) craze in the US was a marketing triumph that convinced many Americans of the need for "off-road" capability in a nation that had spent billions to construct four-lane interstates and paved secondary roads. The British-built Land Rover, originally designed for extremely rugged terrain, became the fashion outside shopping malls and country clubs across the US. One of its strongest American-built competitors was a converted military vehicle called the Hummer, a petrol-guzzling colossus that set new benchmarks for motoring excess.

Still, heavy dependence on Middle East oil left consuming states vulnerable to OPEC price shocks and periodic supply disruptions. And in the case of the US, it also led to a heavy military commitment in the Persian Gulf region. The 1991 Gulf War was prompted by a desire to prevent one autocratic leader, Saddam Hussein of Iraq, from taking control of the lucrative Kuwaiti oil fields and possibly threatening the Saudi monarchy. America's growing postwar influence in the region was deeply resented by many Muslims, especially when it involved US support for repressive regimes. The Iranian Revolution of 1979 set the precedent for successful resistance, empowering prospective insurgents throughout the region. In the 1990s, terrorist organizations like al-Qaeda successfully recruited angry and desperate youths to a plan of action that involved attacks aimed at US interests around the world. Any chance that the US, the world's largest consumer of oil, would wean itself from its dependency faded with the election of George W. Bush in 2000. Both the president and his vice-president, Richard Cheney, had reaped millions from their connections to big oil companies. During his first term in office, the president called for intensified coal and oil exploration, and recommended that drilling begin in Alaska's Arctic National Wildlife Refuge. Even national security advisor and later Secretary of State Condoleeza Rice brought considerable oil connections to her respective posts, having served during the 1990s on the board of directors of the Chevron corporation.

China's appetite

The US was not alone in its growing oil addiction, for the close relationship between access to cheap sources of energy and political power on the world stage was not lost on developing states after 1945. Communist China's march to throw off the shackles of Western imperialism was initially centered on a Maoist program of economic self-sufficiency. And for the first 30 years of communist rule the mandate of the Great Helmsman was carried out with resolve. Sources of domestic energy seemed adequate to the task, for as late as the early 1990s the country was a net exporter of oil and possessed the world's third largest coal reserves. But the market-based reforms inaugurated by Deng Xiaoping in the early 1980s, and the increasing commercialization of the Chinese economy in the 1990s, resulted in much higher levels of fossil fuel consumption. Between 1980 and 2000 the annual use of commercial energy in China increased by almost 250 percent. Coal production passed these levels in the US in 1991, and by 1995, as more trucks and private automobiles appeared on the newly constructed roads, China became a net importer of oil. Two years later the state-owned oil company began making strategic investments in overseas oil projects. The China National Petroleum Company competed with Western firms for oil concessions in Venezuela, Iraq, Sudan, and

Kazakhstan. In 1998 President Jiang Zemin made a state visit to Saudi Arabia and called for a special oil partnership with the Kingdom. During the 1990s, domestic oil refining capacity doubled, and long-distance oil pipeline projects linking China with Russian Siberia and with Kazakhstan were planned.

In light of the fact that China is projected to emerge as one of the world's largest importers of oil by the year 2010, these recent political moves to become more involved in the affairs of producing states make sense, but they also signal the end of China's tradition of autarky. Like the US, China's energy future became tied to the success of foreign relations. Other former colonial states in the Asia-Pacific region also developed a greater reliance on imported fuels. By 2000 almost 27 percent of total oil world consumption was attributed to countries in the region, up from 17 percent 20 years earlier. Some forecasts point to a 50 percent increase in world energy demand by 2025, with most of the added requirement coming from just two countries: China and India. In China's case, even the government's massive investment in hydroelectricity, best represented by the Three Gorges project along the Yangtze River, offered but a partial solution to rising demand for cheap energy.

The promise and perils of nuclear energy

In December 1953, President Dwight Eisenhower addressed the UN on the subject of harnessing nuclear energy for peaceful purposes. In an effort to arrest the growth of nuclear arsenals and to lessen the prospect of an all-out nuclear exchange between the US and the USSR, Eisenhower affirmed that "peaceful power from atomic energy is no dream of the future. That capability, already proved, is here – now – today. Who can doubt, if the entire body of the world's scientists and engineers had adequate amounts of fissionable material with which to test and develop their ideas, that this capability would rapidly be transformed into universal, efficient, and economic usage?" The US government had already established the Atomic Energy Commission in 1946 in order to oversee the development of power reactors, and in 1954 Congress relaxed legislation in order to allow private companies to own and operate nuclear reactors. When the first nuclear power plant began operations in

Shippingport, Pennsylvania in 1957, representatives of the Atomic Energy Commission spoke optimistically of power "too cheap to meter." Others predicted a Cold War race to bring nuclear power technology to the developing world. For the next two decades, great hopes were placed in nuclear power as a viable no-toxic alternative to the "dirty" fossil fuels that released so much harmful carbon dioxide into the atmosphere. Public support for "clean" and efficient nuclear power was strong in the wake of Eisenhower's address; a Gallup Poll of 1956 in the US indicated that most respondents were confident in the safety of nuclear plants. Few probably realized that the government had limited industry liability for accidents and had provided hazard insurance at public expense. Even the respected Sierra Club endorsed nuclear power over dirty coal-fired plants. By the end of the twentieth century almost 17 percent of the world's electric power (343,000 megawatts) was generated by over 430 nuclear power plants.

There were disturbing setbacks in the nuclear industry, however, and by the 1990s the pace of development had slowed. Safety concerns, costs related to building and operating reactors, and the failure to develop a permanent method of disposing of nuclear waste all contributed to the slowdown in new construction. There were 109 reactors producing electrical power in the US in 2000, but not a single new facility had been built in over 20 years. When the number two reactor at Three Mile Island in Middletown, Pennsylvania nearly melted down in March 1979, public opinion turned sharply against the industry. No one was killed at the site, and there was very little release of radioactivity, but the accident signaled the demise of commercial nuclear power generation in the US. The second Bush administration resurrected the idea of nuclear power as a central component of its national energy policy, but in the wake of 9/11, fear of terrorist attacks against the country's nuclear facilities dampened the administration's initial enthusiasm.

Similarly in the Soviet Union, the 1986 meltdown of a nuclear reactor at Chernobyl in the Ukraine – that killed 31 workers and forced the evacuation of 130,000 people living within a 20-mile radius of the plant – alerted the international community to the dangers of nuclear power production. The WHO estimated that the Chernobyl reactor released 200 times more radiation than the two bombs dropped on Japan in 1945. The fact that the Gorbachev government hesitated to report the disaster, even as a cloud of radioactive dust was carried across Europe by prevailing winds, only strengthened calls for the abandonment of nuclear power. In France, the developed state most committed to the possibilities of nuclear energy, almost 75 percent of all energy produced in 2000 relied on reactors scattered across the country. But even here a moratorium was placed on further construction. The German government closed nuclear plants in the eastern part of the country after reunification, and plans were drawn up after 1998 to phase out the remaining plants in the western half of the country. Construction of new plants continued in South Korea, Japan, China, Taiwan, and India, but the pace of development was well below the heyday of construction in the West during the 1960s and 1970s.

GOODS, SERVICES, AND CULTURE
Electronic communications

The importance of satellite technology to the postwar communications revolution was scarcely anticipated when the Soviets launched Sputnik, the first artificial earth satellite, in October 1957. The successful launch, propelled into orbit by the first intercontinental ballistic missile, bolstered the morale of Soviet leaders and caught US policy makers off guard; within two years the Soviets scored another impressive victory in the propaganda war against the US when a Soviet satellite successfully orbited the moon. The "space race" was on, and when American President John Kennedy pledged in 1962 to land a man on the moon within a decade, the focus of public interest shifted away from the humble satellite. But research and launches continued, until by the end of the Cold War there were over 3000 military and commercial satellites in operation, beaming back information as diverse as atmospheric data, surveillance images, navigation coordinates, radio broadcasts, and, most pervasively, television pictures. As in so many areas of technology, superpower rivalry had spurred the development of multiple applications for satellites, but it was private and state-owned television that reaped the greatest financial and political benefits.

The first television broadcasts had aired just before the war, but development was arrested due to the global conflict, and it was not until the 1950s that the full potential of the new medium began to be exploited. At the start of the 1960s, televisions were operating in about half of all homes in the US and were becoming more commonplace in Europe. In North America an entire industry related to television broadcasting, involving electricians and technicians, producers, actors, manufacturers, and advertisers, claimed an increasing share of the service economy. Further technical refinements led to the introduction of color broadcasts and inexpensive portable units in the 1960s. The main focus of television in the West was entertainment, with viewers keen to be distracted from both the pressures of the workplace and the looming threat of superpower conflict. Variety shows, dramas, comedies, and sports competitions commanded the largest audiences, and thus attracted the biggest advertisers. Television celebrities were the subject of inordinate public attention, and by the 1970s the celebrity lineup included professional sports figures. Funding all of these productions was a nonstop barrage of commercial advertising whose unifying message was the propriety of consumption. Manufacturing needs, transforming what were once luxuries into essentials of a civilized lifestyle, shaped the parameters of popular culture.

Television news broadcasts began to overtake the print media as the principal source of information about local, national, and international issues for most citizens. By the mid-1960s television news organizations were dispatching crews overseas; their sometimes dramatic images of conflict, hope, and despair were beamed around the world instantaneously by satellite, shaping public opinion in ways never before anticipated by political leaders in open and democratic countries, and raising grave concerns for leaders of closed societies. Outside of the US most television production and broadcasts were subject to varying degrees of state control and public ownership. In authoritarian societies the medium became little more than a tool of indoctrination. Before the end of the Cold War, political leaders in the Soviet bloc countries maintained tight control over television, using it to inculcate loyalty to the state and bombarding viewers with stale propaganda. Satellites enabled these leaders to spread the message of working-class solidarity into remote regions of the country, fostering a prescriptive view of national identity. But as consumer access to small satellite dishes widened, international broadcasts and multiple perspectives threatened the state's monopoly on power. In the 1990s China's communist rulers and Iran's hard-line clerics sought to curb the spread of degenerate Western ideas by outlawing private ownership of satellite dishes. Neither effort met with much success.

The range (if not the quality) of programming available, and the origin of broadcasts, spread quickly in the late 1980s as satellite technology was embraced by additional developing countries. Underrepresented perspectives now began to find their electronic voice in a global marketplace. The Arab satellite news network Al Jazeera, for example, was begun in 1990 in an effort to offer a Muslim perspective on world affairs. On occasion the network unwittingly served as a propaganda arm of Islamic terrorist groups who forwarded controversial video material to the station for broadcast. And there were other, equally problematic uses. Closed-circuit television was marketed as a sophisticated security option beginning in the 1970s. By the close of the century, however, not only private properties, but public spaces of all types, from automobile traffic intersections, to sports complexes, to public schools, could be effectively watched by private contractors at modest cost. Fears over the loss of privacy heightened in democratic states as new technologies intruded themselves into the public square.

Personal computers

The first computers were designed during World War II in order to carry out complex mathematical calculations at rapid speed. After the war, several British and American companies undertook research into the potential commercial applications of the machines, and by the early 1950s the International Business Machine (IBM) corporation began its rapid march to market domination. The company enjoyed significant revenues from military contracts during the 1950s, and a focused research and development program allowed IBM to develop a reputation for innovation and market savvy. By the mid-1960s IBM computers were in operation around the world, and the bulk of the giant company's profits were generated through private-sector commercial contracts. There were approximately 70,000 IBM computers in the US by 1968, with virtually all of the machines owned by large businesses and the military. Only with the advent of microprocessor technology in the late 1960s was the stage set for the personal computer revolution. The first unit, the Apple II, appeared on the market in 1977, with IBM joining the retail sector in 1981. Joining forces with a small Seattle software firm called Microsoft, IBM sold its machines with Microsoft's MS-DOS operating system preinstalled.

Sales of personal computers surged during the 1980s, with IBM enjoying the lion's share of profits. Newer companies then secured modest market share by offering cheaper "IBM-compatible" units aimed at householders. The new desktop PC quickly replaced the typewriter as the compositional tool of choice since it allowed for easy formatting, revisions to text, and storage of multiple drafts. Small and medium-sized businesses took advantage of the enhanced computational and record-keeping power of the new technology. And just as the rage for personal computers reached its height, yet another stage in the unfolding information revolution started with designs to link personal computers in a wider electronic network. By the mid-1980s hundreds of hosts had been established on the fledgling Internet, and in the early 1990s, breakthroughs in fiber optics and microchip technologies made the Web available to millions of users. Electronic mail enabled individuals to communicate with colleagues down the hall, across continents, and around the world instantaneously. And the "Web" swiftly became the first-stop source for millions of users in search of products and information. By the early twenty-first century, "online" sales of goods and services registered a significant and growing percentage of overall commercial transactions in the developed world.

The benefits of the new "information society" were transparent and profound, most especially in the power of the Internet to make geography irrelevant and to further the integration of global markets. Financial institutions and investment firms examined the latest data online and moved millions of dollars across borders in a global market environment that operated around the clock. Instant access to information became the precondition for success in the dynamic financial markets. Students and scholars could access valuable research materials from their dormitory, laboratory, or office; teachers could introduce an enormous array of documents and illustrations in the classroom setting; and consumers could book airline flights; apply for a mortgage; join a hobby group; and purchase a astonishing range of creature comforts without ever leaving their home. Notions of community were quickly redefined in the 1990s as services available over the Web expanded; the online environment fostered "virtual" communities of people with similar interest across international borders, people who might never meet one another in person but whose familiarity was made possible by the new technology.

The Web also posed new challenges. For educators, easy access to information of widely varying quality left the uncritical student with a false sense that all online materials constituted legitimate sources. Library and book culture was severely tested by instant "authorities" and "research papers" that could be downloaded instead of composed. The popularity of email occasionally reduced opportunities for face-to-face contact at large institutions, while some users even detected a decline in prose style and civility in the new communications environment. Authoritarian governments viewed the Web with enormous apprehension, especially since personal websites of every description could be uploaded by individuals and groups who lacked the considerable financial resources needed to deliver their message of dissent on television. Taking issue with those in power, offering alternative views on every conceivable subject, and communicating with individuals of like mind on another continent all became possible in a remarkably short period of time. For governments dedicated to the principle that stability rests on efficient censorship, the Internet was an insidious threat to state power.

Air travel

The first daily passenger airline service began in 1919 with flights linking London and Paris. Although commercial airline service grew in the 1920s, the experience of flight was limited to the affluent and adventuresome. Even in the 1930s most people did not consider air travel as a viable or particularly safe option; when Franklin Roosevelt flew to the Democratic National Convention in

Detroit in 1932, it was considered an act of derring-do by many observers. In Nazi Germany, the young film maker Leni Reifenstahl shot footage of Hitler in his airplane cabin surveying the countryside below as the plane transported the dictator to the Nuremberg rallies. Transatlantic air travel began just before World War II, but it was not until the advent of the commercial jetliner in the 1950s that mass air transport began in earnest.

Research into the possibility of building a jet-propelled aircraft had begun just before the war, and this too was speeded up owing to military priorities. Nazi Germany, Britain, the Soviet Union, and the US all had programs devoted to jet propulsion during the war years. Within seven years after the defeat of Hitler, the first commercial jet aircraft, Britain's de Havilland Comet, was put into service. Not surprisingly, large commercial jet manufacture was initially dominated by two US firms, Boeing and McDonnell Douglas, but in the 1980s Europe's Airbus consortium began to win an increasing market share. Boeing's 747 jumbo jet, capable of carrying over 500 passengers on long-distance routes, debuted in 1970; by 2000 this one model had flown over three billion passengers, the equivalent of half of the world's population. The speed and range of the big jets enabled the travel industry to offer intercontinental holiday packages at prices within the reach of the middle class in the more favored countries. It also opened the possibility of new migration flows. Between 1950 and 1998 the total number of kilometers flown by commercial passengers grew from 28 billion to 2.6 trillion annually. A comparable rise in air freight meant that more goods were moving more rapidly across international borders than at any time in history.

National carriers proliferated along with the growth in civilian traffic. In countries recently liberated from colonial domination, establishing a national airline, even if the entire fleet was leased from a former colonial power, became a prized symbol of sovereignty and collective self-respect. In the 1980s a push toward deregulation and privatization in the US and Britain led to the formation of new low-cost carriers and greater competition. But just as traffic increased in the wake of deregulation, security issues began to loom ever larger. Hijackings and hostage taking became a tactic of choice for desperate and disturbed individuals, and headline-grabbing assaults on innocent civilians pointed up the vulnerability of powerful countries to terrorist attacks. In December 1988, a Pan American flight en route from London to New York exploded over Lockerbie, Scotland, killing all 356 passengers and crew. An additional 47 residents of Lockerbie village died as the wreckage of the massive Boeing 747 plunged to earth. No group claimed responsibility for the murders, but after two years of painstaking investigation, officials alleged that the perpetrators of the bombing were Libyan nationals. Breaches in airport security continued during the 1990s, and even after the terrorist attacks of 9/11 governments struggled to eliminate lapses.

DEBATE OVER THE ENVIRONMENT

Humans have always been catalysts in environmental change, but during the twentieth century, and especially after 1945, the intensity and comprehensiveness of their role as agents of modification in the biosphere, the space inhabited by living things, was unprecedented. While it is true that for millennia humans polluted the atmosphere by burning wood and scarred the landscape by generating waste, the overall impact of these activities was nominal. Populations were too small, and animate (human muscle and animal) power insufficient to make much headway against natural ecosystems. What was different about the relationship between humans and their environment over the twentieth century was its scale. In the view of historian J. R. McNeill, human-induced changes to the environment will in time emerge "as the most important aspect of twentieth-century history, more so than World War II, the communist enterprise, the rise of mass literacy, the spread of democracy, or the growing emancipation of women."

Human factors in environmental change are intimately related to economic activities, and dynamic economic growth since the 1950s, while considered normative in capitalism, has contributed to a series of fundamental ecological disturbances that put at risk the very climatic conditions essential to human life. World GDP, or the total value of goods and services brought to market, stood at approximately $2 trillion in 1900. This figure jumped to $5.37 trillion in 1950 and then soared to almost $30 trillion in the early 1990s. And while growth in economic activity was mirrored by a surge in global population, the bulk of the economic expansion took place in areas of the globe where population increases were modest. For these inhabitants of the industrialized North who became so accustomed to cheap and abundant fossil-fuel energy, and ready access to plentiful clean water, any disruption to these resources led to major political, foreign policy, and military crises.

Experts disagreed over the timeline for the exhaustion of fossil fuels, but few believed that the crucial role played by oil, coal, and natural gas in powering the economic transformation of the twentieth century would be repeated in the twenty-first. Despite this consensus, government-sponsored research into possible alternatives to fossil fuels was quite modest. Relatively little investment was made, for example, in the development of renewable sources of energy such as wind or solar. Instead, most policy makers in favoured countries, and particularly in the US, focused their efforts on the foreign policy and military fronts, making sure that access to overseas sources of fossil fuels was secure. But perhaps the greatest threat to environmental sustainability at the end of the century was in the realm of ideas. The exultant market culture of the 1990s was predicated firmly on the notion of endless development and growth, the promotion and internalization of new consumer wants, the use and easy disposal of goods, and the drive for more energy-dependent conveniences. The transformation in the popular mind of what for centuries were thought to be exotic luxuries into the essentials of "civilized" living represented both a triumph for the marketing firms and their corporate clients, and a burden for citizens, scientists, and public policy experts who recognized the many dangers inherent in the culture of growth.

The unforeseen costs of progress

Prior to the 1970s, most people in the world's favoured nations thought very little, if at all, about the impact of human activity on the environment. The popular tendency to equate economic development with human progress and personal happiness, together with the penchant in Western science to unlock the secrets of nature in the service of human physical betterment, contributed to an intellectual climate where concern for the carrying power of ecosystems was of little moment. In the communist countries, the exploitation of nature became a law of historical development that undergirded the class struggle and the inevitable triumph of the proletariat. And for committed nationalists the world over, industrialization and economic development were the only paths to respectability in the international community. The prospect that the aggressive manipulation of the biosphere for human ends might entail limits became the perspective of defeatists who lacked the imagination to envision appropriate technological solutions to potential exigencies in nature. Postwar economic theory, capitalist and communist alike, did not accept the argument, made famous – or infamous – by Thomas Malthus in the early nineteenth century, that nature was circumscribed.

In reality, the application of scientific technique to the goal of development and the enhancement of human life often traded short-term benefits for the few in exchange for long-term dilemmas for the many. The quest for enhanced food production is illustrative of the problem. Nitrogen, potassium, and superphosphate fertilizers were in use prior to World War II, but their widespread employment occurred only after 1945. From a global total of about four million tons in 1940, artificial fertilizer production rose to 40 million tons in 1965 and 150 million tons in 1990. More than any other single factor, these fertilizers made possible the great expansion in world population during the second half of the century. Unfortunately, upward of half of all dispensed fertilizers entered the water source of farming communities, leading to excessive levels of nutrient supply. In addition, the manufacture of artificial fertilizers was energy-intensive, and most required energy that was fossil fuel-based. As more intensive agriculture was adopted by developing countries, levels of soil erosion and exhaustion climbed irrespective of the use of fertilizers. By the end of the 1970s erosion had led to the abandonment of almost one-third of all arable land in China, while in Africa erosion rates were nine times the level of that in Europe. In 1991 the UN estimated that erosion was destroying 0.5 percent of the world's arable land each year. The intensive use of chemical fertilizers, together with development of genetically engineered crops beginning in the 1970s, had raised world output at a very high price.

A similar paradigm surfaced in the chemical industry. The production of synthesized chemicals began in the early twentieth century, but problems with chemical disposal only emerged as a serious public policy issue in the 1970s. The burgeoning number of hazardous chemical compounds utilized by large industries – and by the military – after the war enhanced the quality of finished products, but large quantities of toxic waste found their way into landfills, parks, rivers, and ponds. The first large-scale political response to this irresponsible practice occurred in the US between 1976 and 1980. In a residential neighborhood outside of Buffalo, New York, high levels of certain cancers and birth defects were recorded in the 1960s and 1970s. Investigators learned that the previous owner of the property, Hooker Chemical Co., had dumped dangerous organic solvents, pesticides, and acids into the so-called "Love Canal" between 1942 and 1953. The company later capped the canal with clay in hopes of keeping moisture away from the chemicals and forming a seal. These hopes went unrealized. In 1980 the federal government evacuated thousands of families from the area, buying homes, fencing off the entire site, and declaring it a national disaster area. In the wake of Love Canal, the Environmental Protection Agency (EPA) was charged with cleanup activities at a growing number of so-called "superfund" sites across the country. Politicians suddenly became aware of the fact that the over 50,000 toxic waste dumps in the US posed a significant threat to the health and safety of thousands of citizens.

As toxic waste-site cleanups progressed, the favored countries turned overseas for the disposal of dangerous materials. Mexico became a alternative dumping site for US waste products, while West African nations stepped forward to sell landfill rights to Europe and America. Communist East Germany was an especially attractive endpoint for chemical waste from capitalist Western Europe. Since their Soviet overlords were indifferent to indigenous industry-generated air and soil pollution, earning a bit of extra revenue from the Cold War enemy was evidently of a piece with the larger vision of Marxist solidarity. During the 1980s a robust international trade in toxic waste was underway, a peculiar aspect of increasing globalization and one that clearly reflected the complex and disturbing North–South divide.

Air pollution was perhaps the most noticeable and broad-reaching environmental challenge of the postwar era. A problem for humans since the advent of fire, the Industrial Revolution and its attendant massive urbanization raised the stakes of exposure to airborne particulants. Coal-powered engines were the principal culprits, spewing large quantities of smoke and sulphur dioxide into the atmosphere until as late as the 1950s. Some early industrialists equated the sight of smokestacks and soot with human progress and inventiveness, but by the mid-twentieth century the burning of coal triggered major public health crises in a number of major cities. For six days in December 1952, for example, London was blanketed by a thick haze that led to the deaths of 4000 inhabitants. Subsequent legislation helped to facilitate a transition to gas and electric heat in the city, and air quality began to improve before it was once again challenged by the growing concentration of automobiles powered by lead-burning gasoline.

The transition from coal-fired plants and cleaner oil and natural gas installations in the West was spurred by growing public anger over polluted cities, but the automobile posed an equally menacing agent in the form of smog. Caused by the reaction of sunlight to the nitrogen oxides or hydrocarbons discharged by vehicle exhaust, large, sunny cities enveloped by mountains were most susceptible. By the 1970s the expanding populations of cities like Los Angeles, Mexico City, and Athens were facing repeated smog alerts and health hazards. Although the abandonment of lead additives in petroleum during the 1980s helped to mitigate the dangers of smog, the WHO continued to insist at the end of the decade that almost 1.8 billion urban residents were exposed to dangerous levels of sulfur dioxide. One especially dangerous and politically divisive element of air pollution involved the transboundary movement of sulfur and nitrogen oxides known as acid rain, both of which degraded the environment in countries that contributed nothing to the problem. It was not until the fall of communism that serious efforts to control air pollution were undertaken in the former Soviet bloc, and air pollution levels declined in most developed states during the 1990s. But the problem became more acute in developing countries that were eager to "catch up" with the North.

Environmental awareness

Only in the 1960s, and only in those affluent democratic countries where challenges to orthodoxy and conventional authority were permitted, did the modern environmental movement emerge. The very intensity and breadth of economic development in the postwar West, and the growing affluence of these societies, afforded the educated middle class the opportunity to consider some of the less sanguine features of consumer culture. The aquatic zoologist Rachel Carson first sounded the alarm with her controversial bestseller *Silent Spring* in 1962. Carson, who was an employee of the US Bureau of Fisheries, indicted domestic manufacturers of commercial pesticides for their failure to consider the harmful effects of their products on bird populations. President Kennedy appointed a special panel to investigate the allegations, and the results confirmed Carson's principal thesis. For the first time, the frenetic pace of humankind's efforts to master nature were called into question by a public that was finally awakened to the potential dangers associated with the effort to shape the natural environment.

Carson's work spurred a nascent literature of dissent from the prevailing economic orthodoxy. In a pivotal 1968 article published in the journal *Science*, Garrett Hardin described a growing "tragedy of the commons" where decisions made by free individuals to improve their personal quality of life inevitably degraded the quality of life for the community at large. Hardin used the example of a village herdsmen who elects to allow one additional sheep on to the common lands. The single sheep may contribute to overgrazing, but since the cost is shared by all of the village herdsmen, the overall impact is minimal. But if other herdsmen were to make the same "rational" decision and add additional sheep, the commons eventually would be destroyed. In this and in many other cases, personal material interest conflicted sharply with the interest of the commons, and when it came to the natural environment, it was up to the commons – or the state – to regulate individual behavior for the good of the whole.

During the second half of the twentieth century the tragedy of the commons was played out by a small number of favored countries whose citizens expended the bulk of the world's energy while simultaneously compromising the environment of their neighbors across international borders. In the mature capitalist economies, 20 percent of the world's population consumed 80 percent of available resources in the year 2000. Highly productive industries and technologies placed a tremendous strain on the world's ecosystems, and while the prospect of the rest of the world achieving the same level of consumption as the North was appealing in terms of social justice, it was also frightening with respect to the potential environmental impact. Natural resource depletion, waste disposal, the replacement of products of nature with synthetics such as chemical fertilizers for enhanced food production, pesticides for insect control, and nonbiodegradable plastics for natural materials in construction and clothing, all opened up the possibility that market-driven economic development and ecological balance were hopelessly at odds.

As America's economy boomed and the country became more reliant upon imports of cheap foreign oil, a small number of activists began to raise public awareness of the harmful long-term environmental and human health effects of fossil-fuel emissions. The first sign of reform occurred in the cities, where smog caused by auto and power-plant emissions led to calls for government regulation. Congress finally took action in 1967, passing the first Air Quality Act. The legislation set minimum standards for emissions and took special aim at coal-fired power plants. Companies responded by moving to cleaner burning oil and natural gas, but this only compounded the already growing problem of reliance upon foreign sources of oil. One partial solution was to increase offshore drilling, but a single high-profile failure turned the prospect of increased domestic production into an environmental nightmare.

On January 29, 1969, a large oil-drilling platform owned and operated by the Union Oil Co. malfunctioned, dumping 200,000 gallons of crude oil into the Santa Barbara channel in California. The resulting oil slick covered 800 square miles of ocean and 35 miles of coastline. Seals, dolphins, and birds died in large numbers, and the images were projected on television screens across the state and nation. It took workers almost two weeks to stop the leak, and the cleanup lasted throughout the spring. The president of Union Oil, Fred L. Hartley, blithely remarked that too much was being made of the spill. "I don't like to call it a disaster," he stated with great insensitivity, "because there has been no loss of human life. I am amazed at the publicity for the loss of a few birds." The accident galvanized the nascent environmental movement in the US and led to additional industry regulation. By 1970, Congress had passed a second, tougher Clean Air Act, setting strict deadlines for industry compliance and unwittingly intensifying America's reliance on foreign oil to 30 percent of total consumption. Congress also passed the National Environmental Policy Act, one feature of which required that an environmental impact statement be drawn up whenever federal agencies proposed new resource-related projects.

Growing concerns over the environmental costs associated with the burning of fossil fuels also led to the emergence of a number of international environmental organizations. The first "Earth Day" was celebrated in the developed countries in 1970, drawing 20 million people to events in the US alone, and two years later the UN hosted an international energy conference to promote interest in cleaner sources of power. By the 1990s Earth Day was being marked in almost 150 countries, governments were funding research projects dedicated to the study of global environmental change, and leading energy corporations shifted their advertising rhetoric, if not always their actions, in the direction of greater environmental awareness and "green" technologies. Growing numbers of scientists confirmed that energy generation based on fossil fuels contributed to dangerous levels of carbon dioxide being discharged into the atmosphere. In addition to the fouling of air and urban smog, the heat-trapping effects of these discharges threatened to alter the earth's climate, raise average temperatures, and create a dangerous "greenhouse effect." During the 1990s, some researchers began to associate extreme weather events such as droughts, floods, and excessive heat waves with the effects of global warming. They warned that as the worldwide demand for current energy sources increased, especially in poorer countries, the severity of weather-related emergencies would intensify, causing untold economic hardship for millions.

Despite these developments, "growing the economy" remained the imperative of political leaders around the world, and with the eclipse of communism in the early 1990s, the high priests of market-driven economic development gained additional stature. They claimed that privatization and deregulation would foster new economic partnerships that would lead to global prosperity, economic justice, and technological solutions to virtually all environmental challenges. Political leaders in developing countries rebuked developed states for lecturing them about "the commons," viewing calls for conservation and alternative development models as discriminatory. India's Indira Gandhi, while active in the 1972 UN Conference on the Human Environment, quipped that "poverty is the worst form of pollution." And Chinese leaders continued to employ older sources of power and technology in their quest for great nation status. Coal-fired power plants and vehicle emissions reduced air quality in the cities, while pollution from chemical and fertilizer factories in rural areas degraded water supplies. Widespread conversion of cropland into mixed-use zones meant that the country faced the possibility of losing its ability to feed a population that continued to grow despite the government's intrusive birth-control regulations.

UNCERTAIN FUTURE

At the beginning of the twenty-first century, then, rising concern for the environment had by no means compromised the "growth and development" solution to domestic ills and national security anxieties. Power, and thus security, in the international arena remained inextricably linked to the state's ability to secure, distribute, and consume affordable energy. Social order, meaningful employment, physical and mental well-being, were all deemed unattainable without constant economic development, without further dominion over nature. The environmental movement had heightened public awareness of the dangers inherent in technical efforts to manage and alter nature, but the economic and military imperatives that undergirded the sovereign – and solvent – nation-state continued to take priority over the less immediate challenge of long-term sustainability. Most governments continued to subsidize conventional energy producers at the end of the century. In the year 2000, for example, the US government provided the major oil companies with $1.5 billion in tax incentives, while in that same year the government of India offered over $3 billion in subsidies to electrical consumers.

Although it was common knowledge by 2000 that current practices of getting and using the world's resources were unsustainable, most of the world, and in particular the world's most powerful countries, continued to act as though consumption and global ecology were unrelated phenomena. Given this reality, politicians had little incentive to support bold initiatives that required the electorate to consider the earth's ability to endure the pace and intensity of human activity witnessed during the twentieth century. When the US spent billions of dollars to oust an objectionable autocrat in Iraq in 2003, no one believed that such an expenditure in money and lives would have been politically possible if Iraq had not been one of the world's major oil-exporting countries. The invasion was couched boldly in terms of a broader post-9/11 war against international terrorism, with the advancing armies poised to capture and dismantle weapons of mass destruction. Critics of the war, including the majority of UN member states, saw the whole affair differently, as a monumental distraction from the war on terrorism. The alleged weapons were never located, but the supplies of oil for an eager buying public were secured. What those billions might have meant to researchers working on models of economic well-being free from fossil-fuel dependency, or in educating about the value of conservation, is difficult to say. Only 2–3 percent of America's energy needs were being met by alternatives to fossil fuels in 2000. Renewable, non-polluting sources of energy such as wind, hydropower, geothermal, and solar, accounted for only 14 percent of global energy supply in the year 2000, while nuclear energy provided 6 percent.

Despite a 1992 UN-sponsored conference on environment and development, the so-called "Earth Summit" in Rio de Janeiro, the work of international cooperation was made more difficult by the fact that the developed states had industrialized during an era when environmental concerns were absent. Developing countries, on the other hand, were doubly disadvantaged, both because of the need to compete with established industrial powers, and by a new concern over the environmental impact of traditional technologies and fuels. Although delegates to the "Earth Summit" issued a non-binding convention on climate change, efforts to set specific limits on the emission of greenhouse gases (carbon dioxide, methane, nitrous oxide, sulfur hexafluoride) faltered at a subsequent meeting attended by representatives from 160 nations in Kyoto, Japan, in December 1997. According to the Kyoto protocol, developed states were obliged to cut their emissions by 5 percent of 1990 figures by the year 2012. The countries of the EU signed up, but in 2001 President George W. Bush withdrew American support for the agreement, objecting to generous emissions exemptions for developing states like China and India, and claiming that compliance would "cause serious harm to the US economy." The Senate agreed with the president, voting 95–0 to reject the protocol. Under the terms of the agreement, the protocol would only become binding in international law once countries that together produced 55 percent of greenhouse gases ratified. Russia's acceptance in 2004 enabled supporters to cross that threshold. "There are times when only an act of courage can spur progress in world affairs," wrote UN Secretary General Kofi Annan. "Action to reduce greenhouse gas emissions is largely about changing attitudes and expectations." Whether or not the Kyoto agreement could survive without the participation of the US, which with 4 percent of the world's population produced 20 percent of emissions, remained an open question in 2005. The fact that international meetings on the environment did produce agreements during the 1990s was a hopeful sign, but substantive policy changes still required the endorsement of developed states like the US before equitable enforcement mechanisms could be devised and implemented.

7

RELIGIONS AND CIVIL SOCIETY

KEY TOPICS

Christianity becomes a global faith
Challenges in the Islamic world
Hindu and Jewish confessional politics

East Asian transitions
Women, rights, and religion
Ancient faith and modern values

A chapter dedicated to religious belief and practice may seem misplaced in a book on the postwar world. After all, we often read about the secularization of society during the latter half of the twentieth century, how increasing numbers of women and men explain and order their lives without reference to religion. The experience of two world wars in the space of 30 years, and in particular the suffering of millions of innocent noncombatants in those conflicts, led many influential voices to affirm the death of religion, or at least its displacement to the fringes of human life. Sociologists traced the decline of public religiosity in Western Europe during the postwar decades, and predictions about the rest of the developed world were not sanguine. As distinct religious traditions intersected in a highly mobile age, more people came to share the view that sacred stories were relative to time and place, less the mirror of some absolute reality and more the product of human imagination. Both those who applauded and those who deplored the trend believed that the religious impulse would be confined to the less-developed world at the start of the twenty-first century, a blanching relic of the prescientific mind.

In the West, the rising tide of doubt was anticipated during the Industrial Revolution. Karl Marx had scoffed that religion was "the opiate of the people," foisted upon the underclass by elites in order to buttress economic inequalities and keep the poor content with the status quo. Half a century later Freud dismissed the religious impulse as akin to a childhood neurosis, something to be gotten over in enlightened adulthood. After 1945 communist governments heartily endorsed both perspectives and took steps to hasten the demise of religious institutions, while secularists on both sides of the Iron Curtain dreamed of a world guided by tolerance and pragmatism without premodern myths about the afterlife. Proponents of atheistic existentialism, while perhaps lamenting the fact that there was no suprahuman reality or transcendent truth, urged women and men to forge their own meaningful value system in an otherwise absurd universe. For many intellectuals, the religious worldview, built upon stories of ancient peoples, no longer met the needs of postmodern communities.

None of the predictions has come to pass. In fact, if we examine the power of religious ideals to inform individual behavior and collective political action since the 1950s, it is hard to avoid the conclusion that an unanticipated revival of the sacred, especially within the established traditions of Christianity, Judaism, Islam, Hinduism, and Buddhism, has become one of the dominant features of recent global history. New, nontraditional religious movements have also proliferated, especially among the middle class in the developed West. Perhaps the resurgence should not surprise us. After all, Homo sapiens appears always to have taken a serious interest in the possibility of a larger, supernatural frame of reality. Unique among species in possessing the power of self-consciousness, humans can step outside of themselves and reflect upon their place and function in the world. As religious scholar James C. Livingston has written, humans constantly consider and discuss questions of meaning and value, and in every generation they have been concerned with life's essential questions: Why am I here; whom should I obey; what happens at the moment of death? In the end it appears that most humans cannot be satisfied with the answers provided by temporal existence, even affluent Western existence, and are naturally drawn to a power beyond the everyday, to what is thought to be transcendent and permanent. To borrow Livingston's useful definition, religion is the human response, through beliefs and actions, to a conception of the ultimate or sacred. And since a large part of that response involves the establishment of moral guideposts and values that inform everyday action, the directive role of religion in wider culture remained extremely powerful after World War II, lifting some to the peaks of sanctity while reducing others to the worst forms of barbarity. In a controversial 1996 book titled *The Clash of Civilizations and the Remaking of World Order*, Samuel Huntington argued that religion, and in particular differences between Christianity and Islam, would become the preeminent force in international relations during the twenty-first century. And while many scholars take issue with the particulars of Huntington's thesis, few would deny the centrality of the sacred, for good and ill, in recent global history.

Church and state

The modern Western idea of the appropriate relationship between religion and the state traces its roots to an Enlightenment minimalist argument. Simply put, it calls for the privatization of religion, its removal from the public square and relegation to the realm of personal choice. Exponents of this position argue that the close relationship between church and state during the medieval and early modern centuries provided ample evidence of cruelties and abuses initiated in the name of orthodoxy. Wars, persecutions, inquisitions, crusades, pogroms, the debasement of women – all had been undertaken in the name of a benevolent and merciful God. Citing this ample historical evidence to support a picture of religious agency as a force for inhumanity, Enlightenment thinkers called for a radical separation of church and state, for the creation of clearly defined public and private spheres, placing religion squarely in the latter. The framers of the American Constitution encapsulated this position when they wrote that "Congress shall make no law respecting an establishment of religion, or prohibiting the free exercise thereof". No longer the business of the secular state, religion became an option. Religious persons were free to attempt to influence public policy in a peaceful manner, but the state would restrict itself to temporal matters.

The Western minimalist approach to religion has not, by and large, been embraced by the majority of the world's peoples. Indeed the norm in most religious traditions since the 1950s appears to be quite the opposite. The notion that the authority of the state is not anchored in religion, or that political leaders should not claim religious sanction for their authority, strikes many people in the non-Western world as preposterous. Rather than dissipate the role of religion in civil society, millions of believers continue to justify political policy and action on the basis of sacred mandates. In recent decades, this tension between modernizers and fundamentalists has been especially pronounced in the Islamic world, where submission to God has always involved a total way of life. In addition, religiously motivated groups with little or no formal connection to the state, and sometimes in vocal opposition to it, have managed to impose a religious agenda on public discourse through acts of intimidation and violence. Small groups of well-educated religious militants from all of the major faith traditions have been able to influence domestic and international politics through ready access to modern communications technology. More disturbingly, some religious militants have turned to terrorism, confident that their noble ends justify ignoble means. Dedicated to the notion that the postwar move to privatize and relativize religion is another malevolent feature of Western colonialism, these fundamentalists claim the right to use force in pursuit of a public sphere that is guided by a single religious metanarrative or story. According to this troubled perspective, God has enemies and is in need of human assistance to deal with the problem. By the start of the twenty-first century, as we have seen in earlier chapters, acts of terrorism driven by a religious agenda had become a source of deep concern in countries around the world.

CHRISTIANITY BECOMES A GLOBAL FAITH

In the year 2000 Christianity stood as the largest world religion, with just under two billion adherents, or one-third of the world's population. Catholics formed the most numerous faith community within this tradition, with approximately 800 million people identifying themselves with the Roman Church, while a wide variety of

Protestant denominations, together with Orthodox Christians and Pentecostals, rounded out the total. As Europe's major powers established large overseas empires during the late nineteenth century, Christian missionary activity accelerated. Just as the apologists for empire equated the ascendancy of Western culture with human progress, so too Christian missionaries and their domestic supporters associated their faith tradition with the enrichment of humanity. Some even predicted the inevitable decline of the other major world religions. Two world wars in the short space of 30 years, and the deaths of combatants who, although mortal enemies, shared the same Christian faith, dispelled all such linkages. Institutional churches had done little to oppose Nazism and its anti-Semitic program in the 1930s and 1940s: Pope Pius XII (r. 1939–58) even agreed a concordat with Hitler and declined to speak out in the face of genocide, while only a small number of Protestant churches took a stand against the German state. A handful of Christians in German-occupied Europe attempted to protect their Jewish neighbors – at great personal risk to themselves and their families – but the majority of Christians in the Nazi empire dutifully carried out their wartime orders with little sense of remorse. In the face of enormous injustice and inhumanity, it became apparent that Western democratic states were not the only practitioners of appeasement. It was now very difficult to claim the ethical superiority of Christianity as practiced in the West. After the war, leaders within the various Christian denominations, including even the Roman Catholic Church, became less certain that theirs was the final truth or that salvation was available solely within the confines of one tradition. Under these circumstances, dialogue and empathy across traditions became the compelling focus of Christianity.

The ecumenical movement

Although there had been earlier efforts to unite the various Christian communions, the decline in postwar church attendance in the West prompted a renewed effort to heal the wounds of institutional division that were now some 400 years old. In 1948 the World Council of Churches (WCC) held its inaugural meeting in Amsterdam, and subsequent assemblies in Chicago (1954) and New Delhi

(1961) broadened the appeal of the organization among Protestant and Orthodox churches. While remaining aloof from the WCC, a decree on ecumenism issued by the Catholic Church in the mid-1960s recognized that other Christian denominations were in some measure of communion with Rome, and a series of bilateral dialogues were opened with Protestant colleagues. In 1965 the Roman Catholic and Eastern Orthodox churches lifted the joint excommunications that had been in place since 1054, and three years later the Vatican accepted membership on the Faith and Order Commission of the WCC, a body dedicated to theological reconciliation. The second half of the century witnessed a decided shift toward interdenominational service partnerships, common liturgical reform, and intercommunion. And in some cases the ecumenical movement led to formal union: The Church of South India, for example, was formed in 1947, joining Methodists, Presbyterians, Congregationalists, and Anglicans in one Protestant communion. And while Protestant–Catholic differences remained significant, especially over the issues of abortion, the ordination of women, and homosexuality, by the 1990s even the doctrinally conservative Pope John Paul II was speaking positively about a larger church of Christ that transcended denominational lines.

Watershed at the Vatican

In the early 1960s the Roman Catholic Church, under the leadership of Pope John XXIII (r. 1958–63), moved decisively to reverse almost a century of official church intransigence in the face of modernization. The church's predicament was first made manifest a century earlier when an embattled Pope Pius IX (r. 1846–78) promulgated an official "Syllabus of Errors" in 1864. The pontiff condemned upwards of 80 modern teachings, including rationalism, liberalism, socialism, and religious pluralism. Five years later Pope Pius called 744 bishops (mostly Europeans) to the First Vatican Council in Rome. There the assembled delegates reaffirmed the centrality of revelation to the knowledge of God, and declared that when speaking on matters of faith and morals, the pope was infallible. Significantly, the final canons were issued in the form of positions that were declared anathema by the Church. Vatican I was the face of Roman Catholicism in crisis, its leadership unwilling to come to terms with the implications of modern science and industry, the political empowerment of the working class, the legitimacy of alternate religious traditions, and the appeal of secular nationalism.

There was little movement from these positions for the next eight decades. And when Angelo Giuseppe Roncalli was elected pope in 1958 at the advanced age of 77, many Vatican watchers assumed that his would be a caretaker pontificate. But the energetic John XXIII set an ambitious agenda for Catholic reform, one made more urgent by his predecessor's failure to lead the Church in strong opposition to Nazi atrocities. The pope's call in 1959 for a Second Vatican Council included an invitation to Protestant churches to send representatives and an endorsement of greater lay participation, thus setting the stage for a new era in ecumenism and lay engagement. The sessions began in the fall of 1961 and continued until 1965, by itself significant in reaffirming the deliberative and conciliar traditions within Roman Catholicism. The Council's final decisions (none of which were framed in the traditional form of condemning errors) were far-reaching. The Church was now understood to be the "people of God," not simply the official clerical hierarchy. The universal Latin liturgy was replaced by vernacular translations, and the role of the laity was enhanced by the creation of an order of permanent deacons that could include married men. The Church also formally recognized the integrity of non-Catholic Christianity and attempted to reverse centuries of harmful teachings about Jews and Muslims. Reaching beyond the Western monotheistic faiths, the Council acknowledged the richness of Asian traditions like Buddhism and Hinduism, and it was careful to emphasize points of contact between all the great faith traditions. In sum, the Roman Catholic Church abandoned its exclusionary past and began a serious dialog with its neighbors. The theologian Karl Rahner wrote that Vatican II signaled a decisive moment in history when a European-based communion finally became a "world church."

A wider Christian community

Rahner's observation was instructive, especially in terms of emerging trends in Christian outreach. The postwar decades witnessed a sharp decline in church attendance in Western Europe, while in the communist East state authorities worked assiduously to undermine the appeal of institutional religion by harassing clergy and discriminating against believers. But Christianity has always been a proselytizing faith, and in the postwar period this age-old mandate was followed with renewed vigor outside the West. Sixteenth-century Spanish and Portuguese explorers brought Roman Catholicism to Central and South America, and in the seventeenth century Protestant dissenters from England carried their reformed confessions to North America. But the great age of Protestant evangelism occurred during the late nineteenth century, as white missionaries accompanied colonizers to Africa and Asia. At the start of the twentieth century, just over half of the world's Christians lived outside of Europe, and by the end of the century the overwhelming majority were non-Europeans. Attendance at traditional Christian church services, while declining in West, burgeoned elsewhere. "If we want to visualize a 'typical' contemporary Christian," writes professor of religious studies Philip Jenkins, "we should think of a woman in a village in Nigeria or in a Brazilian *favela*."

And just as the Germanic peoples of the early Middle Ages brought their cultural and political traditions to bear on Roman Christianity (transforming Jesus, for example, into a warrior king), so too non-Western peoples contributed their own unique perspectives and practices to the faith after World War II. As the demographic center of Christianity shifted away from Europe to Africa, Asia, and Latin America – the poorest regions of the world – theological viewpoints stressing the importance of social commitment, racial equality, and economic justice became more important to ministers and laity alike. And while Christianity and Marxism remained firmly at odds, the Marxist economic critique of existing power relations attracted some influential thinkers within the Christian fold who believed that the message of the gospel included an emphatic call for the creation of a more just society. The message of the "social gospel" took on new resonance, particularly in Catholic Latin America.

Roman Catholicism and the state in Latin America

Three trends marked the immediate postwar period in Latin America. The first involved a troubled political and economic relationship with the US. Although most of the 27 countries in Latin

America had secured their political independence in the early 1800s, severe economic problems over the next century hampered the formation of stable civilian governments and compounded existing social inequalities. Throughout the continent, traditional landed elites, together with a small middle class involved in commerce and industry, monopolized political power through their control of the armed forces. Single-product export economies, not unlike those in postcolonial Africa, insured that domestic economic development remained tied to consumer demand in more developed countries.

By the 1930s the US had replaced Britain as the single largest investor in Latin America, and before the end of World War II more than half of the continent's trade was tied to its wealthy northern neighbor. Latin America's postwar economic problems, in many ways more deep-rooted than Europe's, never become a priority for Washington. When the 21-member Organization of American States (OAS) was formed in 1948, the US pressured member nations to adopt a strongly anticommunist resolution. Most complied by 1954, but support for the US position in the Cold War did not translate into significant financial assistance from the North. Endemic poverty throughout much of Central and South America, the main cause of leftist insurgency, was all but ignored by cold warriors in Washington, whose main interest was Soviet expansionism.

The second trend involved an unprecedented rise in population and the movement of people from rural to urban settings. With an overall population of 38 million in 1900, Latin America was home to more than half a billion people in 2000 (one-third of the total live in Portuguese-speaking Brazil). After 1945 massive internal migration turned moderate-sized cities into megalopolises; affluent central areas with new high-rise buildings were enveloped by sprawling shantytowns where the hopes of millions seeking employment were regularly shattered. By the 1990s, Mexico City and São Paulo, Brazil, each had populations of approximately 20 million, most of whom lived in squalor. When combined with ongoing rural poverty (population growth meant that the rural population levels remained steady), the emergence of this large urban underclass further destabilized an already fragile social order.

The third trend, discernible amidst much variety, involved a drift toward more authoritarian forms of government, often with the support of the Roman Catholic Church until the 1960s, and then in opposition to a reform-minded and socially activist Church during the 1960s and 1970s. Only Mexico, Colombia, Venezuela, and Costa Rica escaped the grip of antidemocratic government during this period. The Church had been stripped of its massive landholdings during the revolutionary era of the early 1800s, and it was disestablished in most countries by 1900, but its cultural influence remained strong well into the late twentieth century. By 2000, 35 percent of the world's Roman Catholics lived in Latin America, and for centuries their spiritual leaders had identified closely with the highly Europeanized upper classes who dominated the continent's conservative political regimes. The authoritarianism reflected in the Syllabus of Errors and the papal doctrine of infallibility helped to inform the outlook of a very traditional and conservative hierarchy in Latin America.

Social activism

Given the tradition of elite leadership, the impact of the Second Vatican Council (1962–5) on the Latin American Church was enormous. In a radio address just before the opening of the first session of the Council, the Pope enjoined the delegates to present the Church "in the underdeveloped countries as the church of all, and especially of the poor." Six years later, at a meeting of Latin American bishops at Medellín, Colombia, the hierarchy acknowledged the enormous social and economic injustices across the continent and called for activists within the Church to work for land reform, unionization, the creation of rural cooperatives, and the expansion of basic literacy. Some Catholic intellectuals, influenced by Marxist-oriented dependence theory, began to champion a new "liberation theology," insisting that the early Catholic Church had explicitly linked faith with social and political reform. One of the leaders of the movement, the Peruvian priest Gustavo Gutiérrez, insisted that the poor of Latin America "will not emerge from their present status except by means of a profound transformation, a social revolution, which will radically and qualitatively change the conditions in which they now live." For Gutiérrez, it was the responsibility of the Roman Catholic clergy to inspire that revolution from the pulpit and in the streets.

For the first time, many bishops began to challenge the legitimacy of authoritarian rule in Latin America. They condemned human rights abuses and widespread poverty, and called for the restoration of democratic politics. In Chile during the 1970s and 1980s, for example, the hierarchy supported the formation of organizations dedicated to monitoring human rights abuses that took place under the repressive regime of General Augusto Pinochet. Catholic leaders played a key role in the restoration of democracy in Chile during the 1980s, repeatedly mediating between opposition groups and the government. In Brazil, the world's largest Catholic country, the military regime that came to power in 1964 faced constant criticism from the country's bishops and priests. The latter were instrumental in forming Christian "base communities," small groups that met regularly to study the Bible and consider its implications for daily life. Further north in Central America, the majority of priests and laity in Nicaragua supported the 1979 Sandinista revolt against the Somoza dictatorship, and a pastoral letter from the bishops legitimated the popular leftist rebellion. The Church in El Salvador, on the other hand, suffered mightily for its political activism. Normally supportive of the ruling elite, the hierarchy turned against the corrupt and repressive regime in the mid-1970s. Hundreds of priests and lay activists were tortured and killed in the struggle, and in March 1980, the popular Archbishop of San Salvador, Archbishop Oscar Romero, was murdered by a government-sponsored death squad while celebrating mass.

Conservative restoration

The Church's activism on behalf of social and economic justice in Latin America reached its peak in the 1970s, but even then not all national episcopacies took a reformist stand. In Argentina, Bolivia, Paraguay, Honduras, and Uruguay, Church leaders failed to challenge authoritarian regimes. Liberation theology also had Cold War implications. The US, locked in a global ideological struggle with the Soviets, did not appreciate the fact that activist clergy were siding with leftist reformers and communists. The American military had meddled repeatedly in the internal affairs of Latin American republics since the late nineteenth century, and with the onset of the Cold War the interventionist impulse was revived. In 1954 a CIA-backed uprising had ousted the left-wing president of Guatemala, Jacobo Arbenz Guzmán. The reformist Guatemalan leader had sought to redistribute over 200,000 acres of land owned by the US-based United Fruit Co., shifting control to Guatemalan peasants. Executives at United Fruit appealed to the Eisenhower administration for assistance, and in the aftermath of the military coup the new right-wing government swiftly quashed Guzmán's land reforms.

The 1961 Bay of Pigs fiasco was a decisive setback for anticommunists in the US, but it enabled autocratic right-wing governments across Central and South America to appeal successfully for additional military and financial support from Washington. In 1965 President Johnson sent 25,000 American troops to the Dominican Republic, to prevent the formation of, in Johnson's words, "another communist state in this hemisphere." Eight years later the Nixon administration, alarmed over the election of Chile's Marxist president Salvador Allende, provided covert assistance to military rebels who overthrew the democratically elected government. The successor state under Pinochet banned opposition parties, and jailed, tortured, and "disappeared" thousands of political opponents. During the 1970s the US also backed the brutal Somoza regime in Nicaragua, while the Reagan administration provided financing and military support for thuggish anti-Sandinista "freedom fighters" during the 1980s. The Reagan White House also intervened militarily in Jamaica (1980) and in tiny Grenada (1983), ostensibly to prevent Cuban domination. Roman Catholic liberation theology, while not explicitly anti-American, clearly ran afoul of conservative, and sometimes brutal, governments that enjoyed the unqualified support of the US.

But the decisive turn against clergy activism occurred only with the elevation to the papacy of the staunch anticommunist John Paul II in 1979. The Polish-born pontiff made ten trips to Latin America between 1980 and 1991, and his experiences left him uncomfortable with the left-leaning political commitments of many Church leaders. The pope began to censure a number of liberation theologians for placing too much emphasis on political reform, banned priests from serving in a political capacity, and called for a new commitment to evangelization. In 1981 John Paul demanded that priests serving in the leftist Sandinista government resign their offices, and the head of the Nicaraguan church, Archbishop Miguel Obando y Bravo, became a leading critic of the new political order. During a 1983 visit to this overwhelmingly Catholic country, the pope openly criticized the government's attempt to "coopt" the Church into revolutionary armed struggle.

The passage away from social activism was also guided by the fact that for the first time in its history the Catholic Church in Latin America found itself losing its cultural monopoly. Evangelical Protestant proselytization efforts, especially in states that abandoned earlier agreements with the Roman Catholic Church forbidding non-Catholic missionary activity, yielded significant numbers of converts during the 1980s and 1990s. From a low of 3 percent in Colombia, Paraguay, and Uruguay, to a high of 25 percent of the population in Guatemala, five centuries of Catholic hegemony came under sustained assault. Part of the appeal of Protestant evangelicalism, and especially independent Pentecostal churches, rested with its emphasis on deep personal conversion experiences. A trend toward the restoration of civilian government during the last two decades did little to address the problem of appalling social and economic inequality in Latin America, and for many recent converts to Pentecostal Christianity, the faith healing, exorcisms of malign spirits, and appeals to the Holy Spirit, restored Latin Christianity's historic focus on personal transformation. The charismatic churches also served as vibrant community centers, providing comfort and guidance to the dispossessed living in the anonymity of the sprawling cities. For increasing numbers of poor people, the traditional Roman Catholic Church, with its hierarchy, formalism, and historic association with colonialism, no longer provided the requisite level of spiritual and material support in a continent of declining expectations. By the close of the century the most dynamic churches in Latin America offered a brand of Christianity that was more evangelical, fideistic, and doctrinally conservative than mainline churches in the developed West.

The African imprint

The massive African continent has been central to the recent demographic shift in Christianity: The faithful had established a strong presence in North Africa during the first four centuries of the Christian era, but during the seventh century, Islam became the religion of choice for the overwhelming majority in the North and Northeast. Besides a minority Christian community in Egypt, only Ethiopia remained as a independent Christian outpost on the continent after the dramatic rise of Islam. Imperialism reversed this trend in the late nineteenth century. In 1900 only a handful of Africans were Christian, but in 2000 almost half of the population had embraced the faith and Africa had become the world's most important region for conversions. In 1970 there were an estimated 1.2 billion Christians worldwide, and 30 years later the figure was nearing the 2 billion mark. One-fifth of these people lived in central and southern Africa.

At the time of independence, it was expected that the influence of Christianity would wane in Africa due to its strong association with colonialism. Given their European-dominated leadership structures, it is not surprising that Christian mission churches played a very minor role in the independence movements. In early 1950s Rhodesia, for example, the colony's four Roman Catholic bishops hailed from England, Ireland, Switzerland, and Germany. There were just over 5500 expatriate priests in Africa in 1949 and 8700 ten years later. After independence many of these ministers were replaced by indigenous leaders who moved quickly to end their dependence on mother churches in Europe. However, even with these changes in personnel, the anticipated decline of "colonial" religion did not occur. Many of the rulers of independent African states had been educated in missionary schools, and they were loath to dispense with this important cultural and spiritual resource. African Christians (especially Protestants) appropriated the scriptures and interpreted church teachings on their own terms, often incorporating a range of indigenous values and traditions into the faith. The centrality of dance in African culture, for example, gradually became an accepted feature of congregational worship. In the case of Roman Catholicism, the reforms of Vatican II were especially welcome to the African hierarchy, as new policies affirmed the use of vernacular liturgies, regional music, and native spiritual practices, such as the veneration of ancestors. A native African hierarchy was first established in 1950, and by 1992 there were 15 African cardinals and over 400 bishops who led a continent-wide Roman Catholic Church of 100 million parishioners. And while there have been areas where the infusion of African tradition into Christianity has created enormous friction (debate over polygamy being the most contentious), this has not inhibited the spread of the faith, or the growth of influence on wider church policy. In the worldwide Anglican communion, for example, many African bishops remain deeply opposed to the ordination of homosexuals, and the more permissive policies of the Episcopal Church in the US and the UK threatens to divide the larger family of Anglicans that is nominally headed by the Archbishop of Canterbury. In addition to mainline denominations, thousands of independent Christian churches emerged after independence. Stressing a uniquely African style of preaching and liturgical practice, many of the independent churches were charismatic, featuring prophesy, spiritual healing, and the exorcism of evil spirits.

African church leaders also played a strategic role in opposing regimes that failed to address the pressing social and economic needs of their citizens. In South Africa, the apartheid system prompted the emergence of a powerful theology of resistance that focused on civil rights. The election of Desmond Tutu as the first black Anglican Archbishop of Cape Town in 1986, for example, signaled the start of a peaceful protest offensive that in basic structure mirrored the earlier American social justice movement of Martin Luther King, Jr. Affirming the values of Latin American liberation theology, Tutu wrote in the midst of the struggle against apartheid that "Many people think that Christians should be neutral, or that the Church must be neutral. But in a situation of injustice and oppression such as we have in South Africa, not to choose to oppose, is in fact to have chosen to side with the powerful, with the exploiter, with the oppressor." Tutu was joined by other prominent Christian leaders, including Beyers Naude and Allan Boesak, both ministers of the Dutch Reformed Church, in identifying opposition to apartheid with Christian moral teaching. As many protest organizations were banned by the government in the late 1980s, the churches became the most powerful legal voice of the opposition. After the collapse of the apartheid system and the election of Nelson Mandela to the presidency of a democratic South Africa in 1994, Tutu was appointed to chair the government's Truth and Reconciliation Commission, whose mandate was to further interracial harmony through a generous amnesty program. Victims of apartheid were afforded an opportunity to testify in public about their sufferings, while the white perpetrators of human rights violations who acknowledged their deeds were exempted from criminal prosecution.

African-American liberation theology

In the US, liberation theology converged on three principal issues: race, gender, and poverty. Concentrating on those passages in the Bible that speak of the equality of humans, during the 1950s a growing number of clergy insisted that race-based practices in American society were in fact contrary to the will of God. In 1957 a group of black Christian ministers, under the leadership of a young Southern Baptist, Martin Luther King, Jr., founded the Southern Christian Leadership Conference (SCLC). As leaders in their respective communities, the ministers hoped to mobilize blacks politically to achieve a fully integrated society where equal rights were protected. In 1954 the US Supreme Court ruled that "separate but equal" public facilities were inherently unequal and enjoined the integration of public schools, but the federal government had done little to enforce the landmark ruling. King had led a successful year-long bus boycott in Montgomery, Alabama, in 1957 in order to desegregate the transportation system there, and the leaders of the SCLC hoped to employ the same tactics of peaceful resistance elsewhere. The group's organizational meetings often resembled Sunday religious services, and its political statements and activities frequently employed biblical references. For Rev. King, the struggle for civil equality was also a quest for Christian nonracial unity. But without the strong support of black churches, the Civil Rights movement in the South would not have been successful.

King had studied the life and work of Gandhi, and a 1959 visit to India strengthened his resolve to end racial discrimination in the US through peaceful means. Sit-ins at "whites-only" businesses in hundreds of cities across the southern US followed in the early 1960s, with volunteers (mostly students) quietly enduring verbal and physical abuse while television cameras recorded the depth of racial bigotry on display. Other protesters took to the highways on public buses in what were described as "freedom rides," demanding integration and suffering repeated indignities on their travels. In 1963 King reasserted his leadership over the broader movement for civil rights when he took the struggle to Birmingham, Alabama, a large industrial city with a long history of white racism. The Birmingham sit-ins and marches prompted a violent response from the city's law-enforcement agencies. High-power fire hoses, police dogs, and batons were used against the demonstrators, all in full view of the American public who witnessed the scenes on national television. The Kennedy administration, having vacillated for the better part of two years for fear of alienating white Southern democrats, finally introduced a landmark civil rights bill in Congress in June 1963. In August King was the keynote speaker at a massive march on Washington, where he appealed for the creation of an America where citizens "would not be judged by the color of their skin, but by the content of their character." And at the close of that momentous year King was awarded the Nobel Peace Prize in Oslo, Norway. He subsequently broadened his campaign for racial equality to include issues of economic justice, and before his assassination in 1967 he began to speak out in opposition to the American war in Vietnam.

Confessional politics in Ireland

The example of a successful civil rights campaign informed by religious conviction in the US subsequently helped to shape developments in British-controlled Northern Ireland. Since the imposition of Protestantism under Henry VIII in the mid-sixteenth century, the majority Roman Catholic population in Ireland looked to the Church as a symbol of Irish identity. When self-rule was finally granted in 1922, the six heavily Protestant northern provinces insisted on remaining part of the UK. The island nation was divided, and under the South's constitution of 1937 the Catholic Church was officially recognized as holding a "special position ... as the guardian of the faith professed by the great majority of the citizens." In practical terms this meant that the Church controlled public education and wielded enormous influence over the national political agenda: No politician in the South was willing to ignore the Catholic hierarchy when important legislation was pending.

Northern Protestants condemned what they viewed as the formation of a reactionary "papist" state in the South and freely discriminated against the Catholic minority within their midst. Gerrymandering of electoral districts insured that Catholics would not enjoy equal political rights, while widespread discrimination in employment, housing, and access to higher education pushed Catholics even further to the margins of citizenship. In 1967 a Northern Ireland Civil Rights Association was established, its program of demonstration and protest modeled on the strategy employed by Rev. King in the US. Unhappily in the case of Northern Ireland, violent elements on both sides of the religious divide prompted the intervention of British troops, more sectarian violence, and the suspension of the Ulster parliament in 1972. The worst forms of discrimination were brought to an end in the wake of the struggle, but the larger issue of a divided Ireland remained to polarize the political landscape for the remainder of the century.

Poland's Catholic identity

The place of the institutional Catholic Church in Polish history had been shaped during long periods of foreign domination and occupation. Partitioned and removed from the political map of Central Europe by the Prussians, Austrians, and Russians from 1795 to 1918, invaded and occupied by the brutal Nazi regime from 1939 to 1945, and transformed into a communist surrogate by the Soviet Union from the end of the war until 1989, Poles (like the Catholic Irish) turned to the Church as their repository of national identity, historical memory, and resistance to outside domination. In this heavily Roman Catholic land (made almost exclusively Catholic by the Holocaust), political nationalism remained inextricably linked to religious identity after 1945, and the clerical hierarchy willingly assumed the mantle of leadership in the nonviolent struggle against perceived Soviet imperialism.

Initially, the Church in postwar Poland was willing to cooperate with the Communist Polish Worker's Party that had been imposed on the country by Stalin, but the hierarchy under the leadership under Cardinal Stefan Wyszynski, archbishop of Warsaw, doggedly opposed all government efforts to interfere in religious matters. In 1953 the government imposed an oath of loyalty on all clergy and claimed the right to appoint and dismiss priests and bishops. The Polish episcopacy formally rejected the moves, and in response the government imprisoned the cardinal, along with almost 1000 fellow priests and lay activists. This was followed by an order abolishing religious education in the schools and curtailing the work of various Catholic social agencies. The regime also began a propaganda campaign against the Church, declaring it to be an obstacle to social progress. It now became clear that the communist leadership was committed to the total eradication of religious influences in Polish life, but it completely miscalculated the popular mood.

The mass arrests and imprisonments turned the clergy into popular heroes and martyrs. Almost immediately upon his release from prison in 1956, Wyszyski undertook to make the Church the principal voice of the opposition. The hierarchy supported underground newspapers, erected new churches and seminaries, and mobilized the nation through a nine-year program of spiritual revitalization. It began as priests and laypeople renewed an oath sworn by the seventeenth-century King John Kazimierz's to serve God, the Virgin Mary, and to free the country from foreign occupiers. The political symbolism was transparent. By 1966, the year of the Church's millennium in Poland, Catholic teaching had firmly established the values of the modern Church as the clear choice of its citizens. More than 2000 catechetical centers had been established across the country by the 1970s, the number of priests had risen to 20,000 (double the total in 1945), and over 6000 young men were studying for holy orders.

Church leaders also joined forces with non-Catholic intellectuals, socialists, and members of the fledgling Solidarity movement to further strengthen opposition to communist state policies. Church facilities were placed at the disposal of political activists, despite the hostility of the government. The election of the Polish Pope John Paul II and his triumphal visit to Poland in 1979 provided enormous momentum for the nationalist and anticommunist agenda. By the mid-1980s, after a failed attempt at martial law, the government had become so estranged from its citizenry that General Wojciech Jaruzelski promised the Church unhampered cultural and religious autonomy if it would throw its prestige behind his economic reform program. But the hierarchy, with full support of John Paul II, refused to undercut the Solidarity activists by cooperating with the now thoroughly discredited regime. The brutal murder in 1984 of a popular Warsaw priest, Father Jerzy Popieluszko, by agents of the regime's security forces, further emboldened the hierarchy. The free elections of 1989 in Poland which catapulted Solidarity into political power and put an end to communist hegemony was as much a victory for the Roman Catholic Church as it was for the Solidarity political candidates. The Church had played a key role in defining Polish communism as a foreign imposition that only survived by threat of force.

To the surprise of many, however, the much more fluid and pluralist political environment of postcommunist Poland undermined the once dominant role of the Catholic Church in civil society. Triumphant as an opposition force, the Church now found its ascendancy contested by a variety of competing interests in the political arena. The episcopacy lobbied hard to influence the language of the new constitution, but its only victory here involved a constitutional call for a formal concordat between the Republic of Poland and the Church of Rome. This treaty was drawn up in 1993 and guaranteed the Church's institutional autonomy, established national holidays in keeping with the Church's liturgical calendar, protected Church-run religious schools, and called for compulsory religious instruction in all public nursery schools and kindergartens. Ratified in 1998, one year after the new national constitution was approved in a referendum, the concordat was a victory for the advocates of an ongoing linkage between religion and Polish national identity. Yet in spite of the massive outpouring of grief in Poland at the time of John Paul II's death in 2005, the Church no longer stood as the exclusive voice of the nation as it did under communism. A free press, the proliferation of political parties, opinion polls, NATO membership, and the ongoing quest for full integration into Western Europe have all complicated the once clearly defined role of religion in the public life of the country.

Catholicism at the crossroads

As the oldest and numerically strongest branch of Christianity, the Roman Catholic Church, with its global reach, its rich liturgical traditions, and its significant cultural achievements across many national borders, began the twenty-first century in an enviable position. But in the view of many critics, the achievements of Vatican II have been dissipated under the leadership of Popes Paul VI and John Paul II. Papal encyclicals and Church policies against contraception, the ordination of women, lay preaching, remarriage of divorced persons, and abortion (even in the case of incest or rape) alienated increasing numbers of communicants, especially in the developed West. One century after the papal declaration of infallibility, the influential Catholic priest Hans Kung published *Infallible?* (1970), a searching critique of papal absolutism. Within a decade of the book's publication, Kung's license to teach as a Catholic theologian was withdrawn by Rome, and the renewal of collegiality between popes and bishops was replaced by a return to centralized rule. A new Canon Law issued in 1983 diminished the status of ecumenical councils and conferences of Catholic bishops, while the voice of the laity was attenuated.

The result of these trends was the emergence of a deep chasm between the papacy and the laity that was most noticeable in Europe and the US. While highly respected for his erudition, his lifelong opposition to communism, and his deep sense of personal piety, John Paul's vision for the Church was out of step with the views of many Catholics. In the US, a 1992 Gallup poll indicated that the majority of Catholics favored freedom of choice regarding birth control, and supported the idea of married priests and the ordination of women, the election of bishops by the priests and people of the diocese, the admission of divorced persons into full communion, and the legalization of abortion. By the 1990s the number of candidates for the priesthood had sunk to record lows, and many parishes had to make do with part-time rectors and retired volunteer priests. And at the start of the new century the American Catholic communion was rocked by a series of clergy sex-abuse scandals that also revealed decades of official cover-ups by Church leaders. In the archdiocese of Boston, Massachusetts, Cardinal Bernard Law was forced to resign in 2003 after admitting that he had transferred alleged pedophile priests to new parishes rather than suspend them from office. Enormous legal settlements with victims' families damaged the Church's financial standing, while parishioner donations in affected dioceses plummeted. A sacred bond of trust between clergy and laity had been shattered, and the future seemed uncertain. When the College of Cardinals declined the opportunity to elect a pope from a developing country and instead chose an elderly Vatican insider (and a European) to succeed John Paul II in 2005, the administrative and doctrinal status quo was boldly affirmed, much to the chagrin of those calling for decisive reform.

Alternative religions in the West

In a recent work entitled *Why Religion Matters: The Fate of the Human Spirit in an Age of Disbelief* (2002), Huston Smith observed that "the finitude of mundane existence cannot satisfy the human heart completely." The decline of traditional institutional religions in the postwar West seemed to belie Smith's point, but the rapid growth of alternative religious movements suggested that the individual quest for the transcendent remained strong. Especially in the West, a wide variety of non-Christian and nonorthodox perspectives won the support of individuals who agreed with Smith that "there is within us – even in the blithest, most lighthearted among us – a fundamental dis-ease" which the fruits of modern science and material culture cannot cure. In the US, Eastern religions (especially Buddhism) gained new converts, especially after Asian immigration policies were relaxed in the 1960s. Islam took root in the African-American community during the same decade, while theistic and nontheistic spiritualist groups thrived in many urban settings. The acceptance of pluralism by mainstream Christian churches helped foster these new faiths. By the 1990s there were over 1000 Christian sects and 600 alternative religious bodies reaching out to American citizens, and a similar pattern of "privatized" religion unfolded in Europe. The quest for life's transcendent meaning appeared to remain strong in the postmodern West at the start of the new century, even while the influence of traditional religious institutions over the shape of belief and practice continued to decline.

CHALLENGES IN THE ISLAMIC WORLD

In contemporary discussions of religion and its impact on politics and broader culture, the faith of 1.2 billion of the world's inhabitants, Islam, inevitably takes center stage. Established in the early seventh century by the Prophet Muhammad, the adherents of Islam quickly built a powerful and wealthy empire that stretched from southern Spain to the northwest corner of India. By the year 1000 Islamic civilization, although politically divided, was unquestionably the most advanced in the world. Prestigious universities, scientific sophistication, commercial success, military dominance, high rates of literacy – Muslim culture boasted many remarkable achievements, and the faithful understandably associated their good fortune with the will of Allah. All of this changed after 1500 as the West, from unlikely origins, began its sudden climb to global ascendancy. By the early twentieth century not only was the Muslim world economically underdeveloped, politically unstable, and socially troubled, but the Western imperial powers, particularly Britain and France, had carved up the historic center of Islamic culture in the Middle East. The successor states to the once-great Ottoman empire – Syria, Lebanon, Jordan, and Palestine, were all creations of British and French imperialists who (according to critics) sought to divide and rule the Muslim world. Modern Egypt and Iraq were also compromised by their British connections. The 1948 "intrusion" of the State of Israel into the heart of the Muslim Middle East was the supreme affront against Islam, for many Muslims an illegitimate hangover from the age of Western imperialism. And when the combined Arab forces of the region were crushed by Israel in the Six Day War of 1967, with the resulting loss of the Sinai, the West Bank, Gaza, the Golan Heights, and Jerusalem, the fortunes of the once powerful Muslim Middle East reached their nadir.

Fast-paced modernization, urbanization and its attendant social dislocation, the widening gap between rich and poor, and the rise of authoritarian Muslim states ruled by Western-trained elites served only to exacerbate the tensions within Islam during the 1970s, 1980s, and 1990s. Despite its emergence as the world's fastest-growing faith tradition, the adherents of Islam, especially those living in the Middle East, continued to wrestle with a troubled history. The American historian Bernard Lewis has argued that at the core of the recent revolutionary wave in Islam "is a sense of humiliation: the feeling of a community of people accustomed to regard themselves as the sole custodians of God's truth, commanded by him to bring it to the infidels, who suddenly find themselves dominated and exploited by those same infidels." Increasingly in the late twentieth century, thoughtful Muslims sought a comprehensive explanation for Islam's predicament, and one deeply troubling answer has involved a searching critique of both modern secularism and Western-style political pluralism.

Islamism

Islam has always contained a strong theocratic dimension whereby temporal rule (*regnum*) was joined with leadership of the religious community (*sacerdotium*): This was the model of governance assumed by the Prophet Muhammad and it was continued for centuries under the caliphate. The caliphs served as the viceregents of Allah, leading armies against the unbelievers and forwarding God's rule in history. During the early twentieth century, many Muslim leaders identified the way forward with the creation of secular states complete with personal-status freedoms for all citizens. Mustafa Kemal Ataturk, founder of modern Turkey, was perhaps the most successful proponent of this Western-based paradigm. But with over 55 Muslim countries in the world by the close of the twentieth century, representing a wide variety of languages, tribes, and cultures, it is not surprising that the modernization model was not embraced wholeheartedly, especially in countries where poverty was widespread and social inequalities great. The inaugural Muslim fusion of political, military, and religious leadership was brought to the foreground during the late twentieth century by Islamists (also known as fundamentalists and Islamic militants), a small minority of Muslims who, unaffiliated with any Muslim state, located the source of Islam's difficulties with all things Western.

Calling for the restoration of government that would rule in strict accordance with the teachings of the Quran and Sharia (law based on the Quran), Islamists condemned the dominance of Western culture and opposed all Muslim rulers who embraced the values of the West. In addition to their denunciation of secularism, Islamists also rejected modern nationalism and patriotism as alien concepts, calling instead for the restoration of a universal Muslim community, or *ummah*, under one just ruler. Holy war against those who stood in the way of this restoration – be they infidel or coreligionist – became for Islamists their highest calling. Deploring the erosion of religion in modern public life and the adoption of secular political and cultural values, they looked to the distant past for their model of the proper polity, to the age of the Prophet Muhammad and his immediate successors.

Late twentieth-century Islamists recalled that Muhammad was not only a prophet and teacher, but a soldier who took up arms and led men into battle, and on this ground a small number of Islamists advocated the use of violence to further their vision of the primitive theocratic state. The Egyptian Sayyid Qutb emerged as the leading spokesperson for this extremist perspective during the 1950s. Secularizing Muslim rulers, and those who forged alliances with the West, as did the absolutist rulers of Saudi Arabia in the 1970s, were viewed as dupes and apostates from the faith who were to be rooted out and destroyed. Ironically, the means to achieving the good society often involved the employment of the very tools of the modern West – technology, communications, weapons – that were allegedly at the root of the problem for true Muslims. Whatever the intellectual inconsistencies, Islamists offered their followers a sense of group identity anchored in the memory of past greatness, a world that existed only so long as Islam rejected the culture of the infidel, the civilization of the modern West.

Islamist revolution in Iran

Since the 1950s, political Islam has been the source of numerous reform movements, but perhaps none was as important as the 1979 Islamist revolution in Iran which toppled a Western-backed monarchy and replaced it with a rigid theocracy. The spiritual leader of the revolution, Ayatollah Ruhollah Khomeini, imposed a new Islamic social and political order on a state that had adopted a crash program in Western-style modernization under the leadership of an authoritarian monarch who was closely allied to the US.

Shah Mohammad Reza Pahlavi came to power in 1941, after the British and Americans forced his father, the founder of the regime, from the throne for his pro-Nazi sentiments. After the war the youthful Shah, fearful of growing Soviet support for the Iranian Communist Party, allied himself closely with the US. American and British interests dominated the Iranian oil fields, and when the reformist prime minister Mohammad Mosaddeq challenged the Shah by calling for the nationalization of Iranian oil production facilities in 1953, the American CIA orchestrated a military coup that ousted the prime minister and restored full authority to the monarch. For the next quarter-century, the authoritarian Shah remained a stalwart American ally in the Cold War, providing valuable oil resources to the Western powers and undertaking a rapid and erratic modernization program. The Shah's government rewarded foreign investors and well-placed Iranian businessmen, but in general the wealth generated from the sale of oil did not improve the lot of small merchants, landless laborers, or rural peasants. Spectacular infrastructure projects in the capital boosted the Shah's international reputation as a modernizer, but had little resonance in the Iranian countryside. Like his father, the monarch emphasized the pre-Islamic Persian history of the country, and his indifference to Islamic traditions infuriated the ayatollahs (religious experts) and the mullahs who led local prayer groups and who enjoyed broad support among the common people. In the view of conservative religious leaders, American economic, military, and cultural penetration would continue to undermine the integrity of Muslim culture so long as the Pahlavi dynasty remained in power.

During the 1960s and 1970s, opposition to the monarchy grew on a number of fronts – unemployed peasants who had migrated to the capital city of Tehran in search of work; middle-class nationalists who resented both the presence of thousands of foreign military and technical advisors; critics of the royal family's lavish lifestyle; and especially Shiite clerics who claimed that the Shah had betrayed Islam and the values of traditional culture. Throughout most of this period opponents of the regime were hunted down by the government's dreaded secret police, whose reputation for brutality was well deserved. But in the mid-1970s oil revenues declined and inflation soared. As the Nixon administration continued to sell sophisticated weaponry to the increasingly unpopular regime, ordinary Iranians yearned for a new direction in politics. In early 1978 student street protests in Tehran turned bloody when government forces open fire. By October, nationwide strikes and demonstrations were organized around the country, with participants demanding that the Shah step down. In December a protest in the capital drew over one million participants. Unprepared for such widespread opposition from across a wide political spectrum, the ailing Shah fled Iran in January 1979.

Before leaving Tehran, the monarch had appointed a civilian government under the direction of a moderate prime minister, Shahpour Baktiar. But on February 1, 1979, the militant cleric Ayatollah Ruhollah Khomeini returned home to a hero's welcome after almost 15 years of exile in Turkey, Iraq, and finally France. This inveterate critic of the Pahlavi dynasty and its Westernizing policies had skillfully employed modern technology in order to reach his audience. In the lead up to the revolution, tape cassettes of Khomeini's lectures were distributed through a network of mosques and sympathetic Islamic groups. Through these tapes, in extensive interviews with the Western television media, and in direct phone conversations with his leading supporters inside Iran, the Ayatollah framed the debate in terms of a rich Islamic tradition at war with the poisonous influence of the secularized and debauched West. By the end of March a popular referendum led to the formation of an Islamic republic with Khomeini wielding final authority over elected officials. Secular leaders of the revolution who had called for the establishment of a liberal republic were quickly eliminated. After the Shah was admitted to an American hospital suffering from the final stages of leukemia, enraged university students (with Khomeini's blessing) took control of the American embassy in Tehran and seized 68 hostages in violation of international law. Fifty-two of the Americans were held prisoner for over a year and were not released until President Carter left office on January 20, 1981. By that date the Khomeini-dominated government was firmly in power, applying strict Islamic law to all aspects of life and even erecting its own secret police force that became as fearsome as its Pahlavi predecessor. From an American perspective, the hostage crisis defined the nature of the newest international threat: Islamic terrorism.

Declaring itself to be the rule of the those who had been liberated from "exploitation and imperialist domination," the new clerical leadership in Iran saw itself as setting the precedent for Islamic revolution throughout the Muslim world. The Soviet Union took small comfort in the triumph of the ayatollahs, for the latter coordinated their hatred for capitalist democracy with a full-scale indictment of godless communism. Khomeini rejected the established international order, excoriating the US as the "Great Satan" and dismissing the Soviet Union as the "Lesser Satan" (Israel became "the Little Satan" in this lexicon). And he called for the immediate export of the Islamic revolution and the establishment of a world order shaped by Muslim law as distilled from the Quran. In particular, Khomeini lashed out at Egypt's President Anwar Sadat as a secularizing apostate for agreeing to peace with Israel. Similar rhetorical venom was directed against Saddam Hussein of Iraq. Fearful that Iraq's majority Shiite population would rally to Khomeini's Islamist theocracy, the brutal Iraqi dictator launched a massive military strike against Iran in 1980. Hussein hoped that a quick victory over his non-Arab neighbor would elevate him to a position in the Arab world similar to that enjoyed by Egypt's Nasser during the 1950s. Instead, an eight-year bloody war of attrition ensued. When highly motivated Iranian troops, animated by the ideals of *jihad* or Islamic holy war, pushed the invaders back and took to the offensive on Iraqi soil in 1982, the French, Americans, and Soviets began sending military and intelligence support to Hussein's regime. Before the war ended in stalemate in 1988, some 450,000 Iranians and Iraqis had died and another 750,000 had been injured.

The decision by the Reagan administration to offer assistance to the murderous dictator Hussein came within the context of additional signals that Islamism had emerged as a serious threat to the stability of Western-oriented Muslim states. In November 1979 a group of 400 militants seized control of the Grand Mosque in Mecca, holiest of Muslim sites, and announced the downfall of the Saudi monarchy. The government quashed the rebellion, but not before Saudi credibility was seriously undermined. In Egypt, long a major recipient of US aid and recently at peace with Israel, Islamic militants in league with dissident army officers gunned down President Anwar Sadat of Egypt in September 1981. And to the south in Sudan, the military government imposed rigid Islamic law on the entire population in 1983, a move that led to a brutal campaign of persecution against the country's minority Christian population. And that same year a US marine base was bombed in the city of Beirut, Lebanon. Two-hundred and forty-one soldiers died in that suicide attack, and evidence suggested that the group responsible for the suicide bombing, the Lebanon-based Hizbullah (party of God) terrorist organization, was receiving financial support from Iran.

Egypt

The roots of modern Islamism in Egypt can be traced to the founding of the Society of Muslim Brotherhood in 1928, but it was under the secular–nationalist Nasser regime that the movement intensified. Although he saw himself as the leader of a pan-Arab movement, Nasser distanced himself from the theocratic tendency in Islam and wished to restrict religion to the private sphere. He imprisoned, tortured, and executed leading members of the Brotherhood, including Sayyid Qutb, who had called for the forceful overthrow of the president and the immediate establishment of an Islamic system of government. But after Egypt's humiliating defeat in the 1967 war with Israel, Nasser's secular and socialist regime was discredited in the eyes of many citizens. His successor Anwar Sadat attempted to adopt a precarious middle path with respect to the Islamist minority. On the one hand he adopted the mantle of Islam by emphasizing the Sharia basis of Egyptian law, but he also banned religious political parties and reached a landmark peace agreement with Israel in 1977. Economic activity did not keep pace with Egypt's burgeoning population under Sadat, exacerbating economic tensions between the rich and the growing ranks of the poor, and together with government inefficiencies and widespread corruption, the Muslim Brotherhood and other Islamist groups gained additional support. It was one of these groups, an alliance of civilian, military, and religious discontents calling itself "Islamic Holy War," that was behind the assassination of the president in 1981.

During the 1980s and 1990s, Islamist groups also targeted members of Egypt's Coptic Christian minority and foreign tourists, the latter an important source of revenue for the country. The authoritarian government of President Hosni Mubarak waged a constant struggle against Islamic militants, arresting terror suspects and subjecting them to military trials that drew the ire of international human rights groups. Despite the crackdown, it seemed unlikely that the appeal of Islamism would decline as long as the state (heavily dependent on American aid) was unable to fully address the problem of widespread poverty and its attendant social dislocation. Even with the support of the armed forces and the enormous annual infusion of American dollars, Mubarak's Egypt faced deep challenges at the start of the new century. In the words of historian N. J. Demerath, "one has the distinct sense of the cultural core dissolving." In Egypt today "There is polarization along almost every conceivable continuum."

Islam in the contemporary West

The atrocities of September 11, 2001, committed by terrorists in the name of Islam, made the lives of millions of Muslims in the West especially complicated. In the late 1990s Islam became the fastest growing religion both in North America and in Europe, and it took its place as the second largest religion in France, Belgium, Holland, and Germany. High birthrates indicated that Islam would soon overtake Judaism as the second largest religion in the US. In addition to the social pressures associated with membership in a faith tradition that is claimed by men of violence, Muslims in the West wrestled with questions of identity in states where Islamic law has no place, and where church and state are officially separate. In 2004 the French government, for example, banned female headscarves in the public schools, claiming that the apparel was in fact a religious symbol. The decision pitted the secular state against the claims of tradition, and the political row that followed only further divided public opinion regarding the willingness of more recent immigrants to assimilate. Clearly the adjustment to a pluralist culture, especially in light of a long history of conflict between Christianity and Islam, was complicated. Myths and stereotypes on both sides continued to inform popular discourse, while Muslims struggled to interpret their tradition in light of a social and political milieu that is condemned vociferously by Islamists. As the number of Muslims living in the West grew, the transition to a view of the faith that is restricted to private life proved especially problematic. Western liberal conceptions of human rights, women's rights, and the status of religious minorities often stood at odds with inherited patterns of belief. And the fundamental question of whether one could be a true Muslim in societies where secular law was supreme remained unanswered.

INDIAN AND JEWISH CONFESSIONAL POLITICS

The rise of Hindu nationalism

Under the leadership of Prime Minister Nehru, the Congress Party of India worked toward the formation of a secular, non-sectarian democracy. While the overwhelming majority (82 percent) of Indians were Hindu, the government was dedicated to embracing the minority Muslim (12 percent) and Sikh (2 percent) populations on equal terms, and this was reflected in the Indian constitution of 1951. Muslims had lived alongside Hindus in India for over 1000 years, but during the first half of the twentieth century the level of sectarian conflict between the two communities had intensified. In part the responsibility lay with the British; always suspicious of the Congress elite, imperial authorities had encouraged sectarian politics by allowing "communal" representation and separate electorates. Muhammad Ali Jinnah's use of religious differences to build support for the creation of an independent Muslim state further aggravated tensions. The sectarian horrors associated with partition in 1947 brought Hindu–Muslim relations to the breaking point; thus it was important to Nehru that a new spirit of inclusion be cultivated as an essential prerequisite to nation building. Gandhi's assassination at the hands of a Hindu fanatic who believed that the Mahatma was indulging Muslims pointed to the urgency of the government's task.

Post-partition India was home to the world's fourth largest Muslim population, and Congress politicians were determined to show the world that the creation of a separate state of Pakistan as a refuge for Indian followers of Islam had been unnecessary. Early signs were encouraging, but in 1956, when Muslims were exempted from a civil code respecting marriage, succession, and maintenance, conservative Hindus voiced strong objection, charging that Nehru's government was making indefensible concessions to particular groups solely on religious grounds. The legislation in question guaranteed Indian women specific rights of inheritance, together with alimony and the opportunity to appeal in cases of divorce. Under the government-approved Muslim personal law, however, Muslim men could take up to four wives and enjoyed easy access to divorce. Muslim women, on the other hand, were denied any inheritance or alimony claims. Tensions came to a head 30 years after the legislation was in place, when the Indian Supreme Court ruled in the "Shah Bano" case that a 75-year-old Muslim woman divorced by her husband did indeed deserve alimony. Traditionalist Muslim men were outraged at this direct assault on what they defined as one of their religious prerogatives. When the Congress Party under Prime Minister Rajiv Gandhi quickly passed a new law restoring the Muslim personal law, Hindu nationalist parties, including the Bharatiya Janata Party (BJP; Indian People's Party), capitalized on the growing anti-Congress sentiment by condemning the legislation.

Ethnoreligious communal politics then turned violent as Hindu nationalist parties threw their support behind a call for the destruction of a Muslim mosque located on the site of what Hindus claimed was the birthplace of the Hindu god Ram. A national movement to rebuild the temple at Ayodhya in the northern province of Uttar Pradesh was undertaken in the late 1980s, with marches, donations of money and prospective temple bricks, and much angry rhetoric signaling the recrudescence of religious politics. The leader of the regional BJP even embarked on a month-long "pilgrimage" in a chariot from Gujarat to Ayodhya in a highly publicized effort to remind the Hindu majority of the cruelty and rapacity of earlier Muslim rulers. Regional Islamization campaigns in neighboring Pakistan and in Iran during the 1980s added to the Hindu–Muslim tensions in India, and provided the BJP with an opportunity to stress India's Hindu majority character. In the national elections of 1991, the BJP campaigned on a strident Hindu identity platform and won control of state government in Uttar Pradesh, the country's most populous state. Finally, in December of 1992 Hindu mobs attacked and destroyed the mosque at Ayodhya, precipitating some of the worst communal fighting since independence. In the wake of the violence, which claimed thousands of lives, the national government was obliged to declare martial law in Uttar Pradesh, temporarily stripping the BJP of its power and plunging the country into a crisis of identity from which it has yet to emerge.

After the BJP lost control of Uttar Pradesh and three other states in the November 1993 elections, the party adopted a more mainstream platform, criticizing Congress for corruption and inefficiency and reaching out for the first time to lower castes and dalits. From a mere two seats in the lower house of parliament in 1980, BJP candidates won a remarkable 178 seats in 1998. And in the fall of 1999 the BJP joined with a number of allied parties to secure a strong majority in the lower house. The party's pragmatic leader, Atal Bihari Vajpayee, became the first Indian prime minister who was not associated with the Congress party. And while the BJP moderated its Hindu emphasis in order to maintain the support of its parliamentary allies, Vajpayee continued to appeal to Hindu national pride in political speeches. The ascendancy of a political party that openly celebrated "Hindutva" or Hindu-ness at the start of the twenty-first century suggested that the future of Indian secularism was by no means assured. In February and March 2002, unprovoked attacks against Muslims in the state of Gujarat resulted in the deaths of over 2000 people, raising new questions about the ability, and willingness, of the BJP-led coalition to protect religious minorities.

Sikh separatism

In the prosperous northwest region of Punjab, Sikh separatists tested the resolve of the national government in the 1980s. Founded in the late fifteenth century by a Hindu mystic who embraced monotheism and opposed the caste system, subsequent leaders of the new faith were subject to intermittent persecution by their Muslim overlords. In response the Sikhs adopted a strong martial tradition, arming themselves and resisting their oppressors. Under British rule Sikh martial prowess was much respected: Sikhs held important positions in the armed forces and civil administration, a favored status that was lost after independence. Still, India's 16 million Sikhs continued to enjoy, on average, a higher standard of living than most citizens. Originally the movement for an autonomous Punjabi-speaking Sikh province did not highlight religious differences and was in line with the government's policy in the 1950s to reorganize Indian states along linguistic lines.

Sikh grievances were numerous, and when militant extremists rose to the forefront of the autonomy movement during the late 1970s and 1980s, the government of Indira Gandhi took military action to root out the ringleaders. In June 1984 troops attacked the Golden Temple in Amritsar, sacred temple of the Sikh religion, on the grounds that militants were storing weapons there. Almost 600 people died in the assault, an action which infuriated Sikh public opinion and led directly to the assassination of Mrs. Gandhi by two of her own Sikh bodyguards in October 1984. The assassination led to vicious reprisals against Sikhs in the capital and other cities, and thousands of paramilitary police forces were dispatched to Punjab in an effort to quell Sikh militancy. During the final decade of the century, calls for a separate country diminished in intensity, but continued to threaten the integrity of democratic pluralism in India.

Israel and Judaism

The establishment of the State of Israel in 1948, its admission to the UN one year later, and success in three wars against neighboring Arab states (1948–9, 1967, and 1973) gave to many Israelis a firm sense of no longer being dependent upon the benevolence of others. The state became the guarantor of the faith, its protector in a hostile world. There was no official state religion in Israel, but obviously Judaism was at the core of national existence since the establishment of the modern polity in 1948. Although the modern Israeli state was a postwar creation, most Jewish Israelis think of their small country in terms of the reestablishment of an ancient homeland that was destroyed by the Romans some 2000 years ago. In the long and sorrowful interregnum, diaspora Jews maintained a belief that their historic homeland would someday be restored. Prayers for a return to Jerusalem became a part of the Sabbath liturgy, while ongoing prejudice and persecution reminded European Jews that their security was always fragile and dependent upon the sufferance of outsiders.

At the time of Israel's establishment in 1948, the population of Jews and Arabs was roughly equal at 650,000 to 700,000. The country's declaration of independence promised "freedom of religion, conscience, language, education, and culture" to all inhabitants, and in large measure this has been realized. But in the aftermath of a war with neighboring Arab states in 1948, the character of the country's population changed dramatically. Many Arab residents of Palestine (Palestinians) either fled Israel or were expelled at the end of hostilities. New Jewish immigrants from Arab states in North Africa, and from communist Eastern Europe, when combined with Arab departures, transformed the new state into an overwhelmingly Jewish polity.

Zionists had conceived of the state as a sanctuary for Jews, and during the second half of the century, thanks to an admissions policy favoring Jews, new immigrants arrived from many nations, including Ethiopia and, after 1991, the former Soviet Union. At the close of the twentieth century, 80 percent of Israel's total population of 5.5 million citizens were Jews, while 800,000 were Muslim Arabs and another 150,000 were Christian Arabs. Hebrew became the official language of the country, while Judaism informed the calendar, official ceremonies, and state functions. Despite this numerical imbalance, the Israeli government provided funding for non-Jewish religious groups, including support for Muslim and Christian schools. Traditional Muslim and Christian days of rest were respected and issues concerning family law were regulated by the individual traditions.

Still, for many Arabs in the Middle East, as we saw in Chapter 3, Israel represented an imperialist imposition, an attempt to frustrate legitimate Arab nationalism. But while the language of the Arab–Israeli conflict often betrayed a strong religious divide, the fundamental issue remained land and sovereignty. Thus questions of religious freedom, or the place of religion in public life, were rarely at the center of the conflict. Within Israel, however, the role of religion in the state emerged as a controversial issue almost from the moment of independence, and it remained at the forefront of debate throughout the second half of the twentieth century.

On one level Judaism was essential to successful statehood; it enabled people from disparate geographical roots to bond together into modern nationhood under the banner of a common religious identity. But most of Israel's Zionist founders were comfortable with the European secular tradition and committed themselves to the formation not of a Jewish state but rather a state for exile Jews. They were uncomfortable with the small ultra-orthodox community in their midst, largely because these citizens believed that the state should be based on sacred Jewish tradition, enforcing biblical prescriptions on the entire population. The government made some early concessions to these fundamentalists, agreeing to support Jewish religious schools, affirming Saturday as the traditional day of rest for Jews, enforcing Jewish dietary rules in state institutions, and exempting men from military service if they were enrolled in full-time religious study. But these steps did not assuage a community which was loath to make any accommodation with the forces of secularization.

The initial hope of the founders was that the appeal of ultra-orthodoxy would wane as material conditions improved for average Israelis. But the forecast was inaccurate. By the end of the century almost 10 percent of the Jewish population embraced ultra-orthodoxy, and their political parties became important power brokers in national politics, often courted by the major parties to form coalition governments. In return for their support, important policy concessions were made to the religious parties. Not the least of these involved the building of settlements in lands occupied after Israeli's victory in the 1967 war. Long considered by religious parties as part of Israel's ancient heritage, the lands upon which settlements were constructed served as an impediment to the peace process. Palestinians who opposed these policies were vilified and rebuffed, and even those secular Jews who stood against the settlements were labeled as invoking rights language that was alien to traditional Judaism. In 1994 Prime Minister Yitzhak Rabin was assassinated by a religious zealot who later confessed that he committed the murder because the Prime Minister had agreed to return sacred land (settlements) for peace. He claimed that under Jewish law, Rabin was a tyrant who deserved to be killed. Many ultra-orthodox regard their control over biblical land to be in accord with the will of God, and any compromise was the equivalent of apostasy. According to one recent observer, the current debate over the sacred status of land threatens to undermine the very fabric of Israeli democracy. In 2004 Prime Minister Ariel Sharon earned the displeasure of the conservative religious parties when he announced a unilateral Israeli withdrawal from Gaza. The action forced the relocation of a small number of Jewish settlers who insisted on their right to remain in occupied lands. By the end of 2004 the opposition within elements of his own party had become so strong that Sharon reached out to the Labour leader, Shimon Peres, in an effort to form a Likud–Labour coalition that would carry out the withdrawal.

EAST ASIAN TRANSITIONS
China's crucible

The Chinese imperial government had always claimed the right to control religious establishments, and on more than a few occasions had taken military action to suppress religious expression. In the mid-nineteenth century, for example, a government crackdown on the Christian-influenced Taiping movement precipitated a devastating civil war that lasted for over 12 years and claimed the lives of millions of Chinese. And after the collapse of the imperial order in 1911, radical republicans attacked a number of Confucian, Buddhist, and Daoist temples on the grounds that traditional religion had contributed to China's weakness in the face of Western imperialism. After the triumph of Mao Zedong's Red Army in 1949, the first constitution of the People's Republic of China acknowledged religious freedom, and in 1954 a Religious Affairs Bureau was established to serve as the government's agent in dealing with religious groups.

Despite the constitutional guarantees, however, increasing restrictions were imposed on traditional religious expression. Foreign missionaries were expelled, and their property was transferred to government enterprises. During the 1950s a sustained effort to reshape education was undertaken in order to excise all traces of spiritual or religious training. Private domestic worship and the discreet observance of annual feasts were not proscribed, however, since the communists were convinced that traditional belief would atrophy as material conditions improved under communism. In place of Confucianism, Buddhism, and Daoism, the Marxists erected a new form of civil religion, complete with conversion experiences for the true believer, a body of ideas that gave unity and comprehension to an otherwise chaotic world, a personality cult in the person of the Party leader, a myth of inevitable progress signaled by the creation of a communal and equalitarian society, and a call for orthodoxy and total commitment.

Beginning with the Cultural Revolution in 1966, a brutal assault on traditional religions was launched under Mao's direction. Antireligious zealots from the Red Guard fanned out across the countryside in order to extinguish all remnants of "feudalism." Monastic lands and the endowments belonging to lineage halls were expropriated, while monks and priests were sent to labor camps in the countryside. Peasants were forced to surrender their most precious sacred ritual objects, while religious scholarship was banned. The systematic persecution continued until Mao's death in 1976, when the government finally put a stop to the excesses. At the Eleventh Party Congress in 1978, freedom of religious belief was restored, and public religious services at temples, churches, and mosques were resumed the following year. A new constitution adopted in 1982 included an article on religious freedom that provided protection for Buddhists, Daoists, Muslims, and Protestant and Catholic Christians. All other religious sects continued to be suppressed, however, and the freedoms permitted the mainline religions were restricted to formal places of worship. Religious schools, hospitals, radio stations, and other social institutions remained illegal. For the government, the concession to traditional religion was necessary "because the people's consciousness lags behind social realities." Still committed to the notion that "Religion will eventually disappear from human history," the Party conceded that administrative decrees and other coercive measures were not sufficient to wipe out religious habits.

Tradition and innovation in Japan

Although the Emperor Hirohito was allowed to remain on the throne after World War II, he was obliged by the Americans to publicly renounce his claim to divinity. Shintoism survived the war, as did Buddhism, but both had to overcome their complicity in the rise of the militaristic government of the 1930s and 1940s. Japan's rapid economic rebound from the catastrophe of the war led many intellectuals to declare that the traditional religious impulse had withered in the midst of material abundance. The process of secularization that characterized Western Europe after 1945 allegedly had the same corrosive impact in Japanese society. In the midst of unprecedented affluence, however, the appeal of local Shinto shrines, each one housing deities that are integral to the well-being of the locality, remained strong. Wedding rituals and ceremonies acknowledging the birth of a child, where the deity is petitioned by resident Shinto priests to provide health and success, continued to take place at local shrines. More than 100,000 Shinto shrines served the population at the start of the twenty-first century, each one providing the visitor a forum for ritual activities that complement personal devotion.

In addition to the mainline Shinto and Buddhist traditions, a vast array of "New Religions" emerged in late twentieth-century Japan. By the early 1990s some 230,000 sects were officially registered with the national government, and one-fifth of the Japanese people identified with one or more of them. Many of the new religions emphasized their effectiveness in solving everyday human problems, especially those involving interpersonal relations and economics. The more successful religions established their own schools, hospitals, and residential communities, appealing especially to members of the middle class and small business owners. Embracing one of the new religions did not require a fundamental shift of approach to the sacred, since they affirmed the spiritual value of traditional Japanese virtues such as loyalty, selflessness, filial piety, and ritual.

WOMEN, RIGHTS, AND RELIGION

The widespread discrimination that energized the feminist movement in the West during the 1960s had important implications for religious thought and practice. While most feminists concentrated on economic, social, and political inequalities, the history of oppression faced by women in religious institutions was not ignored. In fact many feminists argued that a wide range of religious texts and practices had for centuries buttressed a patriarchal order that valued men before women, in effect giving divine sanction to larger systems of inequality. In both the Old and New Testaments, for example, an anti-woman temper is adopted in a variety of passages, while leading figures in the medieval Church instinctively assumed the inferiority of women. St. Jerome, for example, spoke of women as "the devil's gateway" and "the first deserter of God's law," while Thomas Aquinas referred to women as necessary helpmates who did not enjoy the same intellectual potential as men. Images of God as male and the parallel association of divinity with maleness had for centuries relegated women to separate and supporting roles in most religious traditions.

Many Christian feminists argued that the privileging of men on religious grounds served to embed and legitimize the legal, occupational, and familial oppression of women in societies around the world. This powerful critique of patriarchalism at the heart of the world's major religions led some women to reject their faith traditions, while others identified an original message of human liberation that was later distorted by male leaders. Changes in the historical profession helped to bring about a healthy reassessment of gender roles. Beginning in the 1970s, for example, medieval scholars began to write about the important function of women in the early Church as missionaries and teachers. They explored the work of highly regarded female mystics and abbesses, while feminist theologians began to consider an inclusive vocabulary that spoke of God as neither male nor female.

This last issue had major implications for the controversy over the ordination of women. Normally based on the belief that women cannot represent God, that their value as spiritual directors is permanently compromised by biology, advocates for the ordination of women argued that biblical passages against women's ordination can no more represent Christ's intentions than its toleration of slavery does. By the early twentieth century the Congregationalists, Universalists, Unitarians, and Adventists ordained women, but it was not until the 1980s that the mainline Protestant churches followed this important lead. The Roman Catholic and Orthodox churches, however, held fast to the notion that the maleness of Christ prohibits the admission of women into the priesthood. Mary's role in the Catholic and Orthodox traditions as obedient servant and intermediary on behalf of sinners was targeted by feminists as legitimizing patriarchal domination. In the 1980s a new emphasis on Mary as co-redemptrix appealed to some Christian feminists who wished to affirm the equality that they discovered at the core of Christian teaching. Their efforts bore fruit, at least within Protestantism, as women assumed important leadership positions both on lay councils and within the ordained ministry.

Women and Islam

The Islamic world remained the most resistant of the great faith traditions to equal rights for women during the postwar era. Polygamy, restrictions on education and employment opportunities, sex segregation in public life, the *talag* or universal male right to divorce – these and many other elements of patriarchy continued to shape the dominant culture, especially in the Arabian peninsula. Speaking of Islam's postwar relationship within the forces of modernization, one leading scholar has observed that "In no area was the force of tradition felt more strongly and the clash of civilizations more apparent than that of the status and roles of women."

Although the Quran teaches that all humans are equal before God in terms of their religious obligations and moral duties, the sacred text of Islam also assumes that women and men perform different functions in the family and in society. The patriarchal elements of Islamic teaching are clearly evident in the reservation of the "public" function for men. Historically, the principal role of women was in the domestic sphere, providing for the household and for the education of children. The assignment or subordination of women to the private sphere was reflected in the judicial system, where the testimony of a women was worth only half that of a man, while male inheritance was double that of a female sibling. Polygamy or plural marriage, where a man could take up to as many as four wives, was also permitted by the Quran, provided that a husband supported each spouse equally. The comparative ease by which men could secure a unilateral divorce and leave an ex-spouse without material support, long a tradition within Islam, also highlighted women's subordinate status.

In contrast to medieval Christianity, Islam was innovative in providing women the right to contract her own marriage, receive and control a dower, and inherit property. But over the centuries male-dominated Islamic societies, and the male religious scholars (*ulema*) who interpreted the law, undermined these first principles. Beginning in the 1970s, as the "Islamic solution" to the challenges of modernity began to gather strength, the restoration of Islamic law (Sharia) had direct and problematic implications for women. They were identified as the principal bearers of culture, the protectors and teachers of children, and as such were viewed by men as needing special protection from the poisonous influence of the West.

In the 1970s, the oil wealth generated in the Arab Gulf states contributed to the strengthening of the cult of domesticity, as an abundance of cheap foreign labor from northern-tier, non-oil-producing states made it less likely that women would be needed in the work force. In Saudi Arabia, for example, the segregation of women and men was enforced throughout society. Under the official Wahhabi interpretation of Islam, women were required to be fully covered and veiled in black robes when in public, and social contact with men was restricted to close relatives. Although, beginning in the 1970s, they were allowed to pursue higher education and enter the workforce, women were segregated here as well. Some companies went so far as the create "family sections" where women could work separately and receive directions from foremen over the telephone. Even highly successful businesswomen were obliged to depend on their male relatives when dealing with government agencies. In the 1970s it became illegal for Saudi women to marry non-Saudi men, and even exogamous marriages outside tribal groupings were discouraged. Transportation remained a challenge for professional women since they are were not allowed to drive automobiles. In 1990 a small group of women violated the ban on female driving and took their family autos to the center of Riyadh. Arrested and interrogated, they were subsequently released to their male guardians. In the wake of this small incident, religious conservatives harshly criticized the government for its close relations with the infidel West. Already in the 1980s the religious police began raiding female businesses and services in search of "immoral behavior," and even succeeded in banning the importation of dolls. Only in 2001 were Saudi women issued their own identity cards; prior to this they were registered on the cards of their brother or father.

The seclusion (purdah) and veiling of women became one of the hallmarks of Islamist regimes in the late twentieth century, with female supporters of these states insisting that their attention to religious detail is in fact a liberating rejection of hegemonic Western cultural forms. The most extreme form of segregation was imposed by the Taliban regime that came to power in Afghanistan in the mid-1990s. Under the Taliban, girls' schools were closed, women were ordered to be fully covered when appearing in public, and female employment outside of the home was banned. Similar antifemale mandates were evident in Pakistan, Algeria, and Sudan. Islamic feminists argued that the return to these harsh traditional forms nullified the principles of human equality embodied in the Quran, but their voices were largely ignored. By the close of the century, a resurgence of traditional family law in many Muslim states meant that Western conceptions of human rights and personal liberties were rejected, and the subjection of women defended under the heading of orthodoxy.

ANCIENT FAITH AND MODERN VALUES

For the great historic faith traditions, the development of postwar consumer culture, the privileging of technological innovation and scientific inquiry, the intensification of rights-based social movements, and the proliferation of sovereign nation-states, all challenged the assumption that temporal existence was but one temporary component of a larger reality. In response to these developments, some religious leaders struggled to elicit contemporary strategies from ancient texts, affirming that greater social engagement and support for human equality were obligatory. They were prepared to allow for the reinterpretation of ancient texts to meet contemporary social and economic needs. As Christianity became a predominantly non-Western religion, the social gospel received new emphasis in developing countries. And as Muslims migrated to the West, the fact of religious pluralism and its privatization obliged a reconsideration of Islam as a total way of life.

A more unyielding response involved the search for "fundamentals" and the imposition of a lifestyle based on sacred texts. In the Christian tradition, fundamentalists accepted the Enlightenment's separation of church and state and worked instead to influence public policy through the political process. In the US, the views of conservative Christians were ignored by political candidates at their peril, and while candidates with an explicitly religious agenda fared poorly at the polls, both major political parties felt obliged to address issues of concern to activist Christian groups. In South Asia, Hindu Nationalist candidates scored important victories at the regional and national levels during the 1980s and 1990s, while in Israel the election of a conservative Likud coalition in 1997 signaled the arrival of orthodox religious parties to national prominence, immensely complicating relations with Israel's Arab neighbors. In the Muslim world, modern fundamentalism meant the affirmation of theocracy where every compartment of life was regulated by the injunctions of the sacred text.

Within all of the great traditions, the "return to fundamentals" invariably translated into the affirmation of patriarchal norms and a concomitant resistance to female equality. The alleged breakdown in morals that fundamentalists identified as the central crisis of modern society was loosely associated with notions of sexual equality that weakened both the family and undermined the proper socialization of children. Adherence to tradition, variously defined but always including some restriction on women's roles, became the rallying cry of fundamentalists who denounced the corrosive effects of modern secular society. Unwilling to accept the modern notion that religions are conditioned by time and place, fundamentalists attacked the postmodern vocabulary that "infected" everything from art and architecture to historical and literary studies. The notion that texts have no absolute meaning, or that definitions of truth are no more than reflections of extant power structures, exasperated the fundamentalists and troubled believers whose faith was predicated upon the reality of universal, discoverable truths.

In the debate between modernizers and fundamentalists, the relevance and immediacy of the sacred to contemporary life was never in doubt. Thus the alleged connection between secularization and a waning of the religious impulse appeared tenuous at best.

Even in those countries where traditional, institutional religions were reporting declining attendance and financial support, new movements emerged to win the backing of women and men who continued to place religion at the very center of their lives. At the beginning of the twenty-first century, the vibrancy of the great historic faith traditions, together with the rise of new religious and spiritual movements, suggested that the intersection between civil society and the sacred would remain dynamic, providing moral guideposts for both those who reject, and those who celebrate, the values of modern material culture.

CONCLUSION: HOPE AND MISGIVING IN THE NEW CENTURY

The post-World War II tension between centralized socialism and market capitalism, between communist authoritarianism and Western-style democracy, ended peacefully during the final decade of the twentieth century. In the interim the world's population more than doubled from 2.5 billion to nearly 6 billion. For four decades the fate of these billions was inexorably linked to the bilateral relations of the two superpowers. With the collapse of the Soviet Union and its satellite states, the costly and dangerous global rivalry between the Cold War opponents was resolved – and the threat of cataclysmic nuclear exchange removed. Regional conflicts between the surrogates of each side in the larger conflict lapsed as military and economic aid decreased. As a new era of cooperation between the erstwhile enemies began, a multipolar international system, led by an increasingly unified Europe but including emerging powers in South and East Asia, quickly took shape. Its focus was the UN, where states that were not permanent members of the powerful Security Council demanded a greater voice in global governance.

China remained as the only potential communist threat to the democratic West, but even in Beijing the allure of market forces was irresistible. By the start of the twenty-first century, China's communist leaders were charting an unprecedented economic course that would have horrified the author of *Das Kapital*. It was uncertain whether a deeply authoritarian political establishment that encouraged the formation of a capitalist economic order could survive over the long term. More certain was the fact that China's economic potential, in terms of manufacturing capacity, the attractiveness of a low-wage labor pool to international business, and worldwide consumer demand for goods produced in China, meant that the last great communist state was positioned to become *the* economic powerhouse in the twenty-first century. In the late 1950s Nikita Khrushchev had intoned that the Soviet Union's Marxist social and

319

economic system would enable communism to "bury" the selfish and self-destructive capitalist West. The claim, in retrospect, was ill-informed, but China's recent experiment, if successful, may serve as an interesting test case in the unfolding Hegelian dialectic, a rough synthesis of the two antithetical world views that had dominated international relations for most of the second half of the twentieth century.

The end of the Cold War and the subsequent dissolution of the Soviet Union meant that the United States remained as the world's only superpower. During the Clinton administration, a reluctance to employ military force, and especially combat troops, to stop religious and ethnic conflict was interpreted by critics of the administration as a failure of nerve. All such critics were silenced after 9/11, when George W. Bush swiftly deployed American forces first to Afghanistan and then to Iraq. The latter operation was originally launched under the heading of the broader war on terror, but after Saddam was removed from power it became a test case in democratic nation-building. A democratic Iraq, the administration hoped, would serve as an shining example of the "New World Order" to the very undemocratic Muslim Middle East. In February of 2005, the president took his message of advancing democracy in the Middle East to Europe, where most governments had opposed the 2003 invasion of Iraq. And although states like Germany and France pledged to assist in the rebuilding of Iraq by training the new Iraqi defense forces, there was a greater sense that Europe was no longer willing to accept the lead of the US in its efforts to spread democracy overseas.

In this changed international environment, President George H. W. Bush's 1989 declaration of a "New World Order" that featured greater democratization and constitutional reform was interpreted during his son's administration as a mandate to universalize Western liberal democracy and market economics. The president took his reelection in 2004 as a endorsement from the American people to advance the notion that free markets and Western-style democratic politics were socially optimal, that they would – over the long term – lead to a better and more just society for peoples everywhere. For neoconservatives in the Bush administration, the oppressed peoples of the world were chafing for liberalism as defined by free expression, religious freedom, political freedom, and free markets. Military action on behalf of freedom, especially in the autocratic (and oil-producing) Muslim world, would be supported by the majority of the inhabitants. This confidence was not shared by most member states of the EU, whose leaders objected not so much to the underlying ideology as to the American administration's efforts to impose by force its worldview on countries like Iraq. For many in Europe, US actions around the world after 9/11 appeared increasingly unilateralist, and as a result much of the goodwill toward the US that was generated after the terrorist attacks dissipated in the sands of Iraq during 2003.

That Iraq was one of the world's largest oil producers was not lost on opponents of Bush's preemptive war. Back in 1973, in the wake of the OPEC oil embargo, President Nixon appeared on television and announced that Americans, in the spirit of the Apollo moon mission and the earlier Manhattan Project, must dedicate themselves to energy independence by the end of the decade. Thirty years later, in the midst of a heated presidential race, both Senator John Kerry and President Bush spoke of the need for energy independence lest, in Kerry's words, future American soldiers be "held hostage to our dependence on oil from the Middle East." The rhetoric, both in 1973 and in 2004, belied the total lack of a coherent policy. Americans, who made up 5 percent of the world's population in 2004, consumed one-quarter of the world's oil supply. The US imported half of the 20 million barrels of oil consumed each day in 2004, and according to the Department of Energy, two-thirds of the total would be imported by 2020. In August 2002, Vice-President Richard Cheney, former CEO of a multinational oil services company, warned that if Saddam Hussein secured access to weapons of mass destruction, he would be in a position to take control of the greater part of the world's oil reserves and blackmail oil-consuming nations worldwide. Under this reading, American military action in Iraq was undertaken to better secure the long-term energy needs of the larger global community.

The employment of military power to assure the flow of oil was but one of a host of transnational challenges facing the peoples of the world at the start of the twenty-first century. Reconciling economic development and population growth with the needs of the environment stood as the greatest test, but the international community had demonstrated little collective resolve despite overwhelming scientific evidence of impending crises. Water usage is illustrative of the global dilemma. Within 20 years, access to fresh water may be the single most important issue facing rich and poor countries alike. It is generally agreed that humans require a minimum of 13 gallons a day of fresh water for consumption, hygiene, and food production. Water covers 70 percent of the earth, but only one percent of the total is both accessible and fresh. In 2004 residents of over 60 of the world's poorest countries were obliged to make do with much less than the 13-gallon minimum per day. Water-borne diseases such as cholera and dysentery take the lives of ten million people each year, and most of the victims are children. Poor people in many countries spend an inordinate amount of time and effort trying to secure enough water to live at subsistence level, curbing their productive capacity in other areas.

In affluent states like the US, where average water use per person has reached a scandalous 132 gallons each day, traditional sources of fresh water for major cities were quickly reaching their capacity. Atlanta, Georgia, for example, had a population of approximately 2.2 million in 1980. By 2004 the metropolitan population was 3.7 million, with projections of five million by the year 2025. Within a few short years, the city's major water source, the Chattahoochee River, will no longer be able to meet the demands of urban sprawl. Rural areas downstream from metropolitan centres are also impacted by excessive urban consumption, with farmers unable to continue irrigation projects at accustomed levels. Global water use grew sixfold during the twentieth century, and much of the increased consumption was directly related to economic development. In countries as diverse as China, Israel, and Mexico, water tables are down and rates of extraction sometimes exceed replacement. If, as predicted, world population grows from six to eight billion by 2025, 40 percent more fresh water will be needed. Where this additional capacity will come from is unknown; what is certain is that when it comes to water, appeals for conservation in most developed countries have fallen upon deaf ears.

States before peoples?

Sovereign nation-states now encompass the globe; the independence and liberation movements of the second half of the twentieth century have seen to that. And with the collapse of communism in the 1980s, nationalism now stands as one of the last comprehensive ideologies to allure millions the world over. At the time of its birth in the late eighteenth century, the nation-state was identified with opposition to monarchy and arbitrary government, with written constitutions and the rule of law, with respect for human rights and free expression. National self-determination was seen not only as an inherent right of peoples who viewed themselves within the context of shared values, but as a force for international betterment where nations would respect each others' inherent equality. For the American and French revolutionaries, the nation-state was a powerful tool of enlightenment, human freedom, and international goodwill. The motto affixed to the currency of the newly established US, *E pluribus unum*, made explicit the goal of finding unity in a diverse culture.

To a certain measure that same quest for unity in diversity animated the political leaders of many postcolonial states after 1945. This was undeniably the case in much of Africa and South Asia. Unhappily, most of them failed, their efforts frustrated in no small part by the arbitrary state boundaries inherited from the imperial powers. In the meantime, the rhetoric of nationalism turned increasingly negative and divisive, a troubling recrudescence of the prewar bigotry that affected parts of Europe. With the collapse of communism, the twentieth century's engagement with the politics of class conflict ended, only to be replaced by a rhetoric of national identity that emphasized arbitrary differences over shared values. By the mid-1990s most of the world's refugees were fleeing from states wracked by ethnic conflict; more than half of the UN's peacekeeping missions were charged with separating ethnic antagonists; and most of the world's military conflicts involved challenges to states by ethnic minorities.

At the start of the new century, the most strident proponents of nationalism and the sovereign nation-state subscribed to an "essentialist" view of origins. According to this creed, nations are naturally or divinely ordained, and therefore ideally fitted to represent the interests of a sovereign people. The inhabitants of the nation share certain commonalities – or at least they ought to – with the most important being religious identity, language, ethnic origins, and/or social practices. During the late twentieth century, the world witnessed painful examples of the "essentialist" position in places like the former Yugoslavia and Rwanda, and to a lesser degree in Northern Ireland and the Basque region of Spain. But it was also recognizable in states like Saudi Arabia and Japan, where strict immigration regimes effectively denied permanent residency to non-natives. Sadly, modern nationalism has to a large degree jettisoned the inclusive standpoint of the Enlightenment. Sovereign nations protect and defend their own, and their first response to common global problems is to calibrate how far transnational cooperation is at odds with the insular, short-term interests of the nation-state. Needless to say, such territorial provincialism is not a particularly functional paradigm for global sustainability over the long term.

In important respects, the formation of the UN in 1945 was designed to counteract the parochialism of the nation-state. And the UN achieved modest successes during its first 50 years, especially in bringing the voices of minor powers to bear on global and regional problems. But as an organization made up of sovereign states, the UN was rarely in a position to force member states into compliance with its mandates. The sovereign state had clearly arrived as the locus of moral authority for the majority of the world's people by 2000, and any perceived or actual infringement of a member state's freedom of action was certain to cause controversy. Indeed the primacy of the nation-state received perhaps its starkest affirmation in the spring of 2003, when President Bush rebuffed a majority in the UN and ordered a military invasion of Iraq. Even after it became clear that alleged weapons of mass destruction were nowhere to be found in Iraq, the administration continued to insist that the toppling of Hussein's regime was key to the national security of the US. In the 2004 presidential election, the Bush campaign skillfully portrayed the president as the candidate who could best guard the nation's security. Despite the fact that the president's opponent, Senator John Kerry, was a highly decorated veteran of the Vietnam War, the Democratic challenger was attacked for being weak on defense and too enamored of multilateral solutions to military threats. And in his inaugural speech at the start of his second term in 2005, Bush declared that his administration would redouble its efforts to extend political freedom overseas, because freedom at home was increasingly dependent on freedom abroad. The "Bush Doctrine" of preemptive war demonstrated that the requirements of the sovereign state directed the global policy of the world's remaining superpower, and no level of international disapproval would alter that reality.

The world as an aggregation of nation-states, where peoples find their core identity in the nation, is, for good or ill, the most powerful Western contribution to global civilization at the beginning of the twenty-first century. With state interests so deeply woven into the fabric of a people's historic identity, with borders and territory becoming the emblems of self-conscious cultural communities, and with the process of cultural self-fashioning on the increase, the prospect of ever returning to the Enlightenment ideal of multiethnic nations has narrowed. There are some ambitious countercurrents, but these present problems of their own. The varied phenomena of economic globalization, for example, has been lauded by its partisans as the most powerful solution to international conflict, and as the best guarantor of internal stability and progress. Nations that have established deep bilateral economic ties, it is argued, have a powerful incentive to avoid conflict. And with the prosperity generated by global trade, domestic ethnic and religious differences are less likely to threaten the political stability of the nation. The spread of market capitalism, in other words, facilitates the creation of bonds of commonality around the goal of material abundance.

But while one might point to a rough correlation between material affluence and the acceptance of multicultural perspectives, both between and within nations, the difficulty resides in the fact of present and egregious disparities. Closing the gap between rich and poor countries, and within most developing countries, will not be achieved through economic globalization, especially given that favored nations began the process of global exchange with the advantage of having mature economies and stable social and political orders already in place. And even if the economic playing field were level, the "material abundance" solution to the natural avidity of nation-states is simply unsustainable. The favored nations cannot afford to allow the rest of the world to consume resources in the same profligate manner as the fossil fuel-dependent North; demographic realities hamper that prospect at every turn. Without a major cultural shift in popular definitions of the good life – and there is no sign that popularly elected leaders are willing to lead in this area – peoples will remain at the mercy of state interests, and state interests will invariably seek to advantage one constructed identity – the nation – over the real needs of the greater whole.

A Meaningful Life

Thus the new century began with more fundamental questions left unresolved, questions about how best to live, about what pursuits made life meaningful, and on what terms individuals and societies might secure the greatest good for all. The fateful challenges of the twenty-first century – the use and allocation of water, food, and energy; the provision of education, housing, and health care; the protection and renewal of the earth's environment; equitable access to the fruits of human invention and production – are deeply related to matters of justice and human rights. How can the peoples of the global community best ensure that geography and the accident of birth do not set the parameters of existence, that a minimum standard of living – one where life is worth living – is available to all? How can a balanced distribution of the world's resources be achieved while at the same time securing the long-term viability of the earth's fragile ecosystem? From 1945 until the late 1980s, the Cold War overshadowed all attempts to address these pivotal questions, while in the 1990s the opportunity to engage them in a meaningful way was hampered by complacency in the developed world, by an economic system that was predicated upon endless growth and dominion over nature, and by a model of political organization that prioritized the needs (real or imagined) of one people over all others.

In the immediate postwar era, existentialist philosophers like Jean-Paul Sartre called for a rebellion against universalizing systems of thought. Insisting that humans lived in a morally indifferent world, they charged each person to employ his or her freedom to define the humane life and to live authentically. Few took up the challenge, however, and as we saw in Chapter 7, the influence of traditional religious forms – where universals were embraced – remained strong in every major civilization. Still, at the turn of the century it appeared that the lure of the contingent and material reigned supreme in many cultures. The mantra of growth and development, of getting and consuming, of ever greater exploitation of limited resources, was communicated incessantly around the world via radio, television, and the Internet. In the 1950s, as consumerism was beginning its long and ultimately successful march toward shaping a conformist culture, the American poet Allen Ginsberg explored themes of rootlessness and alienation at the core of mass society. And playwrights like the Irishman Samuel Beckett investigated the same topics in what became known as the "theatre of the absurd." In perhaps the best-known example of the genre, Becket's *Waiting for Godot* (1952), the main characters wait in vain for a command from the mysterious Godot, filling their time (and the audience's) with trivial exchanges devoid of meaning. The great enemy in the play is loneliness, and it is fear of being left alone that prevents the pitiable characters from hanging themselves in the final scene.

These and other cautionary notes by distinguished artists of the postwar era largely went unheeded, but at some cost to the general well-being of residents of the developed North. During the presidency of Bill Clinton (1992–2000), the world's most affluent country experienced a period of unprecedented economic growth, and most other developed countries enjoyed similar good fortune. Yet the new wealth not only exacerbated the economic chasm between wealthy and poor countries, but appeared to do little to satisfy the inhabitants of the former. The rates of failed marriages continued to climb, workplace dissatisfaction remained high, and teen depression and suicide emerged as troubling social trends. Despite levels of material affluence that would have been unimaginable to most of the world's population just one century earlier, many members of the middle class sought solace for the myriad stresses of modern life in prescription drugs both for themselves, and, more disturbingly, for their children. Critics lamented the burgeoning "therapeutic culture," where mental and physical health-care professionals counseled and prescribed with abandon.

The measure of the good life, the life worth living, that was inherent in the ideology of globalism, did not always include the Socratic caveat that the unexamined life was not worth living. For the form of liberty embedded in the ideology of globalism was what the late philosopher Isaiah Berlin called "negative liberty." It involved the absence of restraint on individual actions, not the provision of opportunities within a range of positive options. Negative liberty concerned the removal of political barriers to freedom of action in the marketplace, and to freedom of expression in the public square. Its founding document comes from the late eighteenth century. In *The Wealth of Nations* (1776), Adam Smith maintained that the individual's pursuit of material self-interest would lead to the social optimum irrespective of place or culture. The minimal function of government involved the enforcement of law and contracts, the preservation of domestic peace, and national defense. It did not take into account differences based on social status, education, family connections, or inherited wealth.

Under classical liberalism, freedom included the freedom to fail, and the obligation to assume responsibility for one's failure. At the start of the twenty-first century, globalism applied these powerful principles of classical liberalism across national borders, across oceans, and across continents. For some in the West globalism became a belief system that transformed utility, rough economic measures of the good life, into an all-inclusive measure of goodness. Under the ideology of globalism, the flourishing life too often was reduced to the arena of getting and spending, of unquenchable economic activity. In the world's haste to follow the imperatives of globalism, the role of culture, of environment, of history and tradition, receded as ultimate ends of human welfare. Restoring the balance between a worldview that reduces humans to units of consumption, and one that takes full account of the variety of human needs, stands as one of the more important trials of the present age. The fact that any durable solution must involve serious discussion of an ecosystem that defies the arbitrary boundaries of nation-states makes the challenge all the more arduous. Discussing limits within the context of global equity is never easy, especially when such a discussion must question many of the economic assumptions behind the "New World Order." But we are left with no alternative.

On December 26, 2004, a massive earthquake centered to the immediate west of Indonesia generated a massive tsunami that smashed ashore throughout the region, wiping out whole villages as far away as southern Sri Lanka. Over a quarter of a million people in 12 countries were killed within minutes, while hundreds of thousands of survivors were left without food, medicine, or shelter. The international community – and particularly the developed countries of the North – responded immediately with an unprecedented outpouring of emergency aid. Swift action prevented additional deaths that could have occurred from the spread of infectious diseases like typhoid. For a moment, a brief moment, an insurgency movement in the affected areas of Indonesia, and a separatist movement in Sri Lanka, became irrelevant as humans struggled together to respond to nature's fury. In the midst of a horrific tragedy where humans were for once not culpable, the potential for good irrespective of borders, for generosity without precondition, for compassion without ideology, was encountered and affirmed. People came before states in the days and weeks after the deadly tsunami, even as states provided a valuable service in organizing and projecting the compassion of their citizenry. In this one instance, the language of human rights was translated into broad international action, and the assets of the industrialized world were brought to bear on a crisis that was beamed around the world through television. Those images of assistance, of selflessness and quiet heroism, were a welcome antidote to the usual fare of suffering caused by human agency under the guise of national interest. And by their actions, the respondents served to underscore the possibility – the hope – that the world might be otherwise, that the potential for collective stewardship of the planet and its inhabitants has been severely underestimated, that peoples can indeed trump states.

FURTHER READING

I have relied on secondary sources for this book, and the following suggestions are designed to assist students and generalists. Each of the books listed below are readily available at most university libraries, and most of the selections include substantial bibliographies.

INTRODUCTION

Excellent general surveys of the period include Daniel Brower, *The World Since 1945: A Brief History* (Upper Saddle River, NJ, 2003); Pamela Kyle Crossley, Lyn Hollen Lees, and John W. Servos, *Global Society: The World Since 1900* (New York, 2004); William R. Keylor, *The Twentieth-Century World: An International History* (New York, 2001); David Reynolds, *One World Divisible* (New York, 2000); Keith Robbins, *The World Since 1945: A Concise History* (New York, 1998), and T. E. Vadney, *The World Since 1945* (New York, 1998). I have relied on each of these books in the chapters that follow.

CHAPTER 1
Cold War theory

Francis Fukuyama, *The End of History and the Last Man* (Toronto, 1992); John L. Gaddis, *We Know Now: Rethinking Cold War History* (Oxford, 1997); Odd Arne Westard, *Reviewing the Cold War* (London, 2000).

US–Soviet relations

Jonathan A. Becker, *Soviet and Russian Press Coverage of the United States* (New York, 1999); Archie Brown, *The Gorbachev Factor* (New York, 1996); Robert A. Divine, *Eisenhower and the Cold War* (Oxford, 1981); H. Feis, *From Trust to Terror: The Onset of the Cold War, 1945–1950* (1970); Max Frankel, *High Noon in the Cold War: Kennedy, Khrushchev, and the Cuban Missile Crisis* (New York, 2004); Thomas Graham, *Disarmament Sketches: Three Decades of Arms Control and International Law* (Seattle, 2002); J. Kleep, *The Last of the Empires: A History of the Soviet Union, 1956–1991* (Oxford, 1995); David Oshinsky, *A Conspiracy So Immense: The World of Joe McCarthy* (New York, 1983); Thomas G. Patterson, *On Every Front: The Making and Unmaking of the Cold War* (New York, 1992); John W. Young, *America, Russia and the Cold War* (New York, 1999).

Europe and Asia

David W. Ellwood, *Rebuilding Europe: Western Europe, America and Postwar Reconstruction* (London, 1992); Stanley Karnow, *Vietnam: A History* (New York, 1984); Jonathan Spence, *The Search for Modern China* (New York, 1999); M. Walker,

The Cold War and the Making of the Modern World (London, 1994); Gerhard Weinberg, *A World at Arms: A Global History of World War II* (New York, 1994).

CHAPTER 2

Decolonization

Franz Ansprenger, *The Dissolution of the Colonial Empires* (London, 1989); R. F. Holland, *European Decolonization, 1918–1981* (Basingstoke, 1985); Mary Fulbrook (ed.), *Europe Since 1945* (New York, 2001); John Springhall, *Decolonization since 1945* (Basingstoke, 2001).

South and East Asia

Geoffrey Ashe, *Gandhi: A Biography* (New York, 2000); Ahron Bregman, *A History of Israel* (Basingstoke, 2002); Judith Brown, *Modern India: The Origins of an Asian Democracy* (Oxford, 1994); Nicholas Dirks, *Castes of Mind: Colonialism and the Making of Modern India* (Princeton, NJ, 2001); Robin Jeffrey (ed.), *Asia: The Winning of Independence* (London, 1981); Alan T. Wood, *Asian Democracy in World History* (New York, 2004).

Middle East

William M. Cleveland, *A History of the Modern Middle East* (Boulder, CO, 2000); Douglas Little, *American Orientalism: The United States and the Middle East since 1945* (Chapel Hill, NC, 2002).

Africa

Prosser Gifford and W. R. Lewis (eds), *The Transfer of Power in Africa: Decolonization, 1940–1960* (New Haven, CT, 1982); John D. Hargreaves, *Decolonization in Africa* (London, 1996); Paul Kennedy, *Preparing for the Twenty-First Century* (New York, 1993); D. A. Low, *Eclipse of Empire* (Cambridge, 1991); Stephen McCarthy, *Africa: The Challenge of Transformation* (London, 1994); Ali A. Mazrui and Michael Tidy, *Nationalism and New States in Africa* (London, 1984); Godfrey Mwakikagile, *The Modern African State: Quest for Transformation* (Huntington, NY, 2001); John A. Wiseman, *The New Struggle for Democracy in Africa* (Aldershot, 1996).

CHAPTER 3

Recent Europe and America

R. Garthoff, *The Great Transition: American–Soviet Relations and the End of the Cold War* (Washington, DC, 1994); Misha Glenny, *The Balkans: Nationalism, War and the Great Powers* (New York, 2000); J. Newhouse, *Europe Adrift* (New York, 1997); David Remnick, *Lenin's Tomb: The Last Days of the Soviet Empire* (New York, 1994);

L. Silber and A. Little, *Yugoslavia: Death of a Nation* (New York, 1996); Robert B. Marks, *The Origins of the Modern World: A Global and Ecological Narrative* (Lanham, MD, 2002); G. Stokes, *The Walls Came Tumbling Down: The Collapse of Communism in Eastern Europe* (Oxford, 1993); H. Turner, *Germany from Partition to Reunification* (New Haven, CT, 1992).

South and East Asia

Paul J. Bailey, *China in the Twentieth Century* (Oxford, 2001); Erich Reiter and Peter Hazdra (eds), *The Impact of Asian Powers on Global Developments* (New York, 2004); R. Keith Schoppa, *Revolution and Its Past: Identities and Change in Modern Chinese History* (Upper Saddle River, NJ, 2002); Martin Stuart-Fox, *A Short History of China and Southeast Asia* (Crows Nest, New South Wales, 2003).

Latin America

John C. Chasteen, *Born in Fire and Blood: A Concise History of Latin America* (New York, 2001); John Peeler, *Building Democracy in Latin America* (Boulder, CO, 2004); Peter Winn, *Americas: The Changing Face of Latin America and the Carribean* (Berkeley, 1999).

Recent Islam

Fawaz Gerges, *America and Political Islam: Clash of Cultures or Clash of Interests?* (Cambridge, 1999); Dilip Hiro, *Holy Wars: The Rise of Islamic Fundamentalism* (New York, 1989); Lester D. Langley, *The Americas in the Modern Age* (New Haven, CT, 2003); Ira M. Lapidus, *A History of Islamic Societies* (New York, 2002); Walter Laqueur, *No End to War: Terrorism in the 21st Century* (New York, 2003); Bernard Lewis, *What Went Wrong? The Clash Between Islam and Modernity in the Middle East* (New York, 2003); Thomas W. Simons, *Islam in a Globalizing World* (Stanford, CA, 2003).

CHAPTER 4

Economic Globalization

Jagdish Bhagwati, *In Defense of Globalization* (New York, 2004); Sheila Croucher, *Globalization and Belonging: The Politics of Identity in a Changing World* (Lanham, MD, 2004); Thomas Frank, *One Market Under God* (New York, 2000); Thomas Friedman, *The Lexus and the Olive Tree* (New York, 2000); John Gray, *False Dawn: The Delusions of Global Capitalism* (New York, 1998); Michael Kitson and Jonathan Michie, "Trade and Growth: A Historical Perspective," in Jonathan Michie and John Grieve Smith (eds), *Managing the Global Economy* (Oxford, 1995); Thomas D. Lairson and David Skidmore, *International Political Economy: the Struggle for Power and Wealth* (Belmont, CA, 2003); Robert Skidelsky, "The Growth of a World

Economy," in *The Oxford History of the Twentieth Century* (Oxford, 1999); Manfred Steger, *Globalism: The New Market Ideology* (Lanham, MD, 2002); Joseph Stiglitz, *Globalization and Its Discontents* (New York, 2002); Theodore Van Laue, *The World Revolution of Westernization* (New York, 1987); Herman Van der Wee, *Prosperity and Upheaval: The World Economy, 1945–1980* (Berkeley, CA, 1986; Daniel Yergin, *The Commanding Heights: The Battle Between Government and the Marketplace that is Remaking the World* (New York, 1998).

Cities, consumers, and energy

Saskai Sassen, *The Global City: New York, London, Tokyo* (Princeton, NJ, 1991); Peter Stearns, *Consumerism in World History: The Global Transformation of Desire* (New York, 2001); Daniel Yergin, *The Prize: The Epic Quest for Oil, Money and Power* (1992).

CHAPTER 5
General surveys

Leonore Loeb Adler and Uwe P. Gielen (eds), *Migration: Immigration and Emigration in International Perspective* (Westport, CT, 2003); Stephen Castles, *Ethnicity and Globalization: From Migrant Worker to Global Citizen* (London, 2000); Stephen Castles, *Ethnicity and Globalization* (London, 2000); Robin Cohen (ed.), *The Cambridge Survey of World Migration* (Cambridge, 1995); Samuel Huntington, *The Clash of Civilizations and the Remaking of World Order* (New York, 1996); Douglas S. Massey et al., *Worlds in Motion: Understanding International Migration at the End of the Millenium* (Oxford, 1998); Leslie Page Moch, *Moving Europeans: Migration in Western Europe Since 1650* (Bloomington, IN, 1992); Daniel Pipes, *Militant Islam Reaches America* (New York, 2002); Veit Bader (ed.), *Citizenship and Exclusion* (Basingstoke, 1997); Nicholas Polunin (ed.), *Population and Global Security* (Cambridge, 1998); Arthur Schlesinger, *The Disuniting of America* (Knoxville, TN, 1991); Ronald Skelton, *Migration and Development: A Global Perspective* (Harlow, Essex, 1997); Thomas Sowell, *Migrations and Cultures: A World View* (New York, 1996); W. M. Spellman, *The Global Community: Migration and the Making of the Modern World* (Stroud, Gloucestershire, 2002).

Refugees

Arthur C. Helton, *The Price of Indifference: Refugees and Humanitarian Action in the New Century* (Oxford, 2002); David Jacobson, *Rights Across Borders: Immigration and the Decline of Citizenship* (Baltimore, MD, 1996); United Nations Commissioner for Refugees, *The State of the World's Refugees: Fifty Years of Humanitarian Action* (Geneva, 2000); Myron Weiner and Sharon Stanton Russell (eds), *Demography and National Security* (New York, 2001).

CHAPTER 6
Medicine and technology

John Krige and Dominique Pestre (eds), *Science in the Twentieth Century* (Amsterdam, 1997); Roy Porter, *The Greatest Benefit to Mankind: A Medical History of Humanity* (New York, 1997); Roy Porter, ed., *The Cambridge Illustrated History of Medicine* (Cambridge, 1996); James C. Riley, *Rising Life Expectancy: A Global History* (Cambridge: 2001); William B. Schwartz, *Life Without Disease: the Pursuit of Medical Utopia* (Berkeley, CA, 1998); Sheldon Watts, *Disease and Medicine in World History* (New York, 2003); Trevor I. Williams, *A History of Invention: From Stone Axes to Silicon Chips* (New York, 2002); John Ziman, *The Force of Knowledge: The Scientific Dimension of Society* (Cambridge, 1976).

Energy and environment

Philip Andrews-Speed, Xuanli Liao, and Roland Dannreuther, *The Strategic Implications of China's Energy Needs* (New York, 2002); Helen Cothran (ed.), *Energy Alternatives* (San Diego, CA, 2002); Paul Farmer, *Infections and Inequalities* (Greenwich, CT, 1988); Howard Geller, *Energy Revolution: Policies for a Sustainable Future* (Washington, DC, 2003); Ramachandra Guha, *Environmentalism: A Global History* (New York, 2000); Martha Hostetter (ed.), *Energy Policy* (New York, 2002); Rob Jackson, *The Earth Remains Forever* (Austin, TX, 2002); Adeline Levine, *Love Canal: Science, Politics and People* (Lexington, MA, 1982); John Robert McNeill, *Something New Under the Sun: An Environmental History of the Twentieth-Century World* (New York, 2000); D. C. Pirages and T. M. DeGeest, *Ecological Security: An Evolutionary Perspective on Globalization* (Lanham, MD, 2004); Václav Smil, *Energy in World History* (Boulder, CO, 1994); R. A. N. Smith, *Energy. the Environment, and Public Opinion* (Lanham, MD, 2002).

CHAPTER 7
General surveys

John L. Esposito, Darrell Fashing, and Todd Lewis, *World Religions Today* (New York, 2002); James C. Livingston, *Anatomy of the Sacred: An Introduction to Religion* (Upper Saddle River, NJ, 2001).

Islam

Madawi Al-Rasheed, *A History of Saudi Arabia* (Cambridge, 2002); Scott Appleby, *The Ambivalence of the Sacred: Religion, Violence, and Reconciliation* (Lanham, MD, 2000); Yvonne Haddad and John Esposito, *Islam, Gender and Social Change* (New York, 1998); Mehran Tamadonfar, *The Islamic Polity and Political Leadership:*

Fundamentalism, Sectarianism, and Pragmatism (Boulder, CO, 1989); Alexei Vasil'ev, *The History of Saudi Arabia* (New York, 2000).

Church and State

Robert Audi and Nicholas Wolterstorff, *Religion in the Public Square* (New York, 1997); M. B. Biskupski, *A History of Poland* (Westport, CT, 2000); Jose Casanova, *Public Religions in the Modern World* (Chicago, 1994); N. J. Demerath, *Crossing the Gods: World Religions and Worldly Politics* (New Brunswick, NY, 2002); Donald E. MacInnis (ed.), *Religion in China Today: Politics and Practice* (Maryknoll, NY, 1989); Ted G. Jelen and Clyde Wilcox (eds), *Religion and Politics in Comparative Perspective* (Cambridge, 2001).

Christianity

John W. DeGruchy, *Christianity and Democracy: A Theology for a Just World Order* (Cambridge, 1995); Anthony Gill, *Rendering Unto Caesar: The Catholic Church and the State in Latin America* (Chicago, 1998); Gustavo Gutiérrez, *A Theology of Liberation: History, Politics, and Salvation* (Maryknoll, NY, 1973); Elizabeth Isichei, *A History of Christianity in Africa* (Grand Rapids, MI, 1995); Philip Jenkins, *The Next Cristendom: The Coming of Global Christianity* (Oxford, 2002); Timothy G. McCarthy, *The Catholic Tradition: Before and After Vatican II* (Chicago, 1994); Hugh McLeod and Werner Ustorf, *The Decline of Christendom in Western Europe, 1750–2000* (Cambridge, 2003); Jacob Neusner (ed.), *God's Rule: The Politics of World Religions* (Washington, DC, 2003); Daniel L. Overmyer, *Religions of China* (San Francisco, 1986); Richard Polenberg, *One Nation Divisible: Class, Race and Ethnicity in the United States Since 1938* (New York, 1980); Sabine Wichert, *Northern Ireland Since 1945* (New York, 1999).

CONCLUSION

Paul Gilbert, *The Philosophy of Nationalism* (Boulder, CO, 1998); Adrian Hastings, *The Construction of Nationhood: Ethnicity, Religion and Nationalism* (Cambridge, 1997); Michael Hechter, *Containing Nationalism* (Oxford, 2000); E. J. Hobsbawm, *Nations and Nationalism Since 1780* (Cambridge, 1991); Michael T. Klare, *Blood and Oil: The Dangers and Consequences of America's Growing Petroleum Dependency* (New York, 2004); Marq de Villiers, *Water: The Fate of Our Most Precious Resource* (New York, 2001).

INDEX